California Votes

California Votes:
The 2002 Governor's Race & The Recall That Made History

Gerald C. Lubenow, editor

Berkeley Public Policy Press
Institute of Governmental Studies
University of California
2003

Library of Congress Cataloging-in-Publication Data

California votes : the 2002 governor's race and the recall that made history / Gerald C. Lubenow, editor.
        p. cm.
Proceedings of the fourth quadrennial symposium on the California governor's race held at the Institute of Governmental Studies, University of California.
   ISBN 0-87772-410-5
   1. Governors--California--Election--Case studies. 2. Elections--California--Case studies. 3. Campaign management--California--Case studies. 4. Political campaigns--California--Case studies. I. Lubenow, Gerald C. II. University of California, Berkeley. Institute of Governmental Studies.
   JK8793 2002
   324.9794'054--dc22   2003015181

Acknowledgement

Over the years, the quadrennial postelection conferences here at Berkeley have come to be one of the few remaining places where Republicans and Democrats can meet and talk politics in a civil manner. There were some sharp elbows thrown in the recent gatherings, to be sure, some testy exchanges, and a few snide comments. But this year's sessions once again produced a remarkable level of candor. Some would argue that one of the downsides of California politics is that campaigns have become professional affairs. The upside is that when the political pros responsible for electing the people who govern California meet they act like professionals. Whatever merit this volume may have derives from the intelligence, passion, and talent they bring to their work—and to our postgame analysis of their efforts. It is their words, their ideas, and their insights that are the heart of this book. Most of the chapters are edited transcripts of the conference panels. We simply try to bring them to you in as clear and unadulterated a form as possible. We are grateful to the campaigns for their continued commitment to this project.

We owe a debt as well to the political press. Some of the state's top political reporters served as moderators for the panel discussions, and their intelligent but firm prodding produced a coherent and clarifying narrative, as well as a number of fresh insights. I would especially like to thank Mark Z. Barabak of *The Los Angeles Times* and Carla Marinucci of *The San Francisco Chronicle* for writing introductions to the primary and general election panel transcripts. Their meaty sketches of the campaigns serve to refresh the reader's recollection and to put the key events in perspective.

We have tried to add value to the discourse by including sections that look at specific issues. I want to thank Dan Morain of *The Los Angeles Times* and Karen Getman, who recently stepped down as head of California's Fair Political Practices Commission to return to the practice of law and to join IGS as our first Executive in Residence, for contributing articles that help us understand the complex role that money plays in politics. And I want to thank California's seasoned crew of political pollsters for once again helping to parse the numbers and divine their deeper meaning. *San Francisco Chronicle* Photo Editor Gary Fong was, once again, generous with his time and resources in helping us find cover photos.

Finally, I want thank Bruce Cain and the Institute of Governmental Studies for providing financial support for this conference in a very difficult budget year, Marc Levin and the IGS staff for their usual first-rate administrative help in seeing that everything ran smoothly, and Maria Wolf, my assistant editor, for her steady hand in bringing the event to print.

John Jacobs

Dedication

This is the fourth in a series of volumes that seek to provide a candid, unspun, inside view of how politics work in California. That is a task to which John Jacobs dedicated his all too brief life. His death, at 49, on May 24, 2000, was a loss to everyone who cares about politics in this state.

A tribute to him in the *Sacramento Bee*, where his thrice-weekly syndicated column had appeared since 1973 when he moved to Sacramento to become political editor of McClatchy Newspapers, was headlined "An honest champion of politics in a cynical age." These days, California politics needs all the honest champions it can get.

John was a San Francisco native and a Cal graduate. He got his start in journalism as a reporter at the *Daily Cal* and returned to Berkeley to earn a master's degree in journalism before embarking on a distinguished career as a political reporter and columnist.

He was the author of two big books, *Raven: The Untold Story of the Rev. Jim Jones and His People* written with *Examiner* colleague Tim Reiterman, and *A Rage for Justice*, a biography of the late Rep. Phillip Burton of San Francisco. It was a towering book about a towering figure. And Burton provided a perfect vehicle for John's passion for politics, his love of history, his diligence as a reporter, and his ability to write with clarity and grace about the most arcane government program or the most tangled political deal.

He spent seven years researching and writing the Burton book, taking a six-month leave from his job at the *San Francisco Examiner* to complete the writing. He spent those six months at IGS, continuing a long relationship through which we had come to know him as a warm, engaging, witty, and inventive colleague.

One of the things he helped invent during his long and productive relationship with IGS was a review of the California governor's race that has become a fixture of California politics. This is the first of four volumes beginning in 1990 that he did not have a hand in shaping. And here, as across the landscape of California politics, his presence is missed.

Contents

III. The General Election Campaign

IV. The Recall

Appendices

Preface

After the 2002 California governor's race, as we have following every gubernatorial election since 1990, the Institute of Governmental Studies held a conference on campus in early January 2003 to review the race and analyze the results. Once again, we assembled all the key players—the campaign managers and consultants, the pollsters and strategists, the media managers and the money people, and, of course, the press.

And once again, the result was a frank and candid exposition of politics as it is played at the highest level. As IGS Director Bruce Cain observed at the start of the conference, "Even though some of it is familiar, we've discovered that with the passage of time people tend to be more willing to speak frankly about the reasons why they did what they did in the heat of the battle, and we have learned a lot of extraordinary things about how decisions are made."

As we had done following the 1990, 1994, and 1998 races, we planned to produce a volume on the 2002 gubernatorial election based on the conference. But through the spring, as we were editing the manuscript, an effort was launched to recall Governor Gray Davis. And as our editing progressed, so did the recall effort. About the time we were ready to send the book to press, it became clear that the recall effort would reach the ballot and, quite possibly, undo the results of the election.

We decided to hold up publication and include the recall as the final chapters in the book. The result is a publication as unique as the recall itself: a book that combines an in-depth look at the 2002 election that put Gray Davis in the governorship with an analysis of the recall election that plucked him from office less than a year later. Reading the two in juxtaposition, one is struck by a sense that the recall's success and Davis' failure were almost inevitable.

The picture that emerges of the election of 2002 reflects an electorate in the winter of its discontent. The $100 million election, one panelist noted, broke all previous records for spending and generated the lowest voter turnout and the largest number of third-party gubernatorial candidate votes in the state's history. Polling showed that a huge cohort of voters remained undecided until the last minute before ultimately opting for minor party candidates. Dissatisfaction was endemic in California, not only with the candidates, but with the campaigns they ran.

"A hallmark for this survey," PPIC's Mark Baldassare told the January conference of a poll done in collaboration with IGS, "was the lack of enthusiasm the voters had for this election, and specifically for this set of candidates. . . . Voters told us they felt that campaigns and elections in California were on a downward spiral." PPIC's findings, added Baldassare, showed, "Overwhelming disgust with negative campaigning."

Gray Davis may have been the last man standing in 2002, but he was mortally wounded. He had won with 1.3 million fewer votes than he received in 1998, narrowly edging an inept and inexperienced opponent who had run a terrible campaign. Bruce Cain told the January conference, "I know from people that were with Gray Davis on election night sitting there as he watched the returns and he watched the commentary, and he was massively depressed by what he was hearing—massively depressed."

Perhaps never before in California history had a candidate been so deeply despised by the voters who had just elected him to office. Many observers seriously questioned his ability to govern. Poll after poll showed that Californians felt their political process was badly broken.

Many voters felt they had been robbed of a reasonable choice by Davis's meddling in the Republican primary to defeat Richard Riordan. "Davis was extremely vulnerable due to his low job-performance ratings and his poor image ratings with the public," observed California Poll Director Mark DiCamillo, "but Simon was never really seen by voters outside his party as a credible alternative to Davis." Republican pollster Steve Kinney agreed, "What I was seeing was so much disgust in our polling. They didn't like either candidate; they didn't like either campaign."

That mood of political negativity reflected a more pervasive sense of foreboding about the economy, the state budget, and almost every aspect of life in the once Golden State that only grew worse as the year and the recall progressed. "How Low Can We Go?" asked the headline on a statewide survey released in August 2003, by the Public Policy Institute of California. "Recall Reflects New Depths of Pessimism in California."

Shortly after the recall qualified, the yes side opened a wide lead and the margin never narrowed. The result was a massive vote of no confidence in Gray Davis. Democratic Attorney General Bill Lockyer chose Berkeley's October recall review to announce that even he had voted for Schwarzenegger. "You know what Arnold represented for me?" he said. "I looked at the list; it was a crappy list. And he represented for me what he did for others—hope, change, reform, opportunity, upbeat, problem solving. I want that. I'm tired of transactional, cynical, deal-making politics."

So, according to the experts at our recall review, are an overwhelming majority of California voters. With the ascendance of Arnold Schwarzenegger, the mood of Californians seemed to rebound. But whether he is that son of York who can end the winter of our political discontent remains to be seen.

Gerald C. Lubenow
University of California, Berkeley

I. Setting the Scene: Pollsters, the Press and the Public, Media and Money

CHAPTER 1

The Voters—
How Does the Public View Campaigns?

BRUCE CAIN: I'm Bruce Cain, the director of the Institute of Governmental Studies, and I want to welcome everybody to the fourth quadrennial symposium on the California governor's race.

When Jerry Lubenow first started this back in 1990, I don't think we envisioned that it would take off the way that it has: we have done it four times, and there are now lots of places that imitate us. USC does one, the *Sacramento Bee* does one, and there are no doubt others out there. We like to think that this one is distinctive. The format, particularly tomorrow, is unique: we go through the blow-by-blow, decision-by-decision moments of the campaign. And even though some of it is familiar, we've discovered that with the passage of time people tend to be more willing to speak frankly about the reasons why they did what they did in the heat of the battle, and we have learned a lot of extraordinary things about how decisions are made, that decisions aren't always made in the most rational way, that emotions figure in, tensions figure in, etc. And we've learned a lot about tactical decisions from these formats. So tomorrow we will go blow-by-blow through the campaign, and we're counting on the chairs to keep people to that format.

But first, we want to do some analysis on the big picture of what was going on. And so today, we have a panel on how the public views campaigns that features a poll that the Public Policy Institute of California, the Pew Foundation, and IGS have done, where we try to ask in some innovative ways, questions about the public reaction to the campaign process per se. Mark Baldassare will present most of that data, and I will talk about the implications of that data, and then we will have some commentary.

We also have a panel on polls. I think we saw a lot of variance on polling. This has been a theme in past conferences, about the differences between public and private polls, and it's a topic that we're going to get into in some detail again here. We have a distinguished panel of pollsters, including public pollsters and private pollsters to talk about it.

And then we'll get on to the issue of debates, my own little hobbyhorse. You will see from the evidence that we had the fewest number of debates of any state in gubernatorial races, and many states had many more debates. While debates are certainly not the be all and end all of campaigns, we can certainly do better than what we did, or at least that's my opinion. And we'll discuss the formats in other states and the possibilities of requiring more debates.

So with that, I want to turn it over to Darry Sragow, who is chairing the first panel. Aside from being a distinguished Democratic consultant who has done statewide campaigns and assembly races, Darry has also been for the last four years an instructor here at Berkeley.

DARRY SRAGOW: What's really going on is that Dan Schnur and I are hoping to create a whole generation of our students who will take over the state. I called Gray Davis's office yesterday to try to get a hold of Lynn Schenk. The phone was answered by one of our former students. So it works, I got right through. I've been to all four of these symposia. And this is the first time I haven't shown up as a representative of a losing candidate, so I feel pretty good about this one. We have a very distinguished panel including Al Checchi's favorite political reporter, Phil Trounstine. Some of you may have noticed that the title of this panel has changed. The original title was, "Are Campaign Consultants Ruining Politics?" Apparently, Jerry decided that wouldn't take the full hour to answer, and so we have a slightly different topic. Mark Baldassare will start off.

MARK BALDASSARE: Yes, the title was going to be something very different from the more sanitized version that we have now. It was "Are Political Consultants Ruining Politics?" Well, we'll see what the public has to say.

The Public Policy Institute of California conducted five surveys between the middle of August and the day before the election this last year. The one I'm going to talk about today was a survey that Bruce and I collaborated on with funding from the Pew Charitable Trust, which took place the last week of the election. A unique opportunity for us; we're not usually in the field at that late date. But what we heard during that last week of the election was pretty much what we heard in the early going, in terms of the public perceptions of the campaign process and elections in California. It's a pretty negative perspective from the public at large. We interviewed about 5,000 likely voters through the course of the campaign. The last week we were in the field, we heard from 1,000 likely voters, and we surveyed 2,000. So we heard from nonvoters as well as voters.

Some of this is reviewed in an article that Dave Lesher was kind enough to publish in the latest *California Journal*, which says, "Voters Nostalgic for a Good Old-Fashioned Campaign." We saw record-low voter turnout. We've been seeing declining voter turnout, of course, in terms of eligible adults throughout the course of the last 10 years, particularly in California. But we set new records in the primary and the general election. And for me, one of the big stories to come out of this governor's race was the lack of participation on the part of both eligible adults and registered voters—only about half of the registered voters turned out in this election at a time when record amounts of money were spent by the two candidates for governor.

In terms of our polling, the race was fairly stagnant until that final poll we took the week before the election, where we saw about a five-point margin. All along, we were seeing Davis ahead by 9 to 11 points. But throughout the election there was an incredible amount of undecided votes; people said they were going to vote for other candidates, which was unique in terms of polling.

For political consultants, one of the most interesting things we found is that from the public's point of view elections aren't necessarily about winning, they're about getting informed about what the candidates have to say about the issues, and particularly the issues that are important to them. Throughout the election cycle voters were telling us there were a set of issues that they could name that were very important to them. Despite the reputation that California voters have for not being particularly attuned to politics, throughout the election we were seeing all kinds of evidence that people were informed. So informing voters about the candidates, that's what people think campaigns should be about.

One of the things that to me was a hallmark for this survey, and this was actually not from our last poll but from a poll we conducted in September, was the lack of enthusiasm the voters had for this election, and specifically for this set of candidates. This should have told us right away that we were in for record low voter turnout, which in the end we had, but six out of 10 Democrats and six out of 10 Independents, and nearly half of the Republicans said they were less enthusiastic about voting in this particular election than they had been in the past.

Something we saw throughout the election cycle, and I know that Susan Pinkus and Mark DiCamillo saw as well in their surveys, was that when we asked people how they felt about the choice of candidates, they were not very excited about the choices that they were making between Davis and Simon and Cameo and the other third-party candidates involved. Fewer than four in 10 likely voters said they were satisfied with the choice of candidates in this election.

With that record $100 million that was spent went a tremendous amount of penetration into living rooms of average Californians and likely voters. And in the four cycles of surveys that we had before the election, we were seeing very large numbers of likely voters saying that they had seen ads by the candidates for governor. Most of them had mentioned Davis ads, of course—he spent considerably more than Simon. In the last week, the numbers went up even more, as you would expect, with huge numbers of people saying that they saw ads, and huge numbers saying that those ads weren't particularly helpful. Less than three in 10 Independents said that the ads were helpful in making decisions, and Independents really dropped off in terms of their participation this year. By the end of the campaign, only three in 10 Democrats said the ads they saw were helpful.

When we asked people what mattered to them most in a campaign, what did they want to hear from the candidates, the standard refrain from Democrats, Republicans, and Independents was it's issues first, and over character, how intelligent the candidates are, what their party platform is, and so forth. About half of Democrats and Republicans said they want most to hear about issues, but in the course of this campaign, what the voters heard did not please them. Two out of three Democrats, Republicans, and Independents said they were not satisfied with the level of discussion of the issues.

We asked about the styles of campaigning, both in general and specific to this race, and we found that many Californians feel that political candidates are too negative and too critical of their opponents. When we asked specifically about this race, we saw even more people feeling that the campaigns were too negative. And we know this turns off voters and discourages them from going to the polls. In the end, lots of voters told us they felt that campaigns and elections in California were on a downward spiral. Nearly half said they felt that this campaign was worse in terms of ethics and values compared to what we've seen in the past 10 years, and campaigns, in general, are worse than in the past 10 years. How many people thought that campaigns had gotten better? Not many. Some people were generous and said the same, but less than 10 percent said that they felt that campaigns were getting better.

What do voters want? They tell us in any number of ways that they want more dialogue, more live discussion of issues, more genuine interaction either between the candidates or between the candidates and the voters. Debates were the top choice. Mailers were way down the list in terms of how they want to hear from the candidates. Call-in shows, speeches, town hall meetings—this was an election that, as Bruce mentioned, was lacking in debates. Two-thirds of likely voters said this would have been a better campaign had there been more than one debate. Two percent said it would have been worse, so not too many people feel that it could have gotten much worse. Bruce wanted to see how people feel about requiring the candidates to do five debates broadcast in prime time. Pretty far from what we saw in 2002, and even in '98. Six out of 10 voters would favor such a requirement. That's a considerable number.

We asked a lot of questions about codes of conduct, and what if people were asked to sign off at the beginning of the campaign to run a more ethical campaign, or one that had less mudslinging, less negativity. Nearly half the respondents said they view a candidate much more favorably, and nearly everybody said that they view the candidate at least somewhat or much more favorably if they signed a code of conduct pledging to run a truthful and clean campaign. We can talk about that later.

Campaign finance continues to be an interesting hypothetical issue. When we look at how people say they prefer candidates to pay for their campaign, a considerable number of people choose answers other than from their supporters, which, of course, is the main source of campaign funding. Three out of 10 said they would favor public money being set aside for campaigns. About half said they would favor a system of public funding for state campaigns. I think that's an indication of the level of discomfort with the current mode of campaigning rather than the generosity of voters. I wouldn't take those numbers to the bank in terms of running an initiative, but it gives us a sense of how the voters feel about the current process.

So, from the voters' perspective, and I'm sure Mark DiCamillo and Susan Pinkus and Steve Kinney and David Binder will talk about this more, this was a campaign that was marked by unpopular candidates, campaigns that didn't inspire, that relied on a medium that people said was not particularly helpful to them in terms of getting to know more about the issues. Bruce and I, and our colleagues both at IGS and PPIC, will be reproducing a full report on this survey, but clearly voters have some expectations about how they feel campaigns should be run, and it's pretty far from what we're doing today in California. And when we point to several areas of reform, there's a considerable amount of support, largely reflecting the fact that people are not happy with the status quo.

CAIN: Thank you, Mark. I want to say a little bit about the poll and the poll analysis, and a bit about the policy implications, and then we'll go to Phil Trounstine, who will calm the waters in his inimitable fashion.

I want to focus on this question of negative campaigning, which I think was a critical part of peoples' reaction to this. It wasn't just the candidates; it was that we got into a downward spiral of personal attacks by both sides. And our evidence suggests that had a real affect. First of all, most people, according to the data, do not feel that the political ads are helpful at all. That doesn't mean it is not in the interest of the consultants to run these ads, it's just to say that for 75 percent of the public, the ads aren't helpful. And the interesting thing is when you break it down in terms of socio-economic status, the people who are better educated find it the least helpful. So, the people who care the most about politics are being punished the most by having these ads on TV all the time. It's an irony, but that's life.

Some work that John Sides did is quite interesting, and one of the things he points out in his analysis is that when you do negative advertising, there's the direct oppositional effect of taking down the other guy—yes, we know all about that. But there's the secondary effect, which we'll call the reflective effect. It's the effect that it has on you. John looked at our data and found that the favorability of a candidate goes down if people are exposed to the ads. So Davis's favorability was higher among people who didn't see the ads than among people who saw the ads. His favorability among people who didn't see the ads was 56 percent, his favorability among the people who saw ads on both sides was 44 percent, and the people who saw more Davis ads than Simon ads also were at 44 percent favorability. In other words, if you were only exposed to Davis ads, you were less likely to have a favorable attitude about Davis. And the same thing for Simon—Simon's numbers when nobody saw any ads were 45 percent favorability, and when you saw both person's ads it was 35 percent favorability, and when you only saw Simon's ads it was 36 percent favorability. When you break it down by party, it's true for Democrats and Republicans—Democrats vis-à-vis Davis's ads, Republicans vis-à-vis Simon's ads. So, it may be a clever strategy of attrition, but it has a real effect in terms of the base of your voters—you're making your voters angry, you're alienating your voters, you're bringing down yourself. When you throw mud, some of the mud gets on you.

Now, I think this is an interesting fact because it's going to lead to where I'm going. We're all bummed-out, and what can you do about it? The answer is not much, because reform, in general, is difficult; reform in the area of political speech is massively difficult, because the Supreme Court is extremely protective of political speech, and well should be. It would be stupid to think otherwise. So it's ridiculous to consider any kind of regulation by prohibitions or bans on certain kinds of ads. That's just ludicrous, we can't even think about that.

But there are some other options for us, when you think about it. Option number one, which I identify with my good friend, Susan Rasky, is what I call the Raskafarian option; and the Raskafarian option is to do nothing. Her response is, "So what? What's your problem, Bruce? You've been around 30 years; don't be a baby. We have a race to the bottom, you know, these guys are racing for the bottom. It's entertaining, like a car crash. Just sit back and enjoy it." And there are many moments of the day when I share the Raskafarian point of view. I, too, enjoy the car crash. I participate in them thanks to people like Carla Marinucci, who call me up and I comment on the car crashes. So I can't be hypocritical, I like car crashes. And maybe Susan is right, maybe we should just relax and enjoy the spectacle and the blood and not worry about it. But it does bother me that the ads are so moronic, and so depressing, and so many people are bummed-out. The car crash with a little less stupidity is what I'm hoping for.

Now, the second possibility is self-imposed regulations, and Mark referred to that when he talked about codes of conduct. The idea is that you can't impose these things on people, but maybe people will adopt these things, and there will be a political cost to not living up to those promises. Now, on the plus side, the voters like them across the parties, across the different levels of political attention, etc. They think it's a worthy experiment; they would like to see it done. And in theory, it might work if somebody has pledged to do something and then they dropped their standard, there would be a political cost to doing that. And people like John Marelius and Carla and Dan Borenstein would point this out, and it would have some bump effect if you did that. On the minus side, there's obviously no way that you can enforce this. It's a matter of interpretation as to whether somebody's really living up to it, and clever consultants like Darry Sragow, and Dan Schnur, and Garry South, and others, will do issue ads, and put character assassination in there, and claim, of course, that they're not doing character assassination, and so we'll argue ad nauseum about whether they're really living up to their pledge. But it may be a worthwhile discussion, and if it makes life a little more difficult for Darry, that would be a valuable thing.

Now, a third possibility is one that I think we're pursuing in this project, which is what I call enlightened self-interest of the candidates and the consultants. And that is, if we can produce evidence that pursuing this route of mutual negativity, the race to the bottom, has some problems for them down the road. And what are the problems? Well, first of all if you are really eroding the base, and you're making people depressed about politics, then it has effect up and down the ticket in terms of turnout. And that can be problematic for the party, so that even if a particular candidate may be benefiting from this, if you're depressing turnout up and down the ticket, then it's a problem potentially for any party that wants to get control of the legislature or win in the lower races. Second, I know from people that were with Gray Davis on election night sitting there as he watched the returns and he watched the commentary, and he was massively depressed by what he was hearing—massively depressed. It is possible that candidates may not like being in the mud. It's okay for Darry and Dan and consultants to do it, because they're not in the mud. Who ever puts mud on the consultants? Nobody. But the candidates do get the mud; it is a personal hit for them. I think if you look, and Mervin Field was saying this just before we started, if you look at Gray Davis, there is some evidence that he is trying to do something different, that he is trying to actually speak the truth and get involved in the policy. Now, it may be a short experiment, but the point is there seems to be something going on in Gray's head, and I think that election night trauma of being so despised and so maligned at the end of the campaign, may well have an arresting affect on candidates. They may not be so willing to delegate everything to the person who doesn't take the hit. They may say, "It's all well and good for you to say that they can attack me, and I'll survive, and I'll still win; but I may not feel good about myself when it's all over." More importantly, from Gray Davis's point of view, "I may not be able to govern as well as a result of everybody thinking that I'm a money-grubbing shallow schmuck. Whereas, if people think of me as having some personal capital, then I'm much more likely to be able to operate in the legislature, and walk up and down the hallways and command some respect and get something that I want; and I might get some credit for things that I'm doing." So I don't think we can leave out that possibility—a better world through better research is definitely a self-serving academic idea, but discount it for what it's worth. It is possible that on the margin better knowledge about the secondary effects of these things may cause some people to hesitate before they go the route of mutual destruction.

Now, the last thing I want to talk about, and it will set up some comments that Phil may get into, is the role of the press. In general, I think press coverage in this state is pretty damn good on state politics. I think you get pretty much what you want, particularly if you survey all the different newspapers that are covering the races. Occasionally, the press gets off on a scent of their own, not on a scent that has anything to do with the public's concerns. And there's some evidence of that in our polls. One of the questions that we asked was how important it was to them to get data on tax returns and contributions and medical records. And to most voters, tax returns and medical records were irrelevant; only about 20 percent cared. And, I plead guilty to this because I was part of the people that said it was a huge mistake. The reality for most voters is that unless there's really something there, he hasn't paid taxes or he really is about to suffer a massive coronary, for the most part, that's not terribly interesting. What was important was the political contribution data, which is a pain in the neck to go through, but I think people do benefit from knowing the connections of interest groups and money to the candidates. So there was irritation with the way Simon handled that whole tax return thing, and it then becomes only too human for a journalist to say, "Well, if I'm irritated, then the world ought to be irritated with me." But I would just leave you with the possibility that that might not be the case, that if you're really irritated, the voters may not be. That's the one question that I would raise about the press coverage.

SRAGOW: I would just add, in answer to the original question, yes, the consultants are ruining politics. Phil, you've been on both sides now, as Judy Collins would say. You have some meat here, go for it.

PHIL TROUNSTINE: As Bruce and Mark were making their presentations, a number of things occurred to me that dovetail with some of my thinking about what happened during this campaign. First, let me say, it's not news to anybody in the campaign world that when a candidate goes up with negative advertising against his opponent, it drives down his own favorability. This is common information. What is new here is we have some academic evidence to demonstrate that that's true, and I think that's a valuable piece of information. But this is old news. What was new a few years ago was when Al Checchi found that his positive ads were driving down his own favorability. Now, that was new. But in this campaign, there were so few positive ads by either side that you probably couldn't have tested that proposition. So I think that's really not news. The folks who made the decision to run negative campaigns and purely negative campaigns knew in advance what the affect would be, that it would drive down the favorability of their candidates, but worst of all they knew and we all knew the proof is in the pudding, it drives down public interest in the campaign altogether. It drives down enthusiasm for the campaign, it drives down interest in politics, and it increases the level of cynicism that exists already throughout the public.

The fact that most people say they don't find ads to be helpful doesn't mean much to me, as somebody who has been a political reporter, someone on the inside of political operation, and now working in a polling operation. The only way it seems to me that you can test that, and campaigns have done this, is to ask what people know about the candidate in advance, show them some ads, and then test what they know about the candidate afterwards. Without that kind of test, the fact that people say that the information doesn't mean anything to them doesn't mean much. I remember going to the American Association of Political Consultants meeting a number of years ago in San Francisco, where a psychologist explained that negative information is processed and held much more deeply than positive information, and that's why negative campaigning works. Psychologists have studied this phenomenon. If I tell you something negative about a person, you are far more likely to remember it than you will something positive. So even though the public says they don't like it, the fact is it sticks, it works, and it has the effect in the long run of driving down the favorability of both sides. The only question in the Davis campaign was did they have an option? And I'm sure that Garry South and others will talk about that tomorrow, but my suspicion is what you will hear them say is that they did what they had to do, given the fact of the unpopularity of the governor going into the race at the very beginning. So that's really not news.

Now, what seems to me is important from a media perspective about all this is, first of all, where do people get their news? It's usually somewhere about 65 to 70 percent of the information the general population understands about politics is from television. For those of us who have been newspaper reporters and those who are newspaper reporters, this is not particularly exciting news, but it's true. It may have been Kam Kuwata who first said that you don't exist in California as a politician until you're on television, and those who cover politics know this is true. You simply do not exist until you're on television. I was educated by Bill Carrick in 1980 or 1984 to the fact that nobody knows anything except what they see on paid TV.

So what the public actually knows about candidates, mostly it knows from the television ads, the same television ads they say they don't like. This is unfortunate because candidates are going to do on television what they think will help them win a campaign. They will put in their television ads what they think will help them win. Dianne Feinstein once wanted to do an ad on growth control policy, and her consultants told her over their dead bodies they would put up an ad on growth policy, it just wasn't going to happen. Now, it would have been a nice piece of public discussion to have a debate over growth policy, but it would have been a huge waste of Dick Blum's money from the campaign's point of view.

So where the print media comes into play here is that the print media drives the agenda for the broadcast media, and they have very few ideas of their own. Mostly, they depend on what they read in the print media to go out and make a film story about. And that's fine, that's pretty much the way it works nationally as well. It's my view that the reporters who cover this campaign were so fascinated by the pay to play allegations, by the whole notion of pay to play, that they distorted the coverage. That gave Simon material that he put in ads, so that everything that anybody knew about Gray Davis was based on the ads they had seen from Simon. I believe your poll shows—and I know of focus groups and other polling that demonstrates this—most people believe that all politicians play favorites with their campaign contributors. This is a commonly held view. It is not news to the public that if you make big campaign contributions, you get favored treatment. What was lacking in the political coverage of this race was any demonstration that a single campaign contribution that was made to Gray Davis ever led to any particular policy outcome, including the very famous Tosco story that the *San Jose Mercury News* did, which became the anchor for the second part of Simon's campaign. There was never any demonstration that the money that was given ever had any connection to any policy outcome.

Now, I understand why reporters become fascinated, and I see from the standpoint of the other side, if I were Sal Russo, I would be putting that information into reporters' hands every minute I possibly could because it's good to get the reporters writing about that. I feel that where the reporters fell down was there were important policy differences between these candidates that could have been made sexier, that could have been made more interesting, that actually creates controversy and makes good news stories that should have been written about in more detail. For example, did anybody, any newspaper really go after the issue of the energy crisis, Gray Davis's role, and what Bill Simon might have done differently? Was there any really great reporting in that regard? I'm not sure there was. Dan, correct me if I'm wrong.

DAN BORENSTEIN: I think there was some good stuff done.

TROUNSTINE: You think there was some good stuff done. Okay. I don't think I ever saw it on TV. And if you want to affect the public, it's got to make it on television. But I do think that it was reporters' fascination with pay to play that was sort of an intellectual cul-de-sac that they decided to go down, and they got stuck there for a lot of the campaign. And I think that had a detrimental affect on campaign coverage in the press, generally, on television, generally, and then gave Simon material to use, which further drove down public interest in both candidates. For example, some Democrats called Gray Davis money-grubbing and shallow. Now, they may not have really thought that but that is precisely the message that Sal Russo and the Simon campaign wanted to make people believe. And in order to be able to do that, they had to have some news clips that they could use for verification. And those news clips actually never showed a connection between money given and policy outcomes.

I do believe it's a reporter's responsibility to talk about the money interests and the interest groups that are tied to candidates. I think that if, however, you want to take the next step and demonstrate that there is a causal relationship between the money given and some policy outcome, that you can't simply imply that, you have to demonstrate it in print. And I don't believe it was done.

The Pollsters—
Polling in the Governor's Race

Mark Baldassare, Mark DiCamillo, and Susan Pinkus

Introduction

The November 2002 election in California had the lowest voter turnout and the largest number of third-party gubernatorial candidate votes in the state's history. In the governor's election on November 5, Democratic incumbent Gray Davis defeated Republican challenger Bill Simon by a five-point margin. This chapter summarizes the pre-election surveys that were conducted by our three polling organizations prior to the 2002 general election in California—the Field Poll, the *Los Angeles Times* Poll, and the Public Policy Institute of California (PPIC) Statewide Survey. We focus our analysis on the political and economic context of this election, insights from a special survey on public attitudes toward the campaigns that was conducted up to the day before the election, the methodologies used in the pre-election surveys to overcome the challenges in this political environment, and a comparison of pre-election survey results to the *Los Angeles Times* exit poll. Taking into account variations in methods, low voter turnout, third-party voting, and voters' ambivalence toward the major party candidates, the pre-election surveys in the 2002 California governor's election were consistent over time and across polling organizations, and reasonably accurate in predicting the election results.

Polling in the Governor's Race in California

The 2002 governor's race in California can best de described as "the season of voter discontent." Political reformers in the Golden State—and the national pundits who argue that something is wrong with the campaigns and elections in the nation's largest state—turned out to be the most prescient observers of last year's statewide elections. The view that the state's voting process is off-track is bolstered by these facts: Major party candidates for governor spent a record-setting $100 million campaigning in 2002, and yet there was a record-low voter turnout in both the primary and general elections.

If the trends in the 2002 election continue, California voters may be headed for the endangered species list. Twenty years ago, seven in 10 registered voters and half of the eligible adults voted in the 1982 governor's race. This past November, about half of the registered voters and about one in three eligible adults cast their absentee ballots or showed up at the polls on election day. California gained 10 million new residents in the past two decades, but more people voted in 1982 than in 2002. National trends offer no excuses for the state's poor voting performance: California finished close to the bottom of the heap in a fall 50-state comparison of election turnout.

In November 2002, California voters re-elected Democrat Gray Davis to a second term, as he defeated Republican Bill Simon by a 47 to 42 percent margin. Davis's vote total of 3.53 million was 1.33 million less than he received in 1998. Low voter turnout, minor-party voting, and voters skipping the top of the ticket race led to a fairly close election, given the 10-point voter registration edge the Democrats hold over the Republicans, and recent trends in elections for governor and president. The voters' negative reactions to the major party candidates and their political campaigns were significant factors underlying the 2002 vote. The recent California governor's race raises a number of important issues about the current challenges of polling in state elections.

In this chapter, we summarize the methodologies and results of the public opinion surveys conducted by our three polling organizations prior to the 2002 general election in California—the Field Poll, the *Los Angeles Times* Poll, and the Public Policy Institute of California (PPIC) Statewide Survey. We focus most of our attention on the results of the late pre-election surveys released by each of our organizations in October. We also use the findings from a PPIC Statewide Survey funded by the Pew Charitable Trusts, conducted in the final days leading up to the November 5th election and released after the elections, to examine public attitudes toward the campaign practices in this election. Lastly, the *Los Angeles Times* exit poll provides a benchmark for us to compare the results of the pre-election surveys to a random sample of voters who went to the polls.

We begin by describing the context of this election season. We draw upon the pre-election surveys that were conducted in the months leading up to the election, as a way of demonstrating an important trait of the 2002 governor's race—the consistently negative nature of public opinion on election-related issues that was evident both over time and across research organizations. We then contrast the survey methods that were used by the three research organizations. Finally, we compare the pre-election survey results with the *Los Angeles Times* exit poll and actual voting in the governor's race.

The 2002 Context
by Mark Baldassare, Public Policy Institute of California

An important backdrop to the 2002 governor's race is that the overall mood in the state's voters had turned sour. During the 1998 and 2000 elections, we typically found that optimists outnumbered pessimists by at least a two-to-one margin, when we asked questions about the overall direction of the state or California economic conditions. But in the months leading up to the 2002 general election, many likely voters reported that the state was headed in the wrong direction in the PPIC Statewide Surveys (August: 53 percent; September: 43 percent; October: 50 percent) and the *Los Angeles Times* Polls (September: 52 percent; October: 53 percent). The majority of likely voters said the state was in bad economic times in the PPIC Statewide Surveys (August: 53 percent; September: 50 percent; October: 53 percent) and the Field Poll (September: 56 percent). Six in 10 likely voters (62 percent) stated that California as a whole was in an economic recession in a *Los Angeles Times Poll* in September. See Table 1.

Throughout the fall election, the incumbent Democratic governor—who had won by 20 points and 1.6 million votes four years earlier—had low job-approval ratings. A majority of likely voters said that they disapproved of Gray Davis's overall performance as governor in the PPIC Statewide Surveys (August: 52 percent; September: 52 percent; October: 52 percent), and comparable disapproval ratings were found in the *Los Angeles Times* Polls (September: 48 percent; October: 51 percent) and the Field Poll (July: 49 percent; September: 49 percent). By contrast, the approval ratings for President George W. Bush—who lost in California by 13 points and 1.3 million votes in 2000—were consistently in positive territory. While the president's sky-high high-approval ratings after September 11 had declined by the middle of 2002, the majority of likely voters approved of the performance of Bush as president in the PPIC Statewide Surveys (August: 62 percent; September: 62 percent; October: 58 percent), the *Los Angeles Times* Poll (September: 54 percent), and the Field Poll (July: 63 percent; September: 57 percent). See Table 2.

Californians were not all that impressed with the candidate choices in the 2002 governor's race. The majority of likely voters in the PPIC Statewide Surveys in August (54 percent), September (55 percent), October (57 percent), and November (62 percent) said that they were not satisfied with their choices in the gubernatorial election. Importantly, the majority of Democrats, Republicans, and independent voters were not satisfied with the candidate choices. As for the im-

Table 2.1. Overall Mood of Californians

"Do you think that things in California are generally going in the right direction or the wrong direction? (PPIC: likely voters)

	August	September	October
Right direction	37%	48%	40%
Wrong direction	53	43	50
Don't know	10	9	10

"Turning to economic conditions in California, do you think that during the next 12 months we will have good times financially or bad times? (PPIC: likely voters)

	August	September	October
Good times	35%	40%	35%
Bad times	53	50	53
Don't know	12	10	12

"How would you generally describe economic conditions in California now? Would you say that economically California is in good times or bad times right now? (Field: voters)

	September
Good times	20
Bad times	56
In between	21
Don't know	3

"Do you think California's economy is in a recession or not?" (*L.A. Times:* likely voters)

	September
Yes	62%
No	34
Don't know	4

Source: PPIC Statewide Surveys, Field Poll, and *Los Angeles Times* Poll.

Table 2.2. Approval Ratings for the California Governor and the U.S. President

"Overall, do you approve or disapprove of the way that Gray Davis is handling his job as governor of California?"

	PPIC (likely voters)		*L.A. Times* (likely voters)	
	August	September	October	October
Approve	43%	42%	42%	46%
Disapprove	52	52	52	51%
Don't know	5	6	6	3

"Overall, do you approve or disapprove of the way that George W. Bush is handling his job as president of the United States?"

	PPIC (likely voters)		Field (voters)	
	August	September	October	September
Approve	62%	62%	58%	57%
Disapprove	36	36	38	34
Don't know	2	2	8	9

Source: PPIC Statewide Survey, Field Poll, and *Los Angeles Times* Poll.

pressions of the specific candidates, a majority of likely voters gave both Simon and Davis unfavorable ratings in *Los Angeles Times* Polls (Davis: 51 percent, Simon: 51 percent in September; Davis: 56 percent, Simon: 58 percent in October), the Field Poll (Davis: 52 percent, Simon: 50 percent in September), and the PPIC Statewide Survey (Davis: 60 percent, Simon: 54 percent in November). According to the *Los Angeles Times* Poll in October, 56 percent of likely voters said they were planning to vote for their candidate for governor "mostly because he is the best of a bad lot." Similarly, the Field Polls indicated that many of Simon's supporters were voting against Davis rather than for Simon (September: 63 percent; October: 67 percent), and a substantial amount of support for Davis came from voting against Simon rather than voting for the governor (September: 37 percent; October: 32 percent). A September PPIC Statewide Survey perhaps best summed up the voters' opinions about the upcoming fall match up: when asked to think about the governor's election, 55 percent reported that they were less enthusiastic about voting than usual. Significantly, more than half of Democrats (57 percent), Republicans (52 percent), and independent voters (60 percent) were less enthusiastic than usual about voting in the 2002 governor's race. See Table 3.

Table 2.3. Attitudes towards the 2002 California Governor's Race

"Would you say you are satisfied or not satisfied with the choices of candidates for governor on November 5?" (PPIC: likely voters)

	August	September	October	November
Satisfied	38%	38%	38%	35%
Not satisfied	54	55	57	62
Don't know	8	7	5	3

"Thinking about the governor's election that will be held this November, are you more enthusiastic about voting than usual, or less enthusiastic?" (PPIC: likely voters)

	September
More enthusiastic	27%
Less enthusiastic	55
Same (volunteered)	15
Don't know	3

"Are you planning to vote for your candidate for governor mostly because you like him and his policies, or mostly because be is the best of a bad lot?" (*L.A. Times:* likely voters)

	October
Like him and his policies	39%
Best of a bad lot	56
Don't know	5

Source: PPIC Statewide Survey, *Los Angeles Times* Poll.

Californians may have been turned off to the gubernatorial candidates, but they were not tuned out to the campaign news and political commercials. Among the likely voters, we found attention to the 2002 gubernatorial race higher than it was at any time in the 1998 governor's race. In the October PPIC Statewide Survey, 75 percent were very closely or fairly closely following the news about candidates in the election, a similar percentage as in August (74 percent) and September (80 percent). In October 1998, 67 percent reported closely following the election news. While nine in 10 likely voters could identify California issues that they wanted to hear the gubernatorial candidates talk about during the election, two in three likely voters said they were not satisfied with the amount of attention the candidates were paying to the issues of most importance to themselves (August, PPIC Statewide Survey: 64 percent; September, PPIC Statewide Survey: 66 percent).

Voter awareness of political commercials was higher than at any time in the 1998 California elections, and it increased over the course of the gubernatorial campaign. Eighty-one percent of voters say they have seen television advertising by the candidates for governor (in the past month) in the November PPIC State-wide Survey, compared to 68 percent in August, 72 percent in September, and 79 percent in October. The *Los Angeles Times* Poll in September found that 85 percent of likely voters had seen commercials by Simon or Davis or both candidates. By contrast, the PPIC Statewide Survey in October 1998 found 64 percent had seen television advertising by the candidates for governor. See Table 4.

While awareness of political commercials was relatively high, few voters said the television advertisements had made a positive impression. In the PPIC Statewide Surveys in October and November, only about one in 10 likely voters described the Davis and Simon commercials as "very helpful" in deciding which candidate to vote for. Similarly, the *Los Angeles Times* Poll in September found that many voters said the campaign commercials left them with less favorable impressions of both Davis (36 percent) and Simon (47 percent). In the PPIC Statewide Survey in the final week of the governor's race, 58 percent said Davis and Simon should not be critical of one another because their campaigns had gotten too negative. Indeed, negative campaigning by Simon and Davis resulted in more negative impressions of those who were on the attack as well as those who were being attacked. For instance, 51 percent of the likely voters said that the Davis claim that Simon had engaged in fraudulent business practices had left them with a more negative impression of Davis. Moreover, 42 percent of the likely voters said that the Simon claim that Davis makes policy based on the interests of campaign contributors had left them with a more negative impression of Simon.

The context of this election contributed to a defining characteristic of the 2002 governor's race in California: a large number of likely voters in pre-election saying they would not vote for the major party candidates or were un-decided in this race. For instance, in the PPIC Statewide Surveys, large numbers of likely voters were undecided (August: 18 percent; September: 17 percent; October: 17 percent; November: 14 percent). The final Field Poll found one in four voters casting votes for minor party candidates (8 percent), deciding not to vote in the governor's race (3 percent), or undecided (14 percent). The *Los Angeles Times* Polls indicated that two in 10 likely voters would vote for minor party candidates (September: 7 percent; October: 11 percent) or were undecided (September: 13 percent; October: 8 percent). The large numbers of likely voters who were undecided, supporting minor party candidates, and saying they would not vote in the governor's race made it challenging to predict the outcome of the 2002 elections through pre-election surveys, despite the fact that Davis consistently held significant leads of seven to 11 points in all of the PPIC Statewide Surveys, the Field Polls, and the *Los Angeles Times* polls taken before the November 5 election.

Table 2.4. Voters' Attention to Election News and Campaign Advertising

"How closely do you follow the news about candidates for the 2002 governor's election?"

	August	September	October	November
Very/Fairly closely	74%	80%	75%	81%
Not Closely	26	20	25	19

"In the past month, have you seen any television advertisements by the candidates for governor?"

	August	September	October	November
Yes	68%	72%	79%	81%
No	32	28	21	19

So far, have the television advertisements you have seen been very helpful, somewhat helpful, not too helpful, or not at all helpful in deciding which candidate to vote for?"

	October	November
Very helpful	10%	9%
Somewhat helpful	19	18
Not too helpful	25	26
Not at all helpful	46	47

Source: PPIC Statewide Surveys, likely voters.

Pre-Election Survey Methodology
by Mark DiCamillo, The Field Poll

We will now describe the survey methodologies used by The Field Poll, *Los Angeles Times* Poll, and the PPIC Statewide Survey. We begin this comparison by highlighting the fact that each polling organization used similar methods in its 2002 pre-election surveys: that is, each poll was conducted by telephone using random digit dial methodology, the interviews were in English or Spanish, and the surveys were completed during the final four weeks leading up to the November 2002 election. After the data were collected, each of the polling organizations weighted their samples and used screening methods to select large numbers of likely voters—between 818 and 1,025 respondents—for further analysis. In looking at this process, public opinion researchers have an opportunity to examine the variations in methods used by these three polling organizations to deal with many of the practical obstacles associated with polling California voters prior to the 2002 gubernatorial election, such as efforts to reach respondents, the weighting of survey samples, and the selection of likely voters.

One of the first challenges that all pollsters must confront when attempting to conduct pre-election surveys in California by telephone is the unusually large proportion of residents who choose not to list their home telephone number. According to the estimates of Survey Sampling Incorporated, of the nation's 100 largest Standard Metropolitan Areas the top 11 unlisted telephone markets are all located in California. In these 11 markets, which include all of the state's largest metropolitan areas, the average proportion of households that are not currently listed in local telephone directories is 68 percent, more than double the national average. This tends to preclude the possibility of conducting reliable pre-election surveys using registered voter lists, since the proportion of voters systematically excluded from such lists would be large. This is the main reason why each of the three major public polls in California conducted their telephone interviews using a random digit dial sampling methodology, since it avoids altogether the problem of unlisted telephone numbers. See Table 5.

Another characteristic of the California voting population is that a substantial proportion of the state's registered voters do not speak English, with Spanish by far the language most frequently spoken by these non-English speaking voters. In addition, these voters are more likely to vote Democratic, thus, not conducting telephone interviewing in Spanish would tend to underrepresent the Democratic vote. As a result, each of the three polls translated their pre-election questionnaires into Spanish and offered all respondents the option of conducting the survey in either English or Spanish.

Each of the polling organizations carried out its data collection by means of computer-assisted telephone interviewing. Because both The Field Poll and the *Times* Poll have their own data collection and processing facilities and staff, they conducted all interviewing and data processing internally. Because PPIC does not have its own telephone interviewing facilities, the data collection was subcontracted, and the data analysis was conducted internally. For its October 2002 survey, PPIC contracted the telephone interviewing with Discovery Research Group, while the interviewing for its November 2002 survey was completed by Schulman, Ronca & Bucuvalas, Incorporated.

Each of the three polling organizations made repeated attempts to reach a person within each household identified from its RDD samples. The Field Poll and PPIC made up to six attempts (original call and five callbacks) to each household, while the *Times* Poll made four to five attempts to identify households. When encountering answering machines, each of the three polling organizations did not leave a message on an answering machine. This is because a respondent first had to be randomly selected from all those living within the household before the interview could proceed and, therefore, messages could not be left for any one individual within the household.

When encountering households with call blocking (which occurs when the telephone number of the calling party is not detected by the telephone equipment

Table 2.5. Issue #1: Sampling/Interviewing Procedures

Field Poll

- Interviews conducted by telephone using purchased RDD samples (Survey Sampling Inc.)
- English and Spanish interviewing
- Calls made from in-house central location facilities using CATI

Los Angeles Times Poll

- Interviews conducted by telephone using purchased RDD samples (Scientific Telephone Samples)
- English and Spanish interviewing
- Calls made from in-house central location facilities using CATI

PPIC Statewide Survey

- Interviews conducted by telephone using purchased RDD samples (Survey Sampling Inc.)
- English and Spanish interviewing
  Calls made by outside field houses using CATI

of the call recipient), The Field Poll implemented a special callback procedure to attempt to include these households into its sample. This procedure involved calling back these households from telephones not a part of its main phone bank or switchboard, using a separate in-house phone that displayed to the caller that the call originated from Field Research Corporation, enabling it to go through unblocked. The PPIC Statewide Survey and the *Los Angeles Times* Poll did not follow up on blocked telephone numbers.

Once a household spokesperson was reached, PPIC and the *Los Angeles Times* Poll used the "most recent birthday" respondent selection procedure for choosing which adult in the household to attempt to interview. This procedure instructs the interviewer to attempt to interview the adult in the household who has had the most recent birthday. The Field Poll used a different method of selecting who to interview, the "youngest male, oldest female" respondent selection procedure. That procedure directs interviewers to first attempt an interview with the youngest male adult, and if this respondent was not available or no male adults resided there, the oldest female adult was selected.

The Field Poll and the *Los Angeles Times* Poll do not use predictive dialers (i.e., computer-assisted telephone dialing) when placing their calls from their in-house telephone interviewing facilities. The October PPIC Statewide Survey conducted by Discovery Research Group also did not use predictive dialers, while the November PPIC Statewide Survey conducted by Schulman, Ronca & Bucuvalas did so in following the procedures they employ with national surveys. See Table 6.

Another of the challenges facing pre-election pollsters in California is the relatively low proportion of adults in the overall population who are registered to vote. In 2002, just 60 percent of California adults were registered to vote, lower than the levels found in most other states. This is due primarily to two factors. First, according to U.S. Census estimates 16 percent of the adults in California are noncitizens and are therefore ineligible to register. Second, of the adults who are citizens, just 71 percent are currently registered to vote according to the California Secretary of State. The Field Poll and PPIC included two questions to identify citizenship, first asking country of birth and asking each respondent not born in the U.S. whether they were a U.S. citizen. The *L.A. Times* Poll asked respondents the U.S. citizenship question with a single direct question.

When asking whether a respondent was registered to vote, both the Field Poll and the *Times* Poll counted as registered voters only those persons reporting that they were registered to vote at their current address (excluding those registered from a prior address), while PPIC did not include this distinction in its voter registration question. See Table 7.

An important characteristic of California's 2002 gubernatorial election was the extent to which the campaign and choice of candidates at the top of the ticket was seen as unappealing to the voting public. This was one of the reasons why voter turnout fell to a record low in the November 2002 election. Out of 15.3 million registered voters in California, just 7.7 million voted, and fewer than 7.5 million actually cast ballots in the gubernatorial contest. This meant that fewer than half (49 percent) of all registered voters ultimately voted for governor, putting a premium on each poll's ability to winnow down its sample to identify voters it considered most likely to vote in the governor's race.

The Field Poll asked a series of screening questions to adults who stated that they were registered to vote at their current address: (1) whether or not a voter had already voted by means of absentee ballot; (2) if not already voted, certainty of voting; (3) if not already voted, past voting history, with an allowance for first-time voters. In addition, it included a category in its gubernatorial preference question allowing likely voters who did not intend to cast a ballot in the governor's race to be coded separately. Coupled with the poll's voter registration questions, the net effect of these screening questions was to reduce the sample from a total of 1,696 adults initially contacted to a sample of 818 likely voters, or 48 percent of all adults.

To ascertain likely voters in its samples, PPIC followed a procedure based on political science research. They established different thresholds above which registered voters were considered likely voters, focusing on the length of resi-

Table 2.6. Issue #2: Reaching People and Respondent Selection

Field Poll

- 6 call attempts to identified households
- No message left on answering machine
- Youngest male/oldest female respondent selection procedure
- Predictive dialers not used
- Callbacks to households with call blocking using nonswitchboard phones, which display the originating phone number

Los Angeles Times Poll

- 4-5 call attempts to identified households
- No message left on answering machine
- Most recent birthday respondent selection procedure
- Predictive dialers not used

PPIC Statewide Survey

- 6 call attempts to identified households
- No message left on answering machine
- Most recent birthday respondent selection procedure
- Predictive dialers not used in the October survey but used in the November survey

Table 2.7. Issue #3: Identifying Adult Citizens Who Are Registered to Vote

Field Poll

- Country of birth
- If non-U.S., citizenship
- If citizen, voter registration status
- Only those registered at their current address are counted as registered voters

Los Angeles Times Poll

- Citizenship
- If citizen, voter registration status
- Only those registered at their current address are counted as registered voters

PPIC Statewide Survey

- Country of birth
- In non-U.S., citizenship
- Voter registration status

dency at their current address. For short-term residents to be considered likely voters, the level of education and interest in politics had to reach higher thresholds than for long-term residents to be considered likely voters. PPIC included the following five variables in its determination of likely voters: (1) interest in politics, (2) past voting history, (3) attention to the current gubernatorial campaign, (4) length of residency at their current address, and (5) level of education. This method produced a likely voter sample of 1,000 likely voters from among the 2,007 adults interviewed in PPIC's October survey (49 percent), and a sample of 1,025 likely voters from among the 2,106 adults interviewed in the November survey (50 percent).

To identify its likely voters, the *Times* Poll established as its threshold the pre-election estimate of the percentage of registered voters expected to vote in the November 2002 election released by the California Secretary of State. Responses of registered voters to a series of five questions were used to score respondents. These included: (1) voting method—early absentee vs. precinct; (2) certainty of voting; (3) voting intentions; (4) interest in voting; (5) past voting history, with a provision for first-time voters. This method produced a sample of 879 likely voters derived from the *L.A. Times* Poll original sample of 1,895 interviews, or 46 percent of the adults it originally interviewed. See Table 8.

The placement and wording of the gubernatorial preference question in the survey was handled differently by each of the three polling organizations. The Field Poll asked the gubernatorial preference question as its first question after the administration of its voter registration and likelihood of voting screening questions. For PPIC, the gubernatorial choice question was the first question asked in the entire survey. The *L.A. Times* Poll asked the gubernatorial preference question after the administration of its voter registration questions. There were subtle differences in the way each poll worded its gubernatorial preference question. The Field Poll read the names, party affiliations, and the official ballot

Table 2.8. Issue #4: Identifying Likely Voters

Field Poll

- Likely voters identified using the following questions:
  - Early (absentee) voters
  - If have not voted, certainty of voting
  - If have not voted, past voting history, with provision for first-time voters
- 44 percent of adults interviewed were "likely voters" (n = 818)
- Preference question included category for those not intending to vote for governor

Los Angeles Times Poll

- Likely voters identified using the following questions:
  - Early (absentee) voters
  - Certainty of voting
  - Intent to vote
  - Interest in voting
  - Past voting history, with provision for first-time voters
- 46 percent of adults interviewed were "likely voters" (n = 879)

PPIC Statewide Survey

- Likely voters identified using the following questions:
  - Political interest
  - Past voting history
  - Attention to campaign
  - Education
  - Length of current residency
- 50 percent of adults interviewed were "likely voters" (n = 1,000) in October
- 49 percent of adults interviewed were "likely voters" (n = 1,025) in November

titles (exactly as they appear on the ballot) of the two major party candidates, and read a third specified alternative "or a candidate from one of the minor parties." If a minor party preference was given, a follow-up question was asked reading the names, party affiliations, and official ballot titles of the four minor party candidates in random order. Undecided voters were not asked any follow-up "how do you lean" type question. PPIC read the names and party affiliations of five of the six candidates in random order, including those whose party accounted for at least one percent of the state's registered voters, followed by a sixth specified alternative "or someone else." PPIC did not ask a "how do you lean" question of undecided voters. The *L.A. Times* Poll read the names and party affiliations of all six candidates in random order, and then followed the preference question with a "how do you lean" type question among undecided voters. See Table 9.

The procedures used by each poll to fine tune or weight their respective sample estimates varied. The Field Poll applied weights to its sample of registered voters. These weights attempted to bring its registered voter sample into conformity with The Field Poll's internal estimates (updated annually) of the characteristics of California's registered voter population by age, sex, region of state, and party registration. It allocated the likely voter sample to the California Secretary of State's estimate of the share of absentee and precinct voters expected for that election. PPIC applied weights to the overall sample of adults interviewed, bringing the sample into conformity with the 2000 U.S. Census-established estimates of California's adults by age, sex, and region, and chose not to weight the voter sample by party registration because the survey samples were comparable to the party registration figures offered by the California Secretary of State and its internal polling database. The *L.A. Times* Poll applied weights to its adult sample based on census-established estimates of the California adult population for age, sex, race, region, and education, and to its registered voter sample using the official party registration estimates of the California Secretary of State. See Table 10.

These comparisons demonstrate that each of three polling organizations, while using a very similar survey approach and obtaining similar results, differed in many respects with regard to the manner in which each sought to overcome the many practical obstacles associated with pre-election polling in the 2002 gubernatorial election.

Pre-Election Surveys and the Exit Poll
by Susan Pinkus, *The Los Angeles Times* Poll

California was one of the only states that had an exit poll in 2002. This allows us to provide some insights into pre-election polling in California by comparing the results of the Field Poll, the PPIC Statewide Survey, and the *L.A. Times* Poll to the *L.A.Times* exit poll. In general, all three polling organizations did reasonably well in their predictions about the 2002 governor's race. While our final published polls were all higher than the five-point margin of Davis over Simon on November 5, all of our polls had Davis ahead and within the margin of error. Moreover, the timing of the surveys seemed to be an impor-

Table 2.9. Issue #5: Placement and Wording of Voting Preference Question

Field Poll

- 1st question after registration and likely voter screening questions
- Names, parties, and the official ballot titles of two major-party candidates and "a candidate from one of the minor parties." If minor-party preference, names, parties, and official ballot titles of the four minor-party candidates asked in random order
- Leaning question not asked of undecided voters

Los Angeles Times Poll

- 1st question after registration questions
- Names and parties of all six candidates asked in rotated (random) order
- Leaning question was asked of undecided voters

PPIC Statewide Survey

- 1st question in entire survey
- Names and parties of five of the six candidates asked in random order, including parties with at least one percent of the state's registered voters
- Leaning question not asked of undecided voters

Table 2.10. Issue #6: Postsurvey Weighting Procedures

Field Poll

- Registered voters weighted to Field Poll estimates of California's registered voter population
- Weighting variables:
  - Age
  - Sex
  - Region
  - Party registration
  - Absentee vs. precinct voting

Los Angeles Times Poll

• Adults weighted to census estimates of California adults. Registered voters weighted to official party registration estimates of the California Secretary of State
• Weighting variables:
  - Age
  - Sex
  - Race
  - Region
  - Education
  - Party registration

PPIC Statewide Survey

• Adults weighted to census-estimates of California adults. Weighting of registered voters was considered but not used since sample was comparable to official party registration estimates of the California Secretary of State
• Weighting variables:
  - Age
  - Sex
  - Region

tant factor. We can see that the dates of the survey show that the closer one got to the election, the closer the poll results came to the actual vote. Considering the low turnout in this election, and the large numbers of voters eschewing the major party candidates, the consistency and accuracy across the surveys is impressive.

It is interesting to note, that while our organizations arrive at likely voters slightly different from each other, ultimately, we all had similar findings. The PPIC Statewide Survey had Democratic incumbent Gray Davis leading his Republican opponent Bill Simon by 10 points (with field dates of Oct. 7–15), the *Los Angeles Times* Poll had Davis up by 9 points (with field dates of Oct. 22–27), and the Field Poll had Davis leading by 7 points (with field dates of Oct. 25–30). However, PPIC conducted another pre-election poll right up to the night of the election—November 4, which was not made public at that time—and that poll showed the Democratic incumbent Gray Davis beating his Republican rival Bill Simon by 5 points (40 percent–35 percent and 12 percent for third-party candidates). See Table 11.

Of course, voter turnout is crucial in determining who is most likely to vote and which candidate will be elected. Conventional wisdom is that in a lower turnout, Republicans turn out more than Democrats and conversely in a higher

Table 2.11. Pre-Election Surveys and the 2002 California Governor's Election

	PPIC Oct. 7–15	Times Oct. 22–27	Field Oct. 25–30	PPIC Oct. 28–Nov. 4	Actual Nov. 5
G. Davis	41%	45%	41%	40%	47%
W. Simon	31	36	34	35	42
Other	11	11	8	12	11
Don't know	17	8	17	13	--

turnout, there is a larger Democratic electorate. The Democratic and Republican strategists, and the California's Secretary of State, knew that the turnout would be low. No one realized in advance how low it would be. The turnout was the lowest ever recorded in California's history—at around 50 percent of registered voters. At the time, the gubernatorial election in 1998 was the all time lowest turnout at 54 percent of registered voters. Publicly, the California Secretary of State's office gave 54 percent as their predicted turnout for the 2002 election.

As mentioned earlier, with a lower turnout, more Republicans come out to vote and that is what happened in California's gubernatorial election in 2002. The 50 percent turnout was a factor in making this a close election. Davis beat his opponent by five points—47 percent to 42 percent and 11 percent for third-party candidates. According to the Secretary of State—35 percent of voters in California are registered Republicans and in the 2002 election their share of the electorate was 40 percent, according to the *L.A. Times's* exit poll.

The minority electorate—Latinos and African-Americans—was surprisingly low, compared to their share in pre-election polls. For example, in *the L.A. Times* pre-election poll, 17 percent of likely voters were Latinos and 7 percent were black. In the Field Poll, 16 percent of likely voters were Latino and 6 percent African-American—and in the PPIC survey, 13 percent were Latinos and 8 percent were black. According to the *Times* exit poll, 10 percent of the electorate was Latino and 4 percent were African-American. Minority voters overwhelmingly went for the Democrat (65 percent of Latinos, 79 percent of African-Americans, and 54 percent of Asian-Americans voted for Davis). The low turnout among minority voters boosted the white vote back up to what their share of the electorate was in earlier elections when they were the preponderance of voters, thereby causing a closer election. For example, in 1994, 81 percent of the electorate was white, and they voted 61 percent for the Republican incumbent Pete Wilson. In the 2002 election, 76 percent of the electorate was white, and, although they didn't vote overwhelmingly for the Republican Simon, they still voted marginally for Simon (at 46 percent, to 43 percent for Davis). Nearly half of the 2002 white voters were Republican, while 71 percent each of black and Latino voters were Democrats. See Tables 12, 13, and 14.

Table 2.12. Share of the Electorate on Selected Demographics: *L.A. Times* Poll (October 22–27) Compared to *L.A. Times* Exit Poll

	L.A. Times Poll		
	L.A. Times Likely Voters	Exit Poll	% Difference Pre-Elect to Exit
Democrats	45%	46%	-1
Independents	11	10	+1
Republicans	38	40	-2
Other parties	6	4	+2
Liberals	34	35	-1
Middle-of-road	30	30	--
Conservatives	36	35	+1
Men	52	49	+3
Women	48	51	-3
Whites	66	76	-10
Blacks	7	4	+3
Latinos	17	10	+7
Asians/Other	10	10	--

Table 2.13. Share of the Electorate on Selected Demographics: Field Poll (October 25–30) Compared to *L.A. Times* Exit Poll

	Field Poll Likely Voters	*L.A. Times* Exit Poll	% Difference Pre-Elect to Exit
Democrats	46%	46%	--
Independents	10	10	--
Republicans	41	40	+1
Other parties	3	4	-1
Liberals	22	35	-13
Middle-of-road	41	30	+11
Conservatives	37	35	+2
Men	49	49	--
Women	51	51	--
Whites	73	76	-3
Blacks	6	4	+2
Latinos	16	10	+6
Asians/Others	5	10	-5

Table 2.14. Share of the Electorate on Selected Demographics: PPIC Statewide Surveys Compared to L.A. Times Exit Poll

Likely Voters

	PPIC 10/7–15	PPIC* 10/28–11/4	*L.A. Times* Exit Poll	% Difference Pre-Elect to Exit 10/15	11/4
Democrats	46%	41%	46%	--	-5
Independents	3	13	10	+3	+3
Republicans	38	40	40	-2	--
Other parties	3	6	4	-1	+2
Liberals	33	32	35	-2	-3
Middle-of-road	29	29	30	-1	-1
Conservatives	38	39	35	+3	+4
Men	48	49	49	-1	--
Women	52	51	51	+1	--
Whites	73	75	76	-3	-1
Blacks	8	6	4	+4	+2
Latinos	13	12	10	+3	+2
Asians/Others	6	7	10	-4	-3

*This PPIC Statewide Survey on campaign practices was funded by the Pew Charitable Trusts, completed the day before the election and not made public until after the election.

We provide some other data in tables showing a few selected demographic subgroups and how they voted in the governor's race according to the *Los Angeles Times* exit poll, compared to the likely voters in the pre-election polls of each of the polling organizations. The results in these tables demonstrate that accurately predicting the preferences of specific subgroups of likely voters in pre-election polls is no easy task. See Tables 15, 16, 17, and 18.

The low turnout was not surprising given the fact that neither candidate—the incumbent Davis nor his opponent Simon—were liked by majorities of voters. Because of the negative tone of the campaign, and the fact that many voters felt they had no reason for really voting for a major-party candidate, more voters in the 2002 election either stayed home or supported a third-party candidate. Eleven percent of all voters endorsed a third-party candidate, including 23 per

Table 2.15. How Some Demographic Groups Voted in the November Election: *L.A. Times* **Poll (October 22–27) Compared to** *L.A. Times* **Exit Poll**

Vote	Likely Voters			Exit Poll		
	Davis 45%	Simon 36%	Others 11%	Davis 47%	Simon 42%	Others 11%
Democrats	74	10	9	81	10	9
Independents*	45	20	22	35	33	32
Republicans	12	75	5	12	82	6
Liberals	76	8	11	74	10	16
Middle-of-road	46	28	15	52	37	11
Conservatives	15	72	5	15	78	7
Men	42	43	11	42	47	11
Women	49	29	9	52	37	11
Whites	36	44	12	43	46	11
Latinos	57	25	6	65	24	11

*Independents include decline-to-state and third parties.
African-American and Asian sample sizes were too small to break out.

Table 2.16. How Some Demographic Groups Voted in the November Election: Field Poll (October 25–30) Compared to *L.A. Times* Exit Poll

	Likely Voters			Exit Poll		
Vote	Davis 41%	Simon 34%	Others 8%	Davis 7%	Simon 42%	Others 11%
Democrats	72	9	4	81	10	9
Independents*	21	18	27	35	33	32
Republicans	12	69	8	12	82	6
Liberals	68	8	11	74	10	16
Middle-of-road	47	19	11	52	37	11
Conservatives	18	67	4	15	78	7
Men	36	39	11	42	47	11
Women	46	30	6	52	37	11
Whites	35	41	10	43	46	11
Latinos	53	16	4	65	24	11

*Independents include decline-to-state and third parties.
African-American and Asian sample sizes were too small to break out.

Table 2.17. How Some Demographic Groups Voted in the November Election: PPIC Statewide Survey (October 7–15) compared to *L.A. Times* Exit Poll

Vote	Likely Voters			Exit Poll		
	Davis 41%	Simon 31%	Others 10%	Davis 47%	Simon 42%	Others 11%
Democrats	67	9	7	81	10	9
Independents*	38	21	21	35	33	32
Republicans	11	64	7	12	82	6
Liberals	63	10	12	74	10	16
Middle-of-road	47	22	7	52	37	11
Conservatives	18	57	8	15	78	7
Men	41	34	11	42	47	11
Women	42	29	9	52	37	11
Whites	34	36	11	43	46	11
Latinos	58	19	8	65	24	6

*Independents includes decline-to-state and third parties
African-American and Asian sample sizes were too small to break out

Table 2.18. How Some Demographic Groups Voted in the 2002 California's Governor's Race: PPIC Statewide Survey (October 28–November 4) Compared to *L.A. Times* Exit Poll

	Likely Voters			Exit Poll		
Vote	Davis 40%	Simon 35%	Others 2%	Davis 47%	Simon 42%	Others 11%
Democrats	70	7	11	81	10	9
Independents**	29	24	27	35	33	32
Republicans	12	69	6	12	82	6
Liberals	63	10	18	74	10	16
Middle-of-road	48	19	14	52	37	11
Conservatives	15	65	6	15	78	7
Men	37	39	13	42	47	11
Women	42	31	11	52	37	11
Whites	34	40	14	43	46	11
Latinos	55	18	7	65	24	11

This PPIC Statewide Survey on campaign practices was funded by the Pew Charitable Trusts, completed the day before the election and not made public until after the election.
**Independents include decline-to-state and third parties.
African-American and Asian sample sizes were too small to break out.

cent of decline-to-state or independent voters, 15 percent of self-described liberals and 14 percent who live in the San Francisco Bay Area. This is the most votes that third-party candidates have received in a statewide election. In California, the record was previously held by the 1978 governor's election between Jerry Brown and Eville Younger, when 7 percent voted for third-party candidates.

Another challenge for pre-election polling in 2002 was the late decider syndrome. This is the group that makes up their mind at the last minute—either they focus on voting in the election later than others, or they truly can't decide who to vote for, or even deciding whether to vote or not in the upcoming election. In the pre-election polls, there were a large number of undecided voters considering the polls were in the last couple of weeks leading up to the election. In the *L.A. Times* poll, eight percent were undecided and two percent said they wouldn't vote for governor (the *Times* leans the voters while the other two survey groups do not); in the Field poll, 14 percent remained undecided and three percent said they would not cast their ballot for governor; and in the earlier PPIC poll, 18 percent had not made up their mind, and the PPIC poll conducted during the last week of the election through November 4 had 13 percent undecided.

In the *Times* exit poll, 11 percent of election day voters decided on the day of the election who they would cast their ballot for, and among those voters 42 percent supported Davis, 37 percent endorsed Simon, and 21 percent voted for a third-party candidate. Of the seven percent who made up their minds over the weekend before the election, 38 percent supported Davis and 43 percent endorsed Simon, while 19 percent went for a third-party candidate. Clearly, this indicates the benefits of polling right up to election day, and the challenges faced in attempting to predict election outcomes on polling that is completed in the week prior to the election.

Conclusions

California elections now pose a number of serious challenges for pre-election surveys. This includes the standard difficulties in selecting a representative sample of adults, coupled with increasing numbers of non-English speaking residents, and low voter-turnout rates. The past election posed additional challenges because of the voters' negative attitudes toward the major-party candidates and their campaigns. The three polling organizations all begin with the assumption that random-digit-dial telephone samples with English or Spanish interviewing provide the appropriate methodology. They vary somewhat in how they attempt to reach households, ask the vote preference question, screen for register voters, define likely voters, and adjust their survey samples through weighting procedures. Taking into account variations in methods, low voter turnout, third-party voting, and voters' ambivalence toward the major-party candidates, the pre-election surveys in the 2002 California governor's election were consistent over time and across polling organizations, and reasonably accurate in predicting the election results. The importance of exit polls as a tool for assessing the usefulness of methods to overcome the obstacles of pre-election polling is demonstrated by the ability to make comparisons between the pre-election survey samples and results and the exit polls.

References

Baldassare, M. *A California State of Mind*. Berkeley: University of California Press, 2002.

Baldassare, M., B. Cain, and J. Cohen. *California Journal* 34:22–25, 2003.

California Secretary of State. *Statement of the Vote*. November 1982.

————. *Statement of the Vote*. November 1998.

————. *Statement of the Vote*. November 2000.

California Secretary of State. *Statement of the Vote*. November 2002.

Field Institute. "Economic Wellbeing." *California Opinion Index*. September, 2002.

Field Poll, Release #2046. July 11, 2002.

Field Poll, Release #2048. July 14, 2002.

Field Poll, Release #2051. September 5, 2002.

Field Poll, Release #2056. September 12, 2002.

Field Poll, Release #2058. September 17, 2002.

Field Poll, Release #2061, November 1, 2002.

Los Angeles Times Poll. "*Los Angeles Times* Poll Alert." October 1, 2002.

————. "*Los Angeles Times* Poll Alert." October 29, 2002.

————. "*Los Angeles Times* Exit Poll Results." November 7, 2002.

PPIC Statewide Survey. "Californians and their Government." August 2002.

————. "Californians and their Government." September 2002.

————. "Californians and their Government." October 2002.

————. "Special Survey on Campaign Ethics." November 2002.

CHAPTER 3

The Consultants—
Is Politics Being Done in by Spin?

MERVIN FIELD: I've often surmised that as soon as that first democratic election was scheduled in Athens some centuries ago, the Delphic Oracle was besieged by people asking the Oracle to predict how the vote would go. The Oracle's pronouncements were usually pretty clear, but there soon developed many different interpretations of what she was saying. And thus was born the age of political spin.

A typical spin nowadays occurs is when a reliable public poll shows candidate A ahead of candidate B by 10 points. Now, the private pollster for candidate B takes issue with that finding, and says that his candidate is behind by much less than 10 points, close to a statistical tie, and if you really based the finding on committed votes, he is ahead.

Then there is reverse spin. Once again, a reliable public poll documents that candidate A is ahead of candidate B by 10 points or more. But candidate A plays down the spread because he is in the midst of raising money and wants to convince donors that it's going to be a tough race, he'll need all the money he can get, his opponent is surging, and things are very tight. Or he doesn't want his staff and supporters to get overconfident, so he maintains that his own poll shows it's a horse race.

Now, despite the reported differences between public polls and private polls, you rarely see the actual results of a private poll before the election. Public poll data is put on record for anyone to examine and to criticize at the time the report is made. Sometimes, after an election, you may see pre-election private poll data sets, which have been adjusted to reflect actual outcomes.

My first involvement in polling in a political race was more than 60 years ago, and at that time spin pronouncements were somewhat primitive. It went like this: "The pollster interviewed a thousand people and found my rival ahead. He probably just talked to a thousand of my rival's supporters; he didn't talk to any of my supporters." That was the spin at that time.

One rather early crude attempt at spin I experienced occurred in the 1960 governor's race. Earl Warren was running against Jimmy Roosevelt. Our polls were showing Warren ahead of Roosevelt something like 65–35. After publication, I got a call from a reporter who told me the Roosevelt campaign had a poll of their own that showed Roosevelt ahead of Warren by about the same margin. It was a complete reversal of our data. Eventually, I learned that there was a private Roosevelt poll that actually had data close to what we were reporting, but a campaign spokesman for Roosevelt didn't have time to fool around with a lot of explanations, so he simply transposed the pollsters numbers.

Today's spinmeisters are more sophisticated. The spin can consist of several pages of data prepared by a private pollster in an election race based on various assumptions. For example, the assumptions can produce a range from a two-point lead to a 12-point lead for a candidate. The data based on the assumptions that serve the purpose of the private pollster or the campaign is leaked or reported, with the basis for those assumptions not clearly spelled out. Now, some of my best friends are private pollsters. But their job is to put their candidate in the best light possible. This requires them to over-emphasize or underemphasize certain findings, to be very selective in what they report or do not report. If some finding needs to be qualified when reported, the qualification frequently gets lost. And like a lawyer defending a client, the private pollster cannot be as forthcoming with the truth as he might like. This session poses these questions: Was there spin in 2002? Is polling being affected by the spin? And why should we care?

DAN BORENSTEIN: Thank you very much, Merv. Before we go on, let me introduce our panel. We have David Binder, of David Binder & Associates, who qualifies both as a public and a private pollster. Mark DiCamillo is Director of the Field Poll; Susan Pinkus oversees polling for the *Los Angeles Times,* Steve Kinney is a private pollster with Public Opinion Strategies; and Mark Baldassare is director of research and senior fellow at the Public Policy Institute of California.

I want to start by setting up a little bit of what we in the press were seeing as we went through this campaign. We have in the first chart the pre-election numbers from July on through the *L.A. Times* exit poll on election day and the PPIC Poll from November 4.

Table 3.1. A Chronology of Public Poll Results

| Date | 7/2 | 8/21 | 9/3 | 9/21 | 9/29 | 10/15 | 10/27 | 10/30 | 11/4 | EXIT |
Poll	Field	PPIC	Field	PPIC	LAT	PPIC	LAT	Field	PPIC	LAT
Davis	41	41	38	40	45	41	45	41	40	47
Simon	34	30	31	32	35	31	36	34	35	42
Davis - Simon	7	11	7	8	10	10	9	7	5	5
Democrats	44	44	45	45	50	46	46	46	41	46
Republicans	42	39	40	36	37	38	39	41	40	40
Male	47	47	49	48	46	48	52	49	49	49
Female	53	53	51	52	54	52	48	51	51	51
White	75	74	75	73	65	73	66	73	73	76
Latino	14	13	14	14	19	13	17	16	12	10
Universe	LV	LV	LV	LV	LV	LV	LV	LV	LV	
Method	RDD	RDD	RDD	RDD	RDD	RDD	RDD	RDD	RDD	

All respondents are likely voters contacted by random digit dialing. The LAT exit poll involved actual voters.

Table 3.2. A Chronology of Selected Private Polls

Date	8/20	9/20	9/26	10/10	10/17	10/30
Poll	Maslin	Public Opinion	Public Opinion	Public Opinion	Public Opinion	Polling Co.
Davis	48	40	43	40	40	39
Simon	32	35	33	36	32	42
Davis - Simon	16	5	10	4	8	-3

The Polling Co. sampled registered voters. All others sampled likely voters.

Of course, what the journalists always want to know is the horse race. Who is in the lead? All the public polls until the very end show the lead between seven and 11 points. It was pretty consistent. In a moment, we'll compare poll to poll rather than between polls and see that there was even less movement. The final PPIC and *L.A. Times* polls give us numbers that show what the actual margin turned out to be, which was five points.

Table 2 shows some of the private polls that we were being spun with, and some that we weren't being spun with, some that we didn't know about at the time. The first poll is the August 20 Maslin Poll: a 16-point lead for Davis. The Davis campaign was constantly telling the press corps their lead was in double-digits—somewhere between 12 and 18 points. Public Opinion Strategies, Steve Kinney's firm, did the next four polls, most of them for the campaigns. They show Davis ahead by four to 10 points. A couple of days before election day, we got a call from the Simon campaign, and they had great news for us. Their candidate was in the lead. A poll done by the Polling Company showed a three-point Simon lead. We were told that the press corps had it all wrong, that this was the story. I remember that conference call fairly well, because Mark Barabak wanted to know why we were taking time with this in the midst of the rush of the campaign. We were looking at the numbers, and we were looking at the demographic that showed an 80 percent white turnout. It was a very tough screen. Somebody from the Simon campaign might want to talk about what went into that. But what is important is that we were being spun by the Davis campaign and by the Simon campaign. And we were being spun with polls.

What I want to do now is take us through some of the questions and get the panelists to help us understand what was going on. Let me start with Mark DiCamillo. Did the poll numbers change with time?

MARK DiCAMILLO: Well, there were changes in the preliminary stages of the general election campaign in the late spring and early summer, as the voters were learning more about Simon. But one of the remarkable aspects of this campaign was that beginning in late summer and continuing on throughout the fall when the campaign was in full force, and when all the money that we were hearing about in the last session was being spent, all this campaigning, at least according to our polls, didn't appear to have any affect on voter preferences. As Dan showed, we had three polls in this period, and each of them showed the same seven-point margin. And the internals of our polls done at this time were showing the same basic architecture of voter preferences. That is, Simon was getting unwavering support among GOP voters. Very few GOP voters were defecting to Davis; I think we were getting between 10 and 14 percent. On the other hand, very few Democrats were going to Simon. Simon was getting even less support among Democrats. It was anemic, in single digits, between seven and nine points. And looking at the other nonpartisan polls, which I obviously do during the course of the campaign, I didn't see any major changes in their own internal polls. PPIC had a +11 for Davis in August, +8 in September, +10 in October. The *L.A. Times* had it +10 in September.

So internal to each of the polls, each of the credible major public polls, there really wasn't any statistical variation between their polls in the final three months. So the main conclusion I would make in interpreting the polls is that the die was cast very early in the fall. Davis was extremely vulnerable due to his low job-performance ratings and his poor image ratings with the public, but Simon was never really seen by voters outside his party as a credible alternative to Davis.

BORENSTEIN: David Binder, were you watching private polls, and were you doing private polling at the time?

DAVID BINDER: Yes.

BORENSTEIN: Were you seeing the same things Mark saw?

BINDER: Yes. The polls we did were right in line with the public poll numbers.

BORENSTEIN: So you were seeing a pretty consistent 7-10-point lead?

BINDER: We had one poll with a 12-point lead right before Labor Day and then seven in late September/early October.

BORENSTEIN: And whom were you polling for at the time?

BINDER: That was for the State Democratic Party.

BORENSTEIN: And how were they reacting to that?

BINDER: The polls were consistent. What this shows overwhelmingly is that most of the polls show the same thing, with the exception of the Maslin poll of August 20 and the Polling Company poll of October 30, which we can talk about if you like. But all the observers of polls know enough to look at various polls. Nobody is looking at one poll as gospel, they're looking at the range of polls that are coming out, privately and publicly, and trying to make sense out of the range of polling data. And people can sense an outlier, and in these polls nothing looks like one. But if there is an outlier, people know they should reject that or take it with a grain of salt, and look at what the polls taken as a whole are saying. The polls were relatively consistent, and our clients looked at them and interpreted them appropriately.

BORENSTEIN: So would you agree from the private poll perspective that there wasn't a lot of movement; that it was all within this fairly narrow range?

BINDER: I think there was some tightening towards the end, but only slight. The exit poll told me that.

BORENSTEIN: Steve Kinney, four of yours polls that we have up here were between four and 10 points. Can you generally tell us what you were finding?

STEVE KINNEY: Was it a big jump? No, I think you saw five to six points. But what I was seeing was so much disgust in our polling. They didn't like either candidate; they didn't like either campaign. I did see some swing when you got down to five percent; the Democratic white males had moved to Simon a little bit, but not all that much. The thing that Simon was having trouble with was that the Republican working women weren't supporting him. They weren't supporting Davis, but they were going to the third-party candidates. And Simon just never gave people a reason to support him.

BORENSTEIN: And you were telling your campaign that?

KINNEY: Oh, yes, with great regularity.

BORENSTEIN: Okay, let's look at this last PPIC Poll. Mark Baldassare, can you tell us a little bit about what happened in your polling in those final days?

MARK BALDASSARE: Well, first of all, we didn't release it because we were in the field literally up until the day before the election. This is a the poll that we conducted with IGS, and for the sake of our own tracking we thought, "Let's see what happened in that last week of the campaign." We're never in the field the last week of the campaign, so it's kind of interesting.

A couple of things really struck me about that last poll. One thing that really changed very little for us, and I think the Field Poll was within the same circumstance, was the high number of "don't knows," the people who still hadn't decided that last week, and the large number of people who said that they were going to vote for somebody outside of the two major-party candidates. That's not captured in these margins. But from our perspective in terms of predicting what the margin of the election is, how are you going to do it when you have that many "don't knows" and more people saying that they're going to vote for other candidates than we had ever seen before, even in that last week?

The thing that did change that last week and accounted for most of that change in the margin was who the likely voters were. We didn't change our screen of what we defined as a likely voter, but that last week there was an increase in the number of people who said they were Republicans and a decline in the number of people who said that they were Democrats among the likely voters. And that's what accounted for the difference between the 9-11-point margin that we were seeing, and that five-point margin.

Another thing that I thought was really interesting was that at no time in the campaign did you ever see any real movement for or against Davis despite all the money and TV ads.

BORENSTEIN: What caused that narrowing in the last couple days? Was it the ads, was it news events, was it swing voters making up their minds? How do you account for that?

BALDASSARE: What Susan Pinkus found in her exit poll that struck me was the relatively small proportion of voters who were Independents. Those marginal voters dropped out. Some of the Democrats must have really gotten disgusted and dropped out. But there was something going on nationally as well, on election night, however you want to explain it. Somewhere along the line the support groups for George W. Bush that were strong everywhere in the nation and also strong in California I think did help Simon to a small degree.

BORENSTEIN: Susan, when you look at the exit poll now, what happened? Did the low turnout hurt one candidate more than the other?

SUSAN PINKUS: I think it hurt Davis more than it hurt Simon, although the outcome did not change. It still was a five-point lead, and that was what the last pre-election polling was showing. In our pre-election polling there was this static share of vote, between seven and 10 points. But a couple of things happened in this election. As Mark was saying, people were voting the best of a bad lot. We asked, "Was this the best of a bad lot or were you voting for your candidate?" And a huge majority said they were voting for best of a bad lot. They liked Davis more than they liked Simon, but that wasn't saying anything, because they didn't like either candidate.

And everything hinged on who turned out to vote. About 46 percent of the Democrats turned out to vote and 40 percent of the Republicans turned out to vote. That was a much higher group of Republicans turning out to vote than is reflected in the registration in the state. And this was the lowest turnout that we have ever seen in California. It was around 58 percent in 1998. And when I looked at turnout scenarios, I used about a 54/55 percent turnout, thinking that was going to be the turnout. This low turnout produced more white voters than minority voters. And in my pre-election poll, I had more minority voters. I had two-thirds of the electorate white, and they went marginally for Davis. But in the exit poll, they were about three-quarters of the voters, and they went marginally for Simon. So with the depressed share of the minority vote, which was going for Davis, it produced a bigger share of votes for Simon.

BORENSTEIN: Susan, you raised a point that I want to hear the panelists talk about. You talked about turnout. Throughout the campaign, we as journalists were being fed numbers that said this is what our poll results show, but if it's a low turnout model then it's this, and if it's a high turnout model it's this. In preparation for this panel, Mark DiCamillo and I had a discussion about this. I gather there are two schools of thought among you. Some of you do a low turnout and high turnout model. Mark DiCamillo, as I understand it, doesn't do that. And we got inundated with this high turnout/low turnout model stuff. Mark, can you explain what you do, and then could somebody defend the other position?

DiCAMILLO: It is a different conceptual view of how you define likely voters. I don't think we need to get to a point where a pre-election poll has to predict the percentage of the turnout in order to have an accurate likely voter model. It really is irrelevant to me whether it's 55 percent or 45 percent if I get the parameters of the electorate right. So what we're continually looking at and when we're asking our likelihood of voting questions is to eliminate people who are not likely to vote. And we do this in a four- or five-stage process, and we don't give people a weight, which I think some other polls do. I don't know if Susan does, but we literally take people out of the sample if, first of all, they're not a U.S. citizen—we start at that basic level, we pull out about 12 percent of the people that we talk to, before we even ask them if they're registered to vote; we get those people out of there. And then we ask people their registration status, and if they're registered to vote where they currently live.

BORENSTEIN: Okay, who wants to defend the other position?

KINNEY: Well, we use the voter file. We take the voting history: Have they shown up at the polls? Do they have a history of voting? We find that this has been far more accurate, that we do not have to take their word for it as far as their participation. And then, of course, the more times they have voted, if it's two out of four or three out of four or four out of four, then that helps equate to their likelihood of voting.

BORENSTEIN: Susan?

PINKUS: I do it somewhat similar to Mark. We start out with U.S. citizenship because California has a large immigrant population. And we have a very strict voter screen, we use anywhere from six to 10 questions, depending on the election. And especially in California, we try to get the first-time voter in, because he would never get into the past voting history; he would be eliminated automatically. And then we score them. They get a score; it's a likely index score. And depending on how they answer these questions, they fall in or out, depending if it's a low turnout or a high turnout election.

BORENSTEIN: So when we're being told as journalists, "This will be the turnout if there's a high turnout model, this will be the turnout if there's a low turnout model," are we being spun?

DiCAMILLO: I think you would have to have the pollster tell you, "Okay, in a high turnout model, here's the share of the Democrats that are going to turn out, here's the share of Republicans, here's the white share. If those turnouts actually correspond to high and low turnout I would be surprised.

BINDER: I think that's much more the issue than high turnout. High turnout and low turnout do not tell you the whole story, because it's not telling you what the partisan breakout is among the turnout. When you look at the total registered voters in California right now, there's a 9.5 percent gap between Democrats and Republican. When you look at everybody who voted in March 2002 in the primary, there's a one percent gap. The Republicans came out in March, the Democrats stayed home. So the registration advantage doesn't tell you who is going to come out and vote, but that is the most important factor in a pollster's judgment to make a poll. A high turnout . . . there's an old rule of thumb that high turnout means more Democrats. Republicans vote every election; Democrats are more wishy-washy. They come out when they're motivated. And that's oversimplistic. What a pollster needs to do is determine motivation. When you're talking about a high turnout model, you've got to do exactly what Mark said. Does that mean the Democrats are voting in the same proportion as Republicans or more or less?

PINKUS: I agree. When I look at my turnout, that's not the only thing I look at. I want to make sure that my demographics look right. I look at past voting demographics. Polling is an art and a science, so you're not only looking at numbers, but you're looking at the numbers to see if they make sense. And what you see determines what you put in the paper or in your analysis. So I don't think it's just a cut and dry, black and white issue. I think there are many things that you have to look at when you're looking at horse race questions.

BORENSTEIN: Mark Baldassare?

BALDASSARE: I agree that citizenship, registration, and past voting behavior are important. We find this to be particularly important based on the political science literature among more recent voters and more recent residents of California—their level of interest in politics in general, as well as their specific level of interest in the campaign as it's going on. But when I compare or when I talk during the course of an election to journalists who want to compare what we have to others, the first thing that I always say is "Let's take a look at what the Democratic and Republican split is, because that's going to tell us a lot about what the differences in the margin might be between one survey and another."

BORENSTEIN: And Mark does say that to me every time. The two people I talk to at the greatest length are the two Marks. And what both seem to say first is look at the demographic split. And they've trained me to do that.

KINNEY: Besides looking at the party split, you've got to look at the geographical split, because certain parts of the state vote much differently. The Bay Area turns out more; other regions don't turn out as much. A Republican in the Bay Area is far more likely to be a swing voter and not a hard core Republican voter as opposed to other parts of the state. After we determine whom we are going to talk to, we determine what percentage of those people come from different areas of the state, as well as the party break, and you've got control of all of those.

BORENSTEIN: Okay, folks I've asked each of you to take two minutes to answer the key questions. Was there spin in 2003? Why should we care? And are polls being done in by spin? Start with Mark Baldassare.

BALDASSARE: Certainly there's been spin in 2002, and there is in every election, in terms of the campaign saying, "We're better off than what the polls are saying." It might not necessarily be the people who are doing the polling but it might be the campaign spokesperson that says it for one reason or another. Do we care? Well, I think we do to a certain extent, but I have to say this time around I was really impressed. I felt that the journalists on the campaign trail used the information in a very responsible manner, for the large part. They reported what they felt fit with what they knew in terms of public polling. Are polls being done in by it? No, public and private polling are part of the story of a governor's race in California, and they are treated accordingly.

BORENSTEIN: Steve?

KINNEY: Well, as Merv was saying, since the days of the Delphic oracle, as it has been, so it was this year. Do we care? Yes, we do care about the accuracy. It gets frustrating from the pollsters point of view when they take your numbers and put them out there, and then you are the one that's called on to defend them when they don't spin it in an accurate way. The Simon campaign used some of my numbers at one point and said Simon was ahead, and a couple of reporters called me and asked, "Is that accurate?" And I said, "Well, if you believe there is a 23 percent turnout, then, yes, they were accurate."

Are polls being done in by spin? I don't think they're being done in by spin. I think there are a few firms—a couple of them from out of state that I can think of—that create numbers on spin. But I think most good polling firms, both private and public, make a genuine effort because there's got to be decision making based on accurate numbers, not on contrived numbers. And from the pollsters' point of view, we really try to give it accurately. And if a reporter hears that you've done a push poll or has questions, call the pollster and ask them. If the pollster is unwilling to tell you what model they used, what the controls were, what all those things were in the polls, then you should really question it. But most of time the spinning comes from the campaign organization, and only occasionally from the pollsters themselves.

BORENSTEIN: Susan?

PINKUS: There's always spin, and it's not necessarily bad. It depends on how it's presented. There is such a proliferation of polls that one has to be able to discern which are good polls and which are bad polls. Reporters should use polling as one of their tools to report an election; it should not be the only tool they use to analyze an election. If a press release crosses your desk, you shouldn't take it as gospel, you should call the campaign or call whomever sent you the release, and ask for a few things: methodology, sampling size, the dates of the poll, question order, question wording. If they won't give it to you, then I would not report it because you don't know how they are using that result. I would hope that the reporters would not be lazy and use this as their only device for analyzing an election. They should be able to look at the internals of a poll; they should dig deeper and see what's behind the numbers; get quotes or whatever. Do we care? We care only if it's reported inaccurately. And are polls being done in by spin? I don't think so. I think we should just use polling very carefully.

BORENSTEIN: Mark DiCamillo?

DiCAMILLO: On some levels, it's fun when you're a close observer of politics to try to make sense of the spin that comes out of the campaign during an election. My problem with spin is not when campaign spokespersons talk about the events of the campaigns and the battles that are being fought. My problem with campaign spin is when it takes up the topic of who is ahead and by how much, and when these accounts begin to penetrate supposedly objective news reports about the race. An unfortunate trend that's going on in California, as it's going on elsewhere, is that each gubernatorial election cycle is getting less and less free media coverage, especially on TV. And as that news hole shrinks, it's even more critical for whatever little remains of the coverage that voters are given information that's accurate, or at least objectively based. And I can give you examples. There are some polls here that I would consider totally spin. In early July, at the same time that the Field Poll was showing a seven-point Davis lead, there was a poll for the Simon campaign reported on the Hot Line and widely distributed, that showed, lo and behold, Simon was actually ahead by eight points. At the other extreme is the poll in mid August by the governor's pollsters, Fairbank, Maslin, and Maullin, showing a 15-point Davis lead, which none of the public polls were ever showing at that level. And then there's that final poll by the Polling Company, where they suddenly see, 'Oh, no, Simon is ahead by three points,' in the final poll. And the final Field Poll has Davis by seven, and you see the final PPIC Poll coming in with a Davis lead of five at the same time.

I don't have any problem with the way campaigns do their polls and spin information about the campaigns, but I do have a problem when the media treat them on the same plane as nonpartisan polls. And I'm concerned about the extent that the central story line that came from the public polls this year was lost or skewed in the media accounts. That storyline is that voter preferences were remarkable stable in this general election, with voters reluctantly, but not overwhelmingly backing Davis. To the extent that storyline was not getting through, then I think in some ways in some reports the polls were being done in by spin.

BORENSTEIN: Before we go to David, I saw Steve shaking his head. And I want to give you 30 seconds to respond.

KINNEY: The eight-point up was a June poll; it wasn't a July poll. It was before all the stuff came out about Simon and his banking troubles and the other stuff. We did have him up by eight points in June; it was not in July.

BORENSTEIN: David?

BINDER: If the panelists here were a focus group, I'd be very disappointed because there's not a lot of range, not a lot of different opinions here. We're all pretty much in agreement. Yes, there is spin. No, we shouldn't care. No, polls aren't being done in by spin. I think the press is very educated; the public is very educated in how to interpret polls. The private polls that I did were in line with the public polls, and the only time to start asking questions is when they're not. And when they're not, an educated person will look at them and say something is going on there because it is an anomaly, it is an outlier. Educated people can note that and make their own decision when polls are out of whack.

I did a poll back in June for Donna Gerber, Assembly candidate in the 15th Assembly District that showed her down four points on a cold ask, even after positive and negative information. Now, everyone out there will ask, "Well, what was that positive and negative information?' And was it pushed on one side more than the other? But we put out a press release on that and the reason for that spin, if you want to call it that, is to let the people in Sacramento, primarily the lobbyists and the contributors, know that this race appears closer than the registration data would indicate. So that these sorts of press releases, and you can call them spin if you want, they're out there to let people know what is in play and what isn't. Now, the data that we put out in our memo was entirely accurate, there was nothing that was hidden. We put out the question, we put out how we worded it, and we put out the results, and we were open with what our assumptions were regarding who was voting.

So when we do that, I believe that pollsters, private pollsters, and public pollsters, as a function of ethics that we all hold in our profession, are not going to put out false information to get a good spin on it. However, when you do see anomalies, and I think only one of those is a real anomaly, people need to ask questions and dismiss it, or take it with a grain of salt.

BORENSTEIN: We're going to go to Merv to conclude. Merv, take it away.

FIELD: I just want to make a couple points. First, I think the recent election refuted the conventional wisdom that a low turnout is always going to help the Republicans. Before an election when you talk about projected turnout, you say, "It looks like a low turnout. That's going to help the Republicans, isn't it?" Or a high turnout is going to help the Democrats. But here we have the lowest turnout in modern California history, and the Republican candidates were not helped.

Another thing that's booted about in these pre-election polls is the undecided, and I would say there are two factors. If you have an unusually high undecided late in the campaign, double-digit undecided, then that's indicative of the fact that the candidates are not getting the attention of the voters, they're not convincing the voters. But if the undecided is in single digits, that would be normal. And if you wanted to make some projection, more times than not, you're better off to say most of these undecided are not going to vote, or if there are going to vote they're probably going to go the way of decided voters.

Now, systematic public opinion polls have been with us for about 75 years. While polling is going on all the time, there is an increased attention, interest, if not fascination, with those polls that are conducted during election seasons. And while election polls still attempt to fulfill the basic function of any poll, and that's to objectively measure opinions, attitudes, and preferences during a campaign, they have taken on other uses. Candidates and campaign organizations have for some time been using polls for strategic purposes. As we've heard today, some of these purposes beyond providing objective measurements are to mitigate or underscore the effects of a favorable or unfavorable polling result, to use poll results to convince financial backers to provide funds, to strengthen the resolve of campaign staffs and supporters, to undermine opponents' attempts at raising funds and gaining endorsements, to get possible rivals to step aside, and to influence reportage that's being done by the free media. Spin is designed to spread or create confusion among those following or reporting on a campaign as to how voters are reacting.

Now, there are many things wrong with today's political campaigns, and the weaknesses of our political parties, the evils of campaign financing, the growing disengagement of voters in the political process are just some of these problems. I don't know where the increased use of polls and the spinning that results would rank in this mix of problems that we have in the political process, but wherever it ranks, we're all better off if we recognize that poll spinning does exist. In some elections there might be more or less. I think actually in this election, there was less spinning going on because the race was relatively stable. Except for a couple of situations it was a very stable race, and it was difficult for contrary data to create much of a spin.

The National Council of Public Polls and the American Association of Public Opinion Research have a simple list of steps to be taken by reporters or anyone in evaluating the validity and the work of a poll. Anyone presenting a poll report for public consumption is required to do these things. Provide full disclosure, and that means of all the poll results and the methods, include sponsorship, copies of the questionnaire, sample design, sample implementation, tabulating, weighting procedures, and the kinds of screens that are used to get likely voters. Now, if these steps were followed more often, we might see a reduction in the extent and volume of misinformation that exists in the reportage of political campaigns when we encounter political spin.

CHAPTER 4

The Media—
Would Meaningful Debates Make a Difference?

SUSAN RASKY: We're going to start this debate on debates with a presentation by Darshan Goux, a political consultant who worked for seven years in the United States, Australia, and New Zealand before she decided to come in from the cold as one of Bruce Cain's graduate students. She has done some wonderful comparative research about what other states do, so that when we start flinging charges at one other, we will actually have a factual basis to go on.

DARSHAN GOUX: In the 2000 election campaign I moderated most of the focus groups for the Gore presidential campaign. Among the focus groups I moderated were dial groups for both the debate prep and the actual debates, so I'm familiar with how actual voters respond to debates, at least immediately after seeing them. I'm not sure of the long-term effects, but I've seen the immediate effects firsthand. That particular election was an interesting example of how debates may not affect vote choice, but certainly affect the tenor of the campaign—the momentum of the campaign. Things began moving in a pretty positive direction for Gore after the convention in August. He was expected to go into those debates and win. And when he didn't, the tenor of the campaign, at least from the inside, changed quite a bit.

So with that said, I want to tell you how I got started on this research. After what Debra Saunders called in one of her columns a "nondebate" here in California, Bruce asked me to look at the question of debates. I worked with Annabelle Chang and Michelle Lee, who did an incredible job pulling together a lot of the data, to look into what happened in the gubernatorial debates across the country last year, whether California was different from other states, what made debates in some states more effective than others, and whether or not it's possible to develop a law here in California that would compel gubernatorial candidates to debate in a meaningful and substantive manner.

There were 36 races for governor last year. We looked at newspaper coverage of all of the states that had gubernatorial races and tried to determine how many debates were held. So, the numbers that I'm talking about might actually be higher. It's possible that not all the debates that were held were actually covered. Every state had a different number of debates. There were nearly 40 gubernatorial debates in Vermont last year. There were none in the Nevada gubernatorial race. There were two dozen in the Minnesota gubernatorial race. So as you can see, the numbers were all over the place.

We looked at the Cook Political Report ratings from August on the competitiveness of the different races. We found that the number of debates didn't seem to vary much whether it was a very competitive race or not. In races that Cook rated as being a toss-up, you had, on average, about 4.3 debates. We pulled out the Vermont and Minnesota data on this because they were so different than any other states, with 39 and 24 debates, respectively.

The races that the Cook Report called somewhat competitive but not super-competitive had an average of about 4.6 debates. They went from one debate to 12 debates, so it varied quite a bit. And, in the states that were estimated to be solid, not very competitive at all, the number of debates ranged from none in Nevada to nine in Colorado. So competitiveness really didn't seem to have much of an effect on how many debates were held.

I want to talk a little bit about the public demand for debates, and whether there is a demand out there for more debates, at least here in California. The PPIC survey that you heard about earlier was conducted with the Campaign Leadership Committee, and they asked a couple different questions about debate. The first one was: "In this year's election the major candidates for governor held one public debate. Do you think having more debates would have made this campaign better, worse, or would it have made no difference?" And 66 percent of respondents said that the campaign would have been improved if there had been more debates. Looking at some of the cross tabs, 64 percent of Democrats said the campaign would have been better; 68 percent of Republicans thought the campaign would have been better; and 67 percent of Independents thought the campaign would have been improved if there had been more debates. So party doesn't seem to make much difference in people's opinions about the need for debates.

Another question we asked was, "What are the top two ways that you prefer to hear candidates communicate their message to you—through speeches, debates, mailers, radio or TV call-in shows, door-to-door, town hall meetings, or some other way?" Thirty-four percent, more than any of the other options listed, said they would prefer to hear a candidate's message through debate. Thirty-eight percent of registered voters held that opinion. More than three out of 10 respondents in every age group surveyed said they would prefer to hear a candidate's message through debates more than through any other means. Forty percent of men and 32 percent of women prefer to hear about a candidate's message through debates. And, again, party doesn't seem to make much difference—40 percent of Republicans said that they would prefer to learn about candidates through debates; while 34 percent of Democrats and 35 percent of Independents said that's the preferred means. Across all the categories, a plurality of voters would prefer to hear a candidate's message through debates.

One last question had to do with the idea of introducing a law here in California that would compel candidates to debate: "Would you favor or oppose an initiative that requires candidates for governor to participate in a minimum of five prime-time publicly broadcast debates?" Sixty percent favored this idea, 33 percent opposed it, and 6.7 percent said they don't know. Sixty percent is a substantial majority, and it was consistent across all the demographic groups surveyed.

Looking at party ID, respondents who said they were more likely to vote for Simon and respondents who said they were more likely to vote for Davis, all said that they would support such an initiative by 57 percent and 60 percent, respectively. So, there's a lot of support across the spectrum for this idea.

As to whether debates actually make a difference in voters' minds, the research is a bit conflicted. Some of the early research that was done in the 1970s and '80s actually indicated that debates have very little effect on vote choice, but they do tend to reinforce viewers' prior political beliefs. They also show, and I think interestingly for the initiative we're talking about, that independent of other media input, debates lead to information gains about candidates, and to a lesser extent about issues. So, whether or not they affect vote choice, they lead to information gains about candidates and about the issues discussed in the debates. More recent research in West Germany and Canada and Britain has shown that perceptions of who won or lost a debate affected individuals' evaluations of the party leaders who debated, which in turn affected their evaluations of the party and ultimately their vote choice. It's not clear whether that's an impact here or not, the data is a bit confused, but certainly the research agrees that it does affect the information that people have about candidates and issues.

Which brings me to Bruce Cain's idea that there can be some kind of law introduced in California that would compel candidates to engage in political debates. One of the things we're thinking about is not only can you compel candidates to debate, but can you compel them to have meaningful debates? Can you compel them to go off message once in awhile, and directly answer what they've been asked? In doing this research, we reviewed 36 states, and regardless of how many debates they had, whether it was nine or 40, the commentary on the debates was similar. There was a lot of, "It was nothing but a glorified press conference"; "It was nothing but name-calling"; "These are ridiculous, we're not learning anything out of that." But some states seemed to do things that received better reviews. And I want to talk a bit about those, because certainly in thinking about whether there could be a law here that would compel meaningful debates, these are some things that might help make the debates meaningful and not just help make them happen.

Currently, there are two states that we have been able to determine actually do compel candidates to debate, and those are New Jersey and Kentucky. Both of those states base public financing decisions on whether candidates agree to debate or not. If they don't agree to debate, public financing for their campaigns is pulled. That's not something we could think about here, necessarily, but it seems to be working in those states. There's a bill before the Michigan legislature that would enact a similar law.

Multiple Debates

Vermont had 39 debates; Nevada had zero. Oklahoma, Nevada, Maryland, and California were the only states that had fewer than two gubernatorial debates last year; everyone else held at least two debates, and in some cases many more. In Vermont, where they held 39 debates, reporters were saying, "There's nothing new. This is the thirty-ninth time we've heard this." But they also said that by the end of the debates people who were paying attention would have no problem understanding how the candidates differed on issues. So that is certainly one of the benefits that comes out of having multiple debates. Let me talk about some other positive results we found.

Vary the Location

In 2002, gubernatorial debates were held everywhere from high school cafeterias, to Chamber of Commerce meetings, to state fairs, to TV studios, and in South Dakota one of the debates was held at the base of Mount Rushmore. So people have experimented with lots of different locations. What's interesting in reading the commentary about these different locations is that one of the primary objectives, when you have multiple debates, is to keep the audience interested. This also allows and encourages the candidates to go to different parts of the state and to use different formats.

Vary the Ground Rules

The debates that we researched utilized a number of different formats. Some of the debates lasted 30 minutes, some lasted two hours. In Tennessee and Maine, the gubernatorial candidates sometimes got the questions ahead of time. In other places, a panel of journalists asked questions. There was answer and rebuttal time. There were town hall style debates. In one case, the moderator handed each of the candidates 10 one-dollar bills, and asked them to explain how they would break it down in their budget plans. So there are some pretty creative ideas about different formats. There were rapid-fire rounds, where candidates were only allowed to answer yes or no and weren't allowed to explain their answers. A very popular format that seems to be on the rise allows the candidates to ask each other questions. That received varying reviews. Some people thought it was effective, others thought it lowered the level of the conversation.

Varying the kind of moderators and panelists is another way to change the ground rules. Last year, gubernatorial debates were led by journalists in many cases, by students in some cases, and by heads of nonprofit organizations like the NAACP. In Oregon, at least one debate was hosted by a prominent area drag queen, Darcel. So sponsors have tried different ways to get people to watch the debates.

Establish Guidelines for Who Participates

In a number of states, including Massachusetts, Wisconsin, and Alabama, the sponsors of the debates faced lawsuits from minor-party candidates who were excluded from the debates. Generally, they were excluded because of low poll numbers. And none of the cases that we were able to find was successful. But certainly one of the things that would need to be considered in developing any kind of guidelines for debates is clear rules about who is allowed to participate and who is not.

Who was allowed to participate varied by state. Vermont, with its 39 gubernatorial debates, had as many as 10 candidates debate at one time; in Alaska, at one point, the Democratic candidate showed up for her debate to find she was the only candidate there. Her Republican opponent called in and they had a debate by speakerphone. So last year there were anywhere from 10 to two candidates actually involved in a debate. We have heard a lot about debates where there were too many candidates on the stage, and there were very critical reviews of whether that was helpful or not. Our research shows that about 23 percent of the gubernatorial debates in 2002 had three candidates, and about 15 percent of the debates had more than three candidates, the rest, at about 60 percent, had only two major party candidates.

Vary the Audience

The audience make-up seems to have an impact on what topics were covered in a debate and how successful a debate was. For example, the tenor and the subject matter of a debate before a student audience were much different from debates conducted in front of a group of rural voters. Sponsors tend to tailor debates to their specific audiences, and that is another way of keeping the debates varied and of keeping different audiences interested.

Broad and Convenient Distribution

As you know, our debate here in California happened at noon on a weekday. Many people didn't get to see that debate because they were at work. California was not alone in that. Other states had problems making the debates available to the public. The first of the two debates in Texas was inaccessible in many areas of the state unless you had digital cable. Clearly, in thinking about any kind of a law, one would want to make it possible for people who don't have access to things like cable to be able to see debates. With one of the four debates in Ohio, many television stations decided at the last minute not to show the debate, and to air a baseball game. People in the southern part of the state didn't get to see the debate at all, whether they were interested in it or not.

Finally, let me mention briefly the viewership of debates. A study in 2000 by the Committee for the American Electorate found that 63 percent of the 155 gubernatorial, senatorial, and congressional debates that happened in 2000 were never aired to the public. A lot of people don't ever have a chance to see gubernatorial debates. It's hard to judge how meaningful debates are if people can't see them. On the other hand, the preliminary research we just finished, shows that 81 percent of the gubernatorial debates held in 2002 were sponsored, at least in part, by a media outlet, whether it was a television station or a radio station or a newspaper. Media outlets continue to have a lot to do with putting these debates together.

DAVID LESHER: Thank you. My name is David Lesher, and I'm the editor of the *California Journal*. Susan Rasky and I decided going into this that there might be a range of opinions about the role of debates in campaigns. So we decided to adopt a format for this panel that might try to see how much of a range there is. Susan and I are going to take extreme opposite positions on whether debates make a difference or not in campaigns, and see what kind of responses we can get from our panel and from the audience. If we get a consensus I'm going to be disappointed because agreement is a very ugly thing in politics.

I'm going to take the position that debates are the last true and honest part of the campaign still remaining, that they are truly the arena that Teddy Roosevelt talked about, where the candidates are face to face and try and match all the charm and wisdom they have while exposing themselves to whatever we want to throw at them. And without debates we'll lose the last opportunity to avoid a completely scripted campaign where the candidates get to decide what it is that we hear. Susan is going to take the opposite position.

RASKY: I am going to introduce the panel, and then throw it open. Kam Kuwata, veteran of a variety of senate campaigns and staffs beginning with Alan Cranston's staff, Dianne Feinstein's campaigns, most recently the mayoral campaign of James Hahn in L.A. and the antisecession campaign. Mary Hughes heads the firm Staten & Hughes and was the victorious consultant behind Nancy Pelosi's rise to the leadership of the Democrats in the House, and a number of congressional campaigns, including Ellen Tauscher and Anna Eshoo. Debra Saunders is a columnist for the *San Francisco Chronicle*. Bill Whalen is a former speechwriter for Governor Pete Wilson and is now at the Hoover Institute as a research fellow. I'm on the faculty at the Graduate School of Journalism, and once upon a time, practiced real journalism at a legitimate newspaper on the East Coast.

I have the opposite view from Dave. I think debates are boring. I think they're a waste of time. I think it is impossible for any of us to out-finesse the candidate handlers, so I think we should stop trying. I think we have a nostalgic view of debates, and we ought to get over it. And before we turn it over to the panel, I want to stipulate that if in 2006 Arnold Schwarzenegger and Rob Reiner run, that would be a debate worth watching, but most of the rest are not. So Dave, why don't you start.

LESHER: Why don't we see what kind of consensus we have on the panel. Fifty-five percent think debates make a positive difference, so we have a scientific sample here on the panel.

RASKY: Mary, if you think debates make a big difference, why don't we require them, or should we require them?

MARY HUGHES: Well, first of all, let's qualify. Sometimes a debate can make a big difference. The last debate in Massachusetts, according to a lot of people, made a big difference in the outcome of that race. Is that common? No. Is it important? It might be. So the question is, should we have them? Yeah, we should because sometimes they matter a great deal. In races where the outcome is not in question, don't have them. But sometimes they matter. To me, they're like field operations, they take up a lot of time, they're not as expensive, but they're expensive in terms of the time to prepare for them and everybody's time. There's usually much more focus in the media on the negotiations about the debate than the debate. All of that is silly. But field operations get you a percent or two in a close race, so it's basically the same thing. So from an operative standpoint, not a good government standpoint, yeah, I think that's important, and it's an option that I like.

RASKY: Kam, is there any kind of debate you can think of in any kind of campaign you can think of that a political consultant could not game? Is there really such a thing as a straight debate?

KAM KUWATA: I think the bottom line is if you're behind in a campaign, you want to debate. If you're ahead, generally speaking, you don't want a debate. The people who run campaigns, whether it is a citizen question, a journalist question, or an academician question, our responsibility is to try to figure out what is going to take place, and then to make sure we know how to respond to that. So I don't mean to sound full of myself, but we will figure out how to make sure that our candidate has the answer.

Now, what you cannot take into consideration is the lights go on, everyone shuts up, the cameras go, and what comes out of the person's mouth you cannot calculate. Who in 1998 could have predicted that Dan Lungren had such a bad perspiration problem? Garry and I were in the back room watching on TV, and we were nudging each other, "Can you believe that?" None of us could predict that Lungren would develop flop sweat. We were not good enough to do that. But by and large, in terms of questions, you can figure out what's going to be asked.

RASKY: Does that mean you think people voted or didn't vote for Dan Lungren because he sweated?

KUWATA: No, I think in 1998, it was the last chance for Dan Lungren to reverse a losing tide, and because of the work that Gray Davis did in those debates, he closed the door, put the last nail in the coffin on the Lungren campaign.

LESHER: But isn't that the point? That debates do make a difference?

KUWATA: Well, I don't think he had much of a chance, because of the campaign that Gray Davis and Garry South, his manager, ran in the 1998 primary. Now, in 2002, I will be honest, I did not watch the debate, even though it was on my local television station. I read the coverage, but I can't tell you what took place in that debate, other than that Simon disqualified himself because he just could not make the argument. Whatever the hell he was trying to say, I guess he was a liar because it wasn't true. That's what I remember, given the context of everything.

So, if Bruce Cain is going to legislate that candidates have to debate, then please have companion legislation that everybody has to watch it, and news organizations and television stations have to put it on prime time air, so that on Los Angeles TV, we have to watch Gray Davis and Bill Simon debate as much as we have to watch car chases and the new fad diet. If you get that legislation through, I will support legislation to require that all candidates debate. Otherwise, forget it; let's not kid ourselves, because viewing these things is habitual. People watch presidential debates, and they are important, because we see Gore, we see Bush, we make a decision. Everyone watches. Everybody covers it. It gets a huge audience. But other than Phil Trounstine, I'm not sure who watches these damn gubernatorial debates.

RASKY: All right, Debra, as a good libertarian, as well as a conservative. . . .

DEBRA SAUNDERS: Registered Republican.

RASKY: Registered Republican, no less, are you prepared to put up with requiring candidates to debate, requiring news organizations to carry debates in prime time?

SAUNDERS: I want a law that says the *L.A. Times* can't sponsor a debate, because I did not like the choices that the *L.A. Times* made. Of course, I wouldn't support a law, because I don't believe in compelling people to speak, and the voters can let their will be known with candidates who don't debate. Now, if you want to have a law that says that public television has to air a debate, and that there will be long questions, so that there's actually time to make an argument between the people, and if one of the major candidates doesn't show up, the chair is empty, or you can put it on network TV if we fund it by paying for it, because as a Republican I don't believe in taking, yeah, I can go with that, that would be a great bill. But, that's really want you would want to have.

You know what I couldn't stand about the last debate, and many debates, was that they don't even try to persuade you. As penance I went through and looked at the columns I've written on debates this morning, and it was all gimmicks. There was the cop thing that the Simon people did. They weren't even relying on the debate; they were relying on the cop story. Of course, they knew people wouldn't be watching, because it was at lunchtime during the week. I was looking at little things. Tom Campbell, who is such a great guy, when he debated Dianne Feinstein wanted to hit her on her money ties to China. It's a "gotcha" show. I'd go to see a debate of ideas. Of course, then we'd have to have candidates who have ideas. Let's face it, another reason why debates have become as bad as they have is that candidates are really running away from what they believe. I'd like to see a format that makes it hard for them to do that.

KUWATA: When Tom Campbell and Dianne Feinstein debated, Dianne Feinstein was up by 15 points in the polls. I would have said, "Let's forget these debates." She said, "No, I made a promise." We did them. Statewide, public access, prime time San Francisco. He made his charge. He attacked her, and she didn't defend herself probably as well as she could have, and she won the election by 20 points. So, boy, they were meaningful in that election.

SAUNDERS: But didn't Gray Davis benefit in the primary in '98 from the debates? Kam, wouldn't you say that that was a turning point for him?

KUWATA: In a strange way it helped Gray because going into the general election debate, people thought, "Oh my God! Lungren is Steven Douglas and Abraham Lincoln rolled into one."

HUGHES: But isn't that the point? I am involved in a bipartisan group that studies women who run for governor. We've looked at the last three cycles, and one of the interesting comments from focus groups is that they're not watching for substance, they are watching to understand an unscripted human reaction.

These debates are valuable for their substance if there is some, but they are valuable without that. And what is valuable is Dianne may not have defended herself as well as you thought she should, but it was well enough. People need to understand how people are in unscripted moments; they want a peek. This is the only peek they get at who they are. Now, sometimes the structure even prevents that peek. So that's what they're looking for if they're looking. Okay, a lot of them don't watch, but some do, and that's why they're watching.

BILL WHALEN: Let me offer an alternative to what we're talking about here. We're talking about creating a government mandate to force people to debate. Let's think in different terms, such as institutionalizing. Not institutionalizing candidates or political handlers, institutionalizing the debates themselves. What is stopping four TV stations and four California State Universities, one in Fresno, one in Sacramento, one in San Francisco, one in Los Angeles, eight people, four news, four academics, getting into a room and saying, "We will block out the time on the following four Tuesdays in October, we'll create one hour of time, an hour-and-a-half, whatever, and we'll create a format, whatever we choose, half local/half statewide, what have you. We'll announce these; we'll give it a fancy name, build it and see if they come." I have a question for the panel. Has there ever been a race in America where both candidates refused to debate, where nobody wanted to show up for the debate? What I'd be curious about is if you had that situation here in California last time around. Let's say you had four debates institutionalized, would Bill Simon have gone to all four debates? Absolutely, Bill Simon needed as much attention as he could get. The question is would Gray Davis have gone to those four debates? Maybe. Maybe not. It would have been a very difficult decision for him. That's what we're getting at here; it's not so much forcing the candidates to be better, it's finding a way to drag them in. And maybe the best way is to create an institution outside of government.

LESHER: What is stopping that institution? Is it the candidates or the hosts of the institutions?

WHALEN: I think you create it, and you let it go down its own natural path. The media will get behind it right away, all the good government types, the academics will get behind it. Let it go on its own, and you challenge the candidates to go along.

KUWATA: In 1998, we agreed to five debates along the lines of that model. The first one was in San Diego, the second one was in Fresno, the third in Sacramento, the fourth in San Francisco, the fifth was scheduled for Los Angeles. I think by the end of the Fresno debate, anybody who had the coverage said, 'Uncle! We don't want any more.'

WHALEN: I thought the fifth one was cancelled in Los Angeles.

KUWATA: It was cancelled.

WHALEN: Who cancelled it?

KUWATA: I think nobody wanted to do it. I don't think Gray cancelled it. I can't remember exactly what happened, but I don't think he cancelled it. But be that as it may, if there's a need for a debate, there will be a debate, forget your legislation. A candidate and a campaign will agree to a debate if there is a general view of the public to have a debate. So you don't have to institutionalize that.

WHALEN: I think you do. Gray Davis made a very good point in his State of the State speech. He said we have to fix state government so it's no longer at the mercy of a fluctuating economy. I've only been in California since 1994, so I defer to you on most California matters.

KUWATA: What did he say about negative campaigning?

WHALEN: I've been through three gubernatorial cycles now, and what I've seen is that you're completely at the mercy of the candidates. Sean Walsh and I worked together with Pete Wilson in 1994 on his campaign. How many debates were there? One. Gray Davis and Dan Lungren had kind of a harmonic convergence. Why? Because Gray Davis wanted a debate and Dan Lungren was cocky enough to want to sit down with him and debate. What happened this time around? Both parties couldn't agree.

KUWATA: But you don't really hear this great roar from the public that, "We want more debate." If you ask the question in a public opinion survey, "Are you for motherhood or not?" "Well, I'm for motherhood. I'm for motherhood." You would look like an idiot if you said no. I'm the only idiot who said I'm not for debates here on the panel, because you have to be. It's almost like motherhood.

SAUNDERS: But Kam, there was not a demand for debates this year because people didn't want to see Gray Davis or Bill Simon. They didn't like them.

KUWATA: But in terms of information, let's be brutally frank. If you're a voter and you want information, you can get information. Hell, we're in the information age. You have to. . . .

WHALEN: No, no. You're getting filtered information.

KUWATA: Are Barabak's stories filtered, are Borenstein's stories filtered?

LESHER: They're covering today's event.

WHALEN: You don't get honest moments like a debate, to actually look somebody in the eye. Would you rather read something from the Simon campaign and talk about Bill Simon's tax returns, or would you rather look at Bill Simon on TV talking about his tax returns? Big difference.

RASKY: I'm still puzzled by the fact that you folks still think we actually get honest moments in debate. What we get are moments of Dan Lungren sweating, Kathleen Brown announcing to the world that her daughter had been raped, Dianne Feinstein looking at her palm for the answer she had written on it. I don't know, is that what you really want people to judge their candidates on?

WHALEN: That's human nature. Yes, you want to see that.

CHAPTER 5

The Money—
Wealthy Candidates Have Changed the Face of California Politics

Pay-to-Play
by Dan Morain, *The Los Angeles Times*

At first glance, California's first-ever recall of a governor was a historic purging of the political establishment. But its populist roots notwithstanding, the recall ran on the same enriched fuel that drives all campaigns—money. Consuming cash at the rate of a million dollars a day, Governor Gray Davis, the candidates seeking to replace him, the major political parties, and special interest groups waging independent campaigns raised and spent $75 million to $80 million in a campaign that spanned a mere 77 days.

All the major donors chipped in: manufacturers, plaintiffs' lawyers, unions, insurance companies, wealthy political patrons, Indian tribes that own casinos, and many more. But without an infusion of money from a single multimillionaire congressman, the recall likely never would have reached the ballot. Once the recall qualified, candidates got into the race or stayed out depending on their ability to raise money. And as generally happens, the candidate with the most money—Arnold Schwarzenegger—won.

"This is business as usual, as far as I can tell," Democratic campaign consultant Bill Carrick told *The Los Angeles Times* after the election. Added political scientist Gary Jacobson, a campaign finance expert at University of California, San Diego, "You can have a popular revolt—if you can find tens of millions of dollars."

Still, there were differences. Money rarely looms large as a campaign issue with most voters. In Davis's reelection campaign a year earlier, political con-

65

sultants directly involved all but dismissed the impact of money on voter attitudes. But in the recall, political money seemed to sway voters.

Lieutenant Governor Cruz Bustamante, the one prominent Democrat seeking to replace Davis, may have fatally damaged his campaign by trying to evade campaign finance restrictions and taking large sums from Indian tribes that own casinos and unions representing public employees. Although he won handily, Schwarzenegger found himself having to explain his initial declaration that he would raise no money with his subsequent decision to tap an array of donors. And the ghost of Davis's fundraising exploits haunted his efforts to hang onto his seat in the recall.

The recall, historic in itself, was also the first statewide campaign in California governed by contribution restrictions. Proposition 34, a ballot measure drafted by legislators and approved by the state's voters in 2000, barred individual donors from giving more than $21,200 to a single candidate.

But as Californians discovered, campaign finance laws don't stop the flow of money. They simply divert it. Donations of $100,000 and more were common. As moneyed interests showed in the recall, well-heeled donors can simply establish independent committees, which are unfettered by spending limits, and shell out unlimited sums for the candidates of their choice.

"No matter what campaign finance scheme you come up with, money is always going to play a role," said Sacramento lobbyist Scott Lay, who created a Web page to track money raised during the recall. "Moneyed interests will find a way to speak out."

Another political truth made clear by the recall: the national media, campaign finance reform advocates, and academic researchers focus on money spent on presidential and congressional races. The Center for Responsive Politics and other nonprofit groups are devoted to tracking money in federal campaigns. Far less attention is paid to money in state politics. That's lamentable. As it is in Washington, money is at the confluence of state politics and policy.

The Institute on Money in State Politics, based in Helena, Montana, counted $1.54 billion spent on campaigns for governor, lieutenant governor, and legislative candidates in all states in 2002, up from $1.03 billion in 1998. In California, campaigns for legislative seats and statewide offices routinely cost a combined $200 million, or more. Campaign spending topped $500 million in 1998, when Californians elected Davis as governor and decided several high-priced ballot initiatives. Retail politics is a quaint concept in California where well-financed campaigns follow predictable patterns. Candidates spend much of their time raising money, so they can influence 15.4 million registered voters by spending $2 million or so per week on television spots.

The recall seemed different. News organizations—including TV outlets—showed an unusual amount of interest, in part because of Schwarzenegger's celebrity, but also because there had never been a recall of a sitting California governor. Given the media attention being paid to the campaign, some political experts thought there would be relatively little need for fundraising. As it turned out, money was a crucial factor from the beginning.

Political gadfly Ted Costa proposed the recall shortly after Davis won re-election in November 2002, and set about gathering the 900,000 signatures of registered voters required to place it before voters. The effort didn't take off until multimillionaire Representative Darrell Issa (R-Calif.) infused the signature drive with nearly $2 million.

The Issa-backed campaign paid petition circulators up to $1.25 for each signature, and funded a direct mail petition drive. Consultant David Gilliard, who oversaw Issa's petition drive, told a postrecall forum sponsored by the Institute of Governmental Studies at the University of California, Berkeley, that Issa's money helped secure 1.3 million of the 2.1 million signatures gathered in the drive. Costa's forces countered that they were on track to secure the necessary signatures even without the infusion of funding from Issa. That may or may not be so, but it is clear that with Issa's support the measure swept onto the ballot.

And money continued to play a key role as the campaign continued. Despite intense news coverage, the top-tier candidates felt compelled to raise huge sums of money. In the process, Proposition 34's infirmities became all too apparent. In the months leading up to the recall, the California Fair Political Practices Commission, which interprets and enforces campaign finance law, carved some loopholes, and the candidates found others.

The FPPC concluded, for example, that Proposition 34's cap of $21,200 per donor to a single candidate did not apply to the recall target, Davis. In his failed attempt to beat the recall, Davis accepted at least 70 separate donations of more than $21,200 and 46 of $100,000 or more. Another loophole involved loans. Backers of Proposition 34 contended that the measure would remove an advantage enjoyed by wealthy candidates by limiting the amount they could loan themselves to $100,000. In the past, winning candidates paid off their loans by raising money after votes had been cast, allowing them to hide the sources of their funding until after the election.

It quickly became clear that Proposition 34 changed few rules covering loans. As Schwarzenegger showed, candidates can legally take out bank loans, so long as the terms are generally available to the public. The movie star borrowed $4.5 million from City National Bank, at four percent interest. And as many winning candidates have done in the past, Schwarzenegger scheduled fundraisers to retire his campaign debt for after his swearing-in on November 17, 2003.

Schwarzenegger's fundraising prompted other questions. Upon entering the race, he said he would take no campaign contributions. He amended that pledge, saying he wouldn't raise money from "special interests." Then he narrowly defined special interests as public employee unions, single interest trade associations, and Indian tribes that own casinos. As it turned out, Schwarzenegger led all candidates in the money race. In addition to writing himself checks and borrowing $10 million, he raised $11.9 million from outsiders. Much of it came from long-time Republican donors, many of whom have a stake in legislative and administrative decisions. Real estate and development interests also were prominent, accounting for about 14 percent of the $11.9 million he raised.

One policy issue that emerged during the recall campaign involved the vehicle license fee, also called the car tax. Car dealers donated $450,000 to Davis during his first term. In 1999, his first year in office, Davis presided over a car tax cut. In 2003, however, facing a $38 billion budget deficit, Davis restored the fee to 1999 levels. The move would cost motorists $4 billion a year, and raise the price of new and used cars. Schwarzenegger promised to roll back the tax, and car dealers responded by giving Schwarzenegger almost $500,000. But Schwarzenegger's fundraising didn't seem to harm his campaign. No single interest group dominated his donors. Perhaps because of his celebrity and his personal wealth, he gave the appearance that he could not be swayed by donations.

Lieutenant Governor Bustamante, by contrast, drew heavy criticism of his fundraising. In a state that leans heavily Democratic, Bustamante led in early public opinion polls. It was short-lived. Using an aggressive interpretation of Proposition 34, Bustamante took $3.8 million in contributions in excess of the $21,200 cap on individual donations. Ten of the donors gave $100,000 or more. One gave him $1.5 million. Bustamante accepted the money into an old campaign committee that he contended was not covered by the new campaign finance law. As he tried to spend it on his campaign, Bustamante's campaign handlers insisted they were relying on advice given by the Fair Political Practices Commission, although they could not cite specific memos or letters.

Much of the money came from Indian tribes that own casinos. Tribes spent more than $10 million to block Schwarzenegger's election. Four tribes spent upward of $1 million each. One was responsible for giving the $1.5 million to Bustamante. Another tribe spent more than $2 million in an independent effort to boost the candidacy of Schwarzenegger's main Republican rival, Senator Tom McClintock.

The tribes' interest was clear. Under compacts struck during the Davis administration, a single tribe cannot have more than 2,000 slots machines. Several tribes want that cap lifted. McClintock and Bustamante embrace the tribes' right to governor their own affairs and operate their casinos as they see fit.

Bustamante's gambit and the tribes' role in it became subplots in the recall campaign, chronicled by the state's major news organizations. Senator Ross Johnson, a Republican from Irvine who co-authored Proposition 34, helped keep the story alive by suing to prevent Bustamante from using the money. A superior court judge ruled that Bustamante violated the law and ordered him to return the money. Bustamante's decline in the polls was widely attributed to questions about his fundraising.

"This may be something you can get away with when you're running a legislative campaign that is below the radar," Davis's chief strategist, Garry South, said at the IGS postrecall forum. "You can't get away with this kind of scam when you're in the most highly covered race in the history of California."

Schwarzenegger seized the issue, portraying it as a metaphor for what ailed Sacramento. His campaign aired tough ads pointing out that tribes had spent $120 million on politics since 1998, that Sacramento politicians catered to their desires, and that tribes pay no state taxes on their casino winnings. Schwarzenegger called on tribes to pay their "fair share." Many tribes balk at the notion, noting that they are sovereign governments, and that no government entity is forced to pay taxes.

"It was an intensely important issue for Arnold Schwarzenegger," said Don Sipple, the Schwarzenegger consultant who produced the Indian casino ad. "The fact is that the entire political establishment in California has been up to this time addicted to their cash. We found that it was one of the best symbols of what's wrong with the status quo in Sacramento out there."

Enter Gray Davis, the target of it all. In Davis, recall advocates had a prime example of the perils of campaign money. Davis's persistent fundraising was a defining characteristic of his tenure as governor. And, ultimately, it played a role in his downfall. In the heady days after Davis's election victory, Garry South, the architect of the 1998 landslide and Davis's closest political advisor, told reporters that the new governor was determined to raise $50 million during his first term. Davis's bottom line was based on his 1998 primary race against Al Checchi, a free-spending, self-financed multimillionaire, and Jane Harman, a wealthy southern California congressional member.

Convinced his reelection race in 2002 could involve a similarly well-heeled opponent, Davis wanted to be in a position to match the $40 million that Checchi had spent and have a $10 million cushion. As it turned out, South's estimate was short of the mark. In fact, Davis amassed more than $70 million. He raised an average of $1.5 million a month during his first term as governor. In the 2002 election year, he stepped up the pace, harvesting $2.5 million per month or nearly $30 million in all. Davis's ability to raise money was his greatest strength as a candidate. It also was the core of much of the criticism of him during his first term as governor.

In September 2002, for example, as he signed a bill authorizing a statewide vote on a $9.9 billion bond issue to finance a high-speed rail system at a press conference in the California Railroad Museum, Republican operatives were calling Capitol reporters to attack Davis's seemingly endless efforts to raise campaign money. Davis's enemies leaked an e-mail copy of an invitation to a fundraiser hosted by a Davis appointee to the High Speed Rail Commission. In the invitation, the appointee urged that contractors and others who "will build, operate, and maintain the system throughout the nation and especially here in California" attend the $2,000 per couple event, to be held the day after Davis signed the bill.

Stories in major newspapers the following day juxtaposed the bill signing with the fundraiser. Davis reacted by canceling the fundraiser. Undeterred, his Republican challenger, Bill Simon, Jr., traveled to the appointee's Santa Clara home and demanded an investigation. "Sadly," Simon told reporters, "we now have the latest chapter of Governor Davis auctioning off state policy to the highest bidder." Nothing came of Simon's call for an investigation. But the Simon campaign viewed the derailing of the bullet train fundraiser as a victory—one more example of how fundraising and policy intersected during Davis's administration.

Still, there were doubts about the overall importance of Davis's fundraising in the 2002 campaign. Public disgust with California's free-spending politics had led to Proposition 34 and four other campaign finance ballot measures dating back to 1974. But Davis's consultants, as well as those running the campaign of his main foe in 2002, contended that fundraising was at best a second-tier issue. At the January postelection panel analyzing the campaign at IGS, South called the pay-to-play issue "a figment of the press's imagination." It simply did not sway voters, he contended.

"This is a generic issue that applies to every politician, whether you raise one cent or a trillion dollars," South said during the general election panel discussion. "If you're in for a dime in the public mind, you're in for a dollar." South invoked more colorful terms during the campaign: "Telling people that politicians raise money is like telling people that dogs drink out of toilet bowls. I'm sure they're shocked, shocked."

Fundraising would seem to be a tailor-made issue for challengers, particularly those who are self-funded. It is, after all, incumbents who must make decisions that sometimes affect donors. But even within Simon's campaign, there was disagreement over the issue. Consultant Sean Walsh and GOP opposition researchers pressed to make heavier use of the issue. But Sal Russo, who as senior advisor to Simon was in a position to make it a pivotal issue, largely agreed with South's assessment that pay-to-play had little impact on voters.

"I have referred to pay-to-play as the heroin of our campaign," Russo said during the panel at Berkeley. "It felt really good; we got a lot of press coverage; the press was infatuated with it. But it was sort of a dud issue with the public, because the public thinks everybody is a crook in politics. And so it had limited value. It had value, but limited value."

While Russo and South discounted the issue, others saw a downside for Davis who received 1.3 million fewer votes in his 2002 reelection than he received in 1998. Overall, turnout fell by 1.1 million votes, even as the number of registered voters in California increased. Pollster Mark Baldassare of the Public Policy Institute of California believes that while no single pay-to-play story registered a blip in public opinion surveys, the weight of the coverage may have helped depress turn-out. "By the end of the day, people were so disgusted with what they heard that half the registered voters stayed home," Baldassare said.

Fundraising had always been an integral part of Davis's public life. He began his political career as finance chairman for Los Angeles Mayor Tom Bradley and later helped Governor Jerry Brown raise money. First elected to the Assembly in 1982, his district included Beverly Hills, a mother lode for political prospecting and an ideal base of long-term donors. Articles parsing his record during the 1998 gubernatorial campaign hammered on his fundraising.

Once Davis became governor, Davis was part of a daily schedule that included multiple events each week. His efforts to keep his events secret piqued the interest of the press. In short order, stories appeared about his practice of holding small events attended by representatives of specific interests, ranging from health care executives and restaurant owners to car dealers and mobile home park owners.

Davis contended he had no choice but to raise large sums. From the start of his tenure, he anticipated facing a wealthy challenger who would fund his own campaign. Simon is a millionaire, but did not spend as freely as many self-funding candidates. He loaned himself $10 million, and gathered donations for the bulk of the $33.5 million he spent in 2002.

As it turned out, Davis needed virtually every nickel he raised to survive the 2002 campaign. He tapped his war chest to attack Richard Riordan in the Republican primary, knocking out the former Los Angeles mayor and setting up a campaign against Simon, who Davis and his managers perceived as the easiest Republican to beat. In the general, Davis turned his relentless attacks on Simon, airing ads questioning Simon's business acumen and ethics. In 2001 and 2002, Davis spent $47 million on television advertising, according to filings with the secretary of state's office. Davis's final total for the 2002 election year was a record $64.2 million.

The money came at a price. Davis repeatedly faced questions about whether there was a pay-to-play system in his administration where individuals had to make donations to do business with Davis and his aides. Almost from the start of his administration, political foes leveled charges about Davis's fundraising practices. Some lobbyists grumbled that access to Davis came at a price. News accounts reported actions by the administration that closely followed or preceded donations by interests that benefited from the actions. As the campaign turned serious, the focus on his fundraising became ever more pointed. By the time voters went to the polls on November 5, 2002, or avoided them, newspapers had devoted hundreds of column inches to Davis's fundraising.

The *San Jose Mercury* reported that his administration approved a permit that allowed an oil refinery to dump dioxin into San Francisco Bay, after Davis accepted a $70,500 donation from the company. The *San Francisco Chronicle* reported that the Davis campaign had offered students at the University of California, Berkeley, a chance to chat with Davis for a mere $100. The *Sacramento Bee* sought to link hundreds of thousands of dollars in donations from the plumbers' union to an administration decision to delay the use of plastic piping in home construction. The *Los Angeles Times* carried no fewer than 23 articles and columns on Davis's fundraising in 2002.

The *Times* reported a decision by Davis to forgo state regulation of a dietary supplement after a leading supplement manufacturer gave him $150,000. Following a *Chronicle* article reporting that Davis had solicited a donation of $1 million from the California Teachers Association, *The Times* revealed that Davis had asked for the money during a meeting in his Capitol office.

Another report detailed a $251,000 donation from the California Correctional Peace Officers Association (CCPOA) in March, two months after Davis signed legislation implementing a five-year contract that could give prison officers a 37 percent raise. The contract gave the union its long-sought goal: pay parity with the California Highway Patrol and the five major local police agencies, including the Los Angeles, San Diego, San Francisco, and Oakland police departments. As a result, prison officers' pay, which was $54,888 a year in 2002, is expected to rise to as much $73,428 by 2006. The union formally endorsed Davis in August. It donated more than $1.4 million directly and indirectly to him during his first term, making it one of his largest donors.

Underscoring the Simon campaign's ambivalence toward the fundraising issue, the Republicans never made an issue of Davis's relationship with the CCPOA, in part because Simon held out hope for the union's endorsement. Indeed, it is hardly in the Republicans' interest to criticize the union, since they receive the union's money, too. Only one Republican legislator—Senator Tom McClintock of Thousand Oaks—voted against ratifying the CCPOA contract.

Money played a part in articles about the administration's decision in 2001 to award a $95 million software contract to Oracle Corp., a deal that Davis rescinded after an unusually blunt report by the Bureau of State Audits and lengthy legislative oversight hearings during the summer of 2002. In one of the more tantalizing facts to emerge, an Oracle contract lobbyist gave an aide to Davis a $25,000 donation in 2001 shortly after the deal was consummated, with instructions that he pass it on to the governor's reelection committee.

By Davis's standards, a $25,000 check was modest. Still, it was an embarrassment. His critics seized on the donation as evidence that there was a pay-to-play ethos in his administration, and that at least one aide believed that the way to get ahead was to help raise money. Davis fired the aide once the incident became public. Legislative hearings into Oracle raised fewer questions about campaign money and politics than about Davis's management style. No fewer than five of Davis's top aides signed off on the deal, even though most of them testified that they had not vetted it. And while Davis cultivated a reputation as a micro-manager, the governor said he hadn't become aware of the contract until well after it was signed.

Davis's fundraising provided material for much of the 2002 campaign's theater. Campaign workers dressed as cash registers appeared at Davis events. Some carried campaign posters featuring two-headed fish, a reference to *San Jose Mercury* articles about the administration's decision to permit the Tosco refinery to dump toxins into San Francisco Bay.

Money also led to the campaign's most notable pratfall, a misfired allegation that Davis accepted a check on state property. In the early months of 2002, Republicans began quietly suggesting to reporters that Davis may have accepted a donation in the state Capitol, something that would have been illegal. Some urged that reporters ask the governor whether he had done so, although the Republican critics never offered evidence on which to base such a question. I, for one, did not ask it. To have done so would have amounted to shilling for Davis's opposition.

The basis for the suggestion became clear in the one debate between Davis and Simon, when Simon posed the question to Davis. Davis told the statewide television audience that he could recall no such incident. After the debate, the Simon campaign amplified the allegation. The California Organization of Police and Sheriffs, a political group that had switched to Simon in 2002 after having endorsed Davis in 1998, released a photo of Davis taking a check from a COPS executive.

With Simon at their side, COPS representatives claimed the photo had been taken in the lieutenant governor's Capitol office. Reporters hustled to the office and quickly concluded that the photo had not been taken there. Simon, a former assistant U.S. attorney, acknowledged that his staff had not checked out the allegation.

"Whether or not it's the lieutenant governor's office, it may or may not be," Simon told reporters as he back-peddled. "That can be determined. That's not my job to determine that."

While no Capitol reporter posed a question about the photo, there is often a symbiotic relationship between opposition researchers and reporters. Researchers pass along tips, such as the one about the high-speed rail fundraiser. Reporters check them out and sometimes write what they find. Campaigns often complete the circle by using the resulting headlines in television ads.

But opposition research is no substitute for basic journalism. As *The Times'* reporter assigned to cover Davis for most of his first term, I built a database of Davis's donors, categorizing them in a variety of ways. The database, which ultimately grew to almost 12,000 entries, allowed *The Times* to keep a running total of Davis's donations, and track amounts given to him by his various supporters, ranging from billionaire Ron Burkle to unions to corporations such as Citigroup, Worldcom, and Enron.

I used the database to document the amount of money that Davis received from his appointees to boards and commissions. (During his first term, his appointees accounted directly and indirectly for about a fifth of all the money he raised). Other reporters at the paper used it to report stories about Davis's national fundraising and from corporate donors who generally lean toward Republicans. Reports about Davis fundraising may not have affected the outcome of the 2002 election, but based on the outcome of the recall, the governor did pay a price for the money he raised.

After riding high in the polls during the first half of his tenure, the governor emerged from the 2002 election so embattled that he became vulnerable to the first-ever recall of a sitting California governor. At the IGS recall forum, South acknowledged that there had been a cost to all the fundraising: "[Davis] has two ears and two eyes, and knows that he was hurt in the 2002 campaign by the perceptions that he was a nonstop fundraiser."

"The problem," said Democratic consultant Darry Sragow, "is not that people think [Davis] is on the take. Most voters think essentially that most politicians are corrupt. But if they see you out there fighting for them, they forgive. The problem is that this is all they know about him. He never developed political body fat. He never allowed himself to become known to voters."

In the end, some of Davis's biggest donors abandoned him. None was more notable by its absence than the California Correctional Peace Officers Association. In addition to the $1.4 million it gave him during his first term, the union spent $2.3 million to help him win election in 1998. The prison officers' union walked a fine line in the recall. They endorsed Davis, but did not give him any money. Donating to the Davis antirecall effort, Executive Vice-President Lance Corcorcan explained, would only feed the perception that the governor was trading favors for money.

Keeping Up with the Simons, and the Checchis, and the Huffingtons, and . . .

by Karen Getman, IGS Executive-in-Residence

Pausing as he welcomed the audience to the panel discussion on the 2002 primary campaign, moderator Mark Barabak added, "or, as it was known in the Davis Camp, 'How to Bury a Millionaire.'" Indeed, no discussion of the 2002 gubernatorial election and 2003 recall would be complete without a discussion of the millionaire candidate. Whatever one may think of the "pay for play" issue that so dogged the Davis campaign in the 2002 general election, it is clear that a major motivation for that ceaseless fundraising lay in Davis's fear of another brutal campaign against self-funded wealthy candidates with limitless checkbooks. And the irony is he got just that in the recall, and then some.

Garry South, campaign manager for Gray Davis, recently told National Public Radio how Davis's experience with millionaire candidates Jane Harman and Al Checchi in the 1998 gubernatorial primary led him to swear he'd never again let himself be vulnerable to an independently wealthy challenger. South explained: "We adopted the Girl Scout motto 'Be prepared,' and we are lucky that we did, because we needed every dollar that we raised to make this campaign work."

That nagging need to "be prepared" for the omnipresent self-funded multimillionaire opponent has become a critical factor in California gubernatorial and U.S. Senate campaigns. But, as experience has proven, while self-funded multimillionaires may be omnipresent, they are far from omnipotent. California's recent political history is littered with defeated multimillionaires who mistakenly believed their wealth and success in other ventures was adequate preparation for a major election contest. Bill Simon is just the latest addition to a growing pile of defeated wealthy candidates. Yet Arnold Schwarzenegger effectively used his wealth to become the favored replacement candidate in the recall election. What made the difference?

To answer these questions it helps to begin with an earlier election, the Michael Huffington/Dianne Feinstein race for U.S. Senate in 1994. Huffington spent $29 million of his own money trying, and failing, to buy a U.S. Senate seat. At the time, Huffington's $34 million total expenditures was the largest sum ever spent in a Senate race. Gray Davis had opposed Feinstein in the Democratic primary for that U.S. Senate race, and saw up close the effect of Huffington's money.

Surely, however, it was the 1998 gubernatorial primary that changed Davis's campaign tactics for 2002. There, Davis faced ex-Northwest Airlines Corp. executive Al Checchi—among the richest men in America, though largely an unknown figure to California voters. Davis's other opponent in the primary was Jane Harman, wife of electronics magnate Sidney Harman. By the end of the 1998 primary, Davis had raised and spent $9 million, a new record for California primaries. But that figure was dwarfed by the $38 million in personal funds Al Checchi gave to his campaign and the $16 million spent by Jane Harman, 80 percent of which came from her own funds.

Davis spent the next four years preparing for a potential assault by another wealthy opponent. Barabak recalled an off-the-record conversation with Garry South just one week after the 1998 election when South said Davis's goal was to have $50 million to run for reelection—$40 million to match what Checchi had just spent, plus $10 million for insurance. To do that, Davis started fundraising immediately after the election, and kept it up for four solid years.

Bill Jones and later Bill Simon turned that continual fundraising into a major attack on Davis through what became known as the "pay to play" issue. But even while criticizing Davis for his nonstop fundraising, Simon and his campaign handlers were exploiting Davis's paranoia about wealthy candidates and adding to Davis's drive for funds.

It began in late 2001, when Simon officially threw his hat in the ring for governor. His campaign chair John Herrington told *S.F. Chronicle* reporter Carla Marinucci: "We have budgeted $60 million through the general election . . . and we are going to spend $60 million." That was *double* the $30 million Davis had raised to date. Herrington also said that while Simon intended to fundraise from others, "(his) money is always there. That's the difference."

Sal Russo later admitted that Simon never intended to spend more than $5 million of his own money in the primary and another $5 million in the general—precisely what he did wind up loaning his campaign. But at the time, neither Russo nor anyone else from the Simon campaign sought to clarify or modify Herrington's remarks.

Had Davis not experienced the 1998 gubernatorial primary, he might have been more willing to listen to his campaign advisers, who were convinced that Simon would not put in a significant sum of his own money. But by then, Davis's past experiences combined with his cautionary nature to create almost a paranoia. South explains it this way:

"[T]he governor was convinced that Simon had far more in resources than we thought he had available. And he was telling us that on the phone, hollering at us saying 'You guys don't get it. You know the guy is going to dump $10 million, $15 million right off the bat.' And my view from day one was that the guy didn't have that much money to put into this thing. . . . I'd been told by very close sources to Simon clear back in February or March 2001, 'Look, I know his financial situation. He doesn't have $25 to $30 million to put into this race.' But the governor never believed that was the case, and he was arguing clear up until the end that somehow there was going to be this huge, huge dump truck show up, dumping $15 million, $20 million out of Simon's own personal resources at the end to try to take us out."

The paranoia may have been fueled by what was happening elsewhere in the country. In 2001, billionaire Michael Bloomberg spent $72 million of his own money on his successful race for the New York City mayor's office. The money flowed so freely that on December 31, after the election was over but before the swearing-in ceremony, Bloomberg gave his campaign staff $850,000 in bonuses. One year earlier, Jon Corzine, former cochair of Goldman Sachs &

Co., spent $30 million of his own money *just in the primary* in his successful bid for a U.S. Senate seat from New Jersey. At its peak, the Corzine campaign allegedly spent $2 million per week on television ads.

In California, self-made dot.com millionaires were becoming increasingly active in ballot initiative politics, spending unheard of sums to qualify or campaign for initiatives. In the summer of 2000, Tim Draper spent $15 million of his own money on advertisements promoting his voucher initiative and simultaneously attacking Davis on education. Others such as Ron Unz (bilingual education) and Reed Hastings (charter schools) showed the impact one wealthy individual could have on statewide electoral politics.

Millionaire money was coming from outside California, as well. In the summer of 2001, more than a year before the election, two previously unknown groups—American Taxpayers Alliance and Americans for Tax Reform—financed a series of devastating television and radio ads and mailings blasting Davis for failing to stop the energy crisis. Davis's campaign committee brought suit, charging that the real source of the money was wealthy conservatives tied to the Bush White House. The lawsuit failed in the courts, but had its intended effect of putting conservative groups on notice that Davis would not stand by quietly. Nonetheless, South said these experiences led to fears by the Davis camp "that somebody may pop up out of the duck blind, spend $40-50 million and try to take us out."

Adding to the money mix in the 2002 campaign was Richard Riordan, Simon's major primary opponent. Riordan, the mayor of Los Angeles, also was a wealthy man able to self-fund a campaign. (Bill Jones, the third contender for the GOP primary, had little of his own money to put in, and no significant fundraising ability once the White House—still angry over Jones's support of John McCain in the 2000 presidential primary—shut him out of the traditional Republican fundraising base.) According to South, people close to Riordan told the Davis campaign that Riordan had taken out a $10 million line of credit to be used to come after Davis unmercifully on the air should Riordan win the primary. Davis thus had good reason to believe that wealthy individuals could greatly influence the outcome of the 2002 gubernatorial election.

The irony, of course, is that many self-funded candidates have failed miserably in California. Campaign manager Sal Russo said he told Simon, "If he wanted to self-finance then I didn't want to do the campaign, that I didn't think he could be successful. I think it's very difficult to finance your own campaign and be successful."

Why is that? Self-funded candidates have significant advantages. A wealthy political novice can spend the money needed to get name recognition among the voters. He or she can buy credibility among the political establishment by hiring high-paid, veteran consultants. With one check, self-funded candidates can neutralize the incumbent's fundraising advantage. South testified at the trial on Proposition 208 that "in 1996, with all our efforts, [the Davis team] raised about 3.5 million dollars. . . . On the last day of that year, December 31, our opponent [Al Checchi] wrote himself a three million dollar check, which nearly cancelled out all the money we had raised with arduous effort during the entire 1996 calendar year."

Self-funded candidates are not restrained by contribution limits. The U.S. Supreme Court ruled in *Buckley v. Valeo* that the federal Constitution prohibits any limit on the amount candidates can spend of their own funds on their own campaigns. Even in elections where contribution limits are not in effect, the self-funded candidate is able to tell voters that he/she will not be beholden to special interests.

Self-funded candidates do not have to spend time on fundraising. Nor do they have to wait until the money comes in before buying television air time or sending expensive campaign mailers. They can write a check whenever they need, even "loaning" their campaign money while waiting for contributions from others to arrive.

Many of the millionaire candidates' "assets," however, have a negative side in the unique world of politics. Davis's successful campaign slogan from 1998—"experience money can't buy"—reveals a lot about self-funded candidates: they often have no idea how to run a campaign for governor, much less how to run a state, and California voters have historically exhibited a healthy skepticism about candidates who try to buy themselves a major public office.

Novice wealthy candidates do not want to start at the bottom of the political ladder. Like Checchi before him, Simon wanted to start at the top—as governor. Both men wound up learning on the job how to be a candidate, making mistakes at a level where there is virtually no room for error, and where every mistake is exploited fully by the press and one's opponents.

Self-funded, novice candidates come into a race with no grass-roots base—no core group of supporters, built up over many years, who through contributions or other ground-level activity demonstrate their loyalty and work to get out the vote for the candidate. Because they are self-funded, wealthy candidates often have a hard time convincing others to contribute to their campaigns. After the 1998 primary, Harman campaign manager Bill Carrick complained that "one of the hazards of being a self-financed campaign is nobody wants to give you any money."

Millionaire candidates often are at the pinnacle of their profession, used to having others bend to their will. They react badly to the California political press corps, which shows no mercy in its questioning and little of the deferential respect such candidates are used to in their business lives. They also are notoriously bad at taking direction from campaign professionals, instead insisting on keeping their own counsel.

As a novice candidate, Simon made mistakes that were legendary—with the press, with his own advisors, with his fundraising. With respect to the press, for instance, Sean Walsh could only offer inexperience as an explanation for Simon's astonishingly bad performance: "We're all around the press all the time. . . . He'd never done this before."

Riordan was more of a threat than Simon, in the eyes of the Davis campaign, not just because of his more moderate positions, but because he was a wealthy candidate *with political experience*. Riordan had money, but he also had other important pluses that Simon did not—a strong fundraising base in the Westside of L.A., support from the White House, and experience in politics. It was for these reasons, South explained, "that we could not allow [Riordan] to come out of the primary unscathed with a lead on us, which we thought and the governor thought would unleash more money than God has on us. If he pumped in his own dough, which we knew he was preparing to do, and if the national Republican forces thought they had the best candidate, they would turn the spigots on for him."

Although Simon was able to defeat Riordan in the primary, his mistakes as a novice campaigner proved fatal in the general election. Ironically, one of Simon's biggest mistakes was in underestimating the amount of his own money that would be needed for a successful campaign. He loaned his committee only $5 million in the primary and a similar amount in the general, meaning he needed to raise an enormous sum from outside contributors in just the few short months between those two elections. Moreover, he was spending an inordinate amount on campaign staff and consultants, leading to even more budget pressures.

As of the June 30 campaign disclosure deadline, Simon had only 1/6 the cash on hand as Davis ($5 million compared with $30 million). By mid-August Simon, plagued by funding problems, fired more than 30 of his 70 campaign staffers. By the end of the campaign, Davis had grossly outspent Simon on paid media, including $48 million on television in the five biggest media markets. Simon consultant Rob Lapsley conceded that the campaign needed to have spent another $10 - $20 million to be effective in the L.A. media market alone.

South's view is that Simon failed not because he was a self-funded candidate, but because he was an *unfunded* candidate. South explained it this way:

> If Bill Simon, in his own mind and in his own meetings with his accountants, could not come up with $25 . . . to $30 million of his own dollars that he had to put in this . . . he was a fool to run. . . . [F]or somebody to come into this thinking that . . . having never run before, having never raised a dime, with no donor base, no existing contact network out there, to think you could raise what it takes to be competitive at a governor's race, is foolhardy, pure and simple. . . . [I]t's one thing to say, "Well, you know, self-funded campaigns don't work." But what about unfunded campaigns? They don't work either.

Ironies abound in the 2002 gubernatorial campaign. Davis thought he would be safe raising $50 million; in fact, he spent nearly $78 million on his reelection campaign, leaving precious little to ward off the impending recall. Simon, whose personal wealth so frightened Davis, spent less than half that—$36 million—on his own campaign, including only $10 million of his own wealth.

Did Davis, worried by the specter of wealthy candidates and wealthy special interest groups, overreact? He won by only five points against a woefully weak opponent, a spread that reflected a growing disaffection among voters. Davis used his overwhelming financial advantage to fund a flood of negative ads in a bruising campaign that produced the lowest turnout in California history, and fed a voter revolt that led to the first recall election for governor in the history of California.

Adding to the irony, the recall itself was funded by a millionaire candidate. Darrell Issa, who made his fortune on car alarms, had come out of political nowhere in 1994 by putting up $10.2 million of his own money in a failed bid for U.S. Senate (he lost in the primary to Michael Huffington). He later won a seat representing the 49th Congressional District in the U.S. House of Representatives. Issa used $2 million of his own money to fund the recall petition drive, hoping to succeed Davis himself.

The field of potential Republican replacement candidates was dominated by wealthy men—Issa, Arnold Schwarzenegger, Bill Simon, Dick Riordan, Peter Ueberroth. Of the group only Schwarzenegger followed through and completed the race. Along the way, however, California gubernatorial politics experienced another first. Approximately $82 million was spent by all candidates and recall committees on the 75-day race, almost as much as was spent on the 2002 elections. This time, however, the biggest single interest group among contributors was *wealthy candidates*. Associated Press reporter Don Thompson calculated a staggering $15.1 million in contributions or loans from Schwarzenegger ($10 million), Issa ($2.3 million), Ueberroth ($1.8 million), and replacement candidate Garret Gruener, creator of "Ask Jeeves" ($1 million). Wealthy candidates spent more on the race than did Indian tribes, labor unions, and trial lawyers.

Schwarzenegger shared many of the negative traits of previous wealthy candidates—including a lack of experience and a reputation for making his own decisions. He assembled an impressive campaign team of veteran consultants, but within weeks newspaper reports were sounding remarkably reminiscent of the Checchi campaign. There was talk of the Schwarzenegger campaign's free-spending ways (private jets, an army of handsomely paid campaign aides, round-the-clock television ads) and "a bureaucratic organization, riven with disputes and slow to make strategic decisions."

But this election, and this wealthy candidate, were different. Schwarzenegger may not have had prior political experience, but his background in self-promotion and film gave him a media savvy that few candidates can rival. His wife, Maria Shriver, herself a veteran campaigner, proved a tremendous asset, especially when the groping charges emerged. Schwarzenegger's status as a movie star brought more than just instant name recognition—it gave him a Teflon coating. Voters, awed by his mere presence in the race, seemed more willing to accept his flaws. He was able to use the nationwide entertainment media to bypass the harsher treatment given him by California political reporters. No mere mortal of a wealthy candidate would have dared refuse to appear in televised debates save for a single scripted event, choosing instead an Oprah appearance. Schwarzenegger's supporters barely batted an eye.

Moreover, although Schwarzenegger poured enormous sums of money into his own campaign, he was not self-funded. Despite declaring on August 6, as he entered the race, "I don't need to take money from anybody," Schwarzenegger in fact accepted a lot of money from a lot of special interest groups—$9.2 million, mostly from businesses and individuals in the real estate, financial services, and transportation industries. His campaign lawyer, Tom Hiltachk, later admitted that the Schwarzenegger campaign "always anticipated raising funds, from day one."

Perhaps most importantly, Schwarzenegger had the advantage of the truncated election schedule. Virtually all wealthy candidates manage to survive and even do well for some period of time after they enter the race. The voters initially are drawn to the magnetism of the self-made man or woman, and like the notion that their candidate won't be susceptible to special interests. It all falls apart, however, as the campaign wears on and the candidate's flaws are exposed to the media glare. Not so in the recall—from his entry to the race on August 6 to the election on October 7, Schwarzenegger had to make it through only 62 days of campaigning. While the media glare was brighter in the recall than during any ordinary gubernatorial election, it was no brighter than a movie premiere, and lasted only slightly longer than a movie promotion schedule.

Schwarzenegger was the right man, at the right time, for reasons that are explored in depth elsewhere in this volume. It thus may be that his election does nothing to break the long-term jinx of the millionaire gubernatorial candidate.

Looking back after the 2002 election, Davis media consultant David Doak said "I think you've got a system designed now where only rich people can play. I don't think average politicians can run in this state anymore." That is an exaggeration—Gray Davis, Bill Lockyer and Cruz Bustamante are not wealthy yet worked their way to the top of elected state government. Nonetheless, one cannot dispute that the wealthy candidate has forever changed the face of politics in California.

II. The 2002 Primary Campaign

CHAPTER 6

The Primary Campaign—
The Unmaking of Richard Riordan

Introduction
by Mark Z. Barabak, *The Los Angeles Times*

When all was said and $130 million was spent, the most important expenditure in the 2002 race for California governor may have been a relative pittance: $10,000.

The March primary was the sort of political contest that lends itself to only-in-California superlatives. There was an astonishing 60-point collapse in the polls by Richard Riordan, the Republican frontrunner. And an unprecedented $10 million ad blitz that incumbent Democrat Gray Davis launched in the *other* party's nominating fight, allowing him to effectively pick his preferred November opponent.

But in the end it may have been a combination of thrift and arrogance that proved Riordan's undoing—and allowed the untested Bill Simon to emerge as the GOP nominee in his first try for public office.

The $10,000 paid for a videotape of a 1991 Beverly Hills public-access cable program in which Riordan, a devout Catholic, equated abortion with murder. To his great misfortune, the purchaser was Garry South, the hammer-wielding mastermind of the Davis reelection campaign.

In 1993, South was working for Riordan's opponent in the race for Los Angeles mayor, City Councilman Michael Woo. Tipped to Riordan's interview, South obtained a copy of the show along with the broadcast rights. Riordan, a Los Angeles businessman and philanthropist, easily won the mayoral contest;

the video made scarcely a ripple when it briefly surfaced in a Woo television spot.

But South held onto the tape—and a grudge along with it—for nearly a decade. And when a snippet showed up in January 2002 in a Davis TV ad in the governor's race, the effect was devastating. Over time, Riordan had changed his public stance on abortion, campaigning for governor as a "pro-choice" moderate. The advertisement, featuring the abortion-is-murder line, not only raised doubts about his stand on abortion, but also called into question his character and consistency. The result, as one Davis aide later put it, "was a killer." Riordan strategists glumly agreed.

The effect might have been mitigated if Riordan's campaign team had seen the attack coming. While the millionaire candidate lavished generous salaries on a few favored aides and spent $6 million on his own TV spots, fairly modest expenditures—like a few thousand dollars for background research—were nixed as unnecessary. Riordan and most of his advisers were convinced the primary was superfluous and the real race was against Davis.

The nature of their folly was demonstrated by the breadth of Riordan's political collapse: a lead of as much as 40 points in the polls evaporated and he ended up losing to the neophyte Simon by a crushing 18 points. (A third Republican candidate, Secretary of State Bill Jones, was essentially out of the running before the race even began, a victim of ill will from George W. Bush's White House.)

Davis's strategy was as ruthless as it was successful. Aides knew that it would be next to impossible to sell the unpopular incumbent in any sort of positive fashion. So they scarcely tried. "We don't have to make Gray Davis into the sweetheart of the rodeo," South explained at one point. "Gray Davis is not going to be judged against himself. He will be judged against his opponent."

And so the mud flew.

Four years earlier, Davis had romped to election in a 20-point landslide over Attorney General Dan Lungren, another hapless GOP opponent. The Democrat was a reasonably popular governor during the first 18 months of his term, thanks to a roaring economy fueled by the dot-com surge. But his political fortunes sank about the same time the economy tanked.

Confronted with an electricity crisis, Davis dithered to a point where the state experienced its first mandatory blackouts since World War II. The energy market eventually stabilized, thanks in part to reluctant federal intervention and a series of long-term contracts negotiated by the Davis administration. By then, however, the political damage was done.

In Washington, White House strategists were searching for a credible Republican to face Davis and, under blue skies, win the statehouse and give Bush a toehold in California's inhospitable terrain. Jones might have been the logical choice, given the GOP's traditionally hierarchical nature. He was the lone statewide Republican officeholder and had the plain-vanilla personality that Californians seem to prefer in their chief executives. But in 2000, he made the politically fatal miscalculation of switching his support from Bush to Arizona Sen. John McCain in the Republican presidential primaries. Bush neither forgave nor forgot, and Jones's campaign was effectively over before it ever started. "There is no way to get past the White House when they send the message to the core donor community that Bill Jones is not the guy," campaign strategist Rob Lapsley lamented afterward.

Casting about, the White House turned to Riordan, an affable, largely non-ideological Republican (one chum was President Clinton) who was leaving the mayor's office on a tide of good will after two fairly successful terms. For many, Riordan's moderate stance on social issues and appeal to women and Latinos in Los Angeles promised an opportunity to remake the sputtering California GOP. Republicans were "looking for something different and someone they thought was a winner," said Kevin Spillane, who coordinated the draft-Riordan movement that helped coax him into the race.

Encouraged by those come-ons, Riordan embarked on a summer 2001 tour of California, to get a sense of the issues he might face as chief executive. There were early signs of trouble. At one stop, in Lodi, Riordan said he knew agriculture (the state's No. 1 industry) was important, but not much else. Still, things went well enough that the former mayor decided to run. And he started campaigning against Davis from the start; oddly, he never even used the word "Republican" during his announcement swing until someone brought it up the second day.

There were other problems. As mayor of Los Angeles, most of Riordan's trusted advisors were Democrats, who declined to follow him into the governor's race. The result was a revolving team of strategists, many of whom quit after Riordan ignored their entreaties to run a more disciplined campaign. Events like a gay rights breakfast and a testimonial dinner for Oakland Rep. Barbara Lee—the lone congressional dissenter against the use of force after Sept. 11, 2001—were placed on Riordan's schedule by young staffers who failed to appreciate the message his presence sent to conservatives.

In the end, the disastrous Riordan campaign boiled down to a single essential failing: a candidate and campaign that took the primary for granted and looked too far ahead to a general election that, as hubris had it, never materialized.

Simon, in contrast, ran a campaign marked until the very end by tentativeness and uncertainty. The candidate, who headed the West Coast office of his family investment firm, had only lived in California for 12 years. He was a political unknown, even though his namesake father has served in the Nixon and Ford administrations. It was the approach of the younger Simon's 50th birthday, and frustration over the state of Los Angeles's public schools, traffic, and other quality-of-life issues, that spurred his entry into politics. (He was also nudged by Riordan, a friend and fellow parishioner at Saint Monica's Catholic Church in Santa Monica who, at that point, had no plans beyond his impending retirement from City Hall.)

In late 2000, Simon happened to meet GOP strategist Ron Rogers at a social event in Los Angeles. Rogers saw Simon as a potential backer for a reapportionment measure he hoped to put on the state ballot. Once they started talking,

Simon dropped "a bombshell," as Rogers later recalled. "What do you think about the possibility of my running for governor?" Simon asked.

A few days later, Simon flew to Sacramento to meet again with Rogers and his partner, Sal Russo. After a daylong session that continued through dinner, Simon was ready to run. He proceeded cautiously, however. He revealed his interest in the governor's race in February 2001, but told reporters there would be no final decision until he completed a lengthy testing of the proverbial waters. "There were lots of different points in the first six months when we would say, 'Does it make sense to consider another office?,'" Simon conceded a day after his surprise primary win.

Simon began traveling the state, speaking wherever a handful of Republicans gathered. He flew to Washington to meet with the state's GOP congressional delegation; most were unimpressed.

By then, Riordan was looming large, having hinted at possibly making a gubernatorial run of his own. On a Sunday in midsummer 2001, Simon and Russo went to visit Riordan at his Brentwood home. Far from discouraging Simon, Riordan encouraged him to "keep going." "We walked out of there convinced he wasn't running," said Russo.

So Simon continued his travels, slowing building his support at the Republican grass roots. He outlined plans—albeit vague—to address the state's energy problems, water and transportation headaches, called for tax cuts and touted himself as "the candidate of ideas." By the fall, he was in the race to stay. He husbanded his considerable personal resources, however, waiting until January 2002 to finally take to the television airwaves. His first spot featured a testimonial from former New York City Mayor Rudolph Giuliani, his old boss in the U.S. attorney's office in New York. Simon happened to be breakfasting in New York City with the mayor when Giuliani learned of the Sept. 11 attack. The embrace by one of the heroes of that horrifying day gave an enormous lift to Simon's rookie campaign.

He also got a lot of help from another, less likely source. In short order, Davis unleashed his own advertising campaign, a relentless television pounding of Riordan. The governor and his strategists never expected to knock the GOP front-runner out of the race; at least not until the very end. The idea was to bloody Riordan a bit, to prevent him from building momentum into the fall campaign. "I still believe, given the fact that Riordan didn't hold up very well over a four-month primary, that we would have beat him in a general election," South said after the fact. "But with him as a nominee . . . it would have complicated our lives."

Davis first spot attacked the avowedly pro-choice Republican by citing his past support of anti-abortion candidates and causes. Riordan responded with a generic ad, filmed weeks earlier, in which he tut-tutted over Davis's harsh tone but crucially never challenged the truthfulness of the governor's claims. It was a gamble: Riordan strategists wagered that in a post-Sept. 11 environment, voters would have little tolerance for the sort of negative campaign Davis was waging. They were wrong. When Davis aired his second attack ad—featuring the "abortion is murder" line—Riordan went into free fall, handing Simon the strategic opportunity he needed. As Riordan's poll numbers dipped, his wealthy rival finally began pouring millions of dollars into his own ad campaign, which boosted Simon's stock as Riordan's continued to plummet.

A turning point came at the state Republican Party convention in February. Gathered for three days in San Jose were 1,000 of the party's most fervent followers. A straw poll was held as a way to draw notice and raise money for the party. The Riordan campaign, fearing embarrassment, worked behind the scenes to kill the popularity contest. When that failed, Riordan announced a boycott. Simon, by contrast, devoted exhaustive time and resources and won the straw poll—and, even more importantly, the favorable press notice that followed.

For Riordan, a bad convention turned worse when he insulted former Republican Gov. George Deukmejian, who had shown up to lend his support to Jones. Hundreds of delegates gasped during a candidates' forum when Riordan dismissed the ex-governor, seated just a few feet away, as small and petulant. (In perhaps the most brazen move of the campaign, strategists for Davis promptly aired an advertisement that quoted Deukmejian—no friend of the governor-- criticizing Riordan)

By then, there was little the former front-runner could do to salvage his campaign. In the final days Riordan abandoned his above-the-fray stance and began attacking Simon, his old friend and fellow parishioner. But with a solid conservative base, Simon easily captured the Republican nomination on March 5. The turnabout in the candidates' respective fortunes was as startling as it was sudden. Indeed, few were more surprised than Simon's own staffers—many of whom had spent the final weeks of the primary contest lining up jobs for the unemployment they anticipated on March 6.

The Primary Campaign Panel

MARK BARABAK: Welcome to this session on the gubernatorial primary campaign, or as it was known in the Davis Camp, "How to Bury a Millionaire." I'm going to start by introducing perhaps the bravest man in all of California, Kevin Spillane. You know the old Kennedy line about "victory having a thousand fathers and defeat being an orphan." Kevin is our orphan this morning. He's the only one from the Riordan camp who showed up, and he deserves credit for doing so on behalf of the Riordan campaign. Joining us on behalf of the ultimate nominee, Bill Simon, are Ron Rogers, Jeff Flint, Sal Russo, Sean Walsh, and Rob Lapsley. From the winning Gray Davis camp we have Garry South, David Doak, Tom O'Donnell, and Ben Tulchin, who is here on behalf of Paul Maslin, the Davis pollster, who could not be here. With that very brief introduction, I'll turn it over to my comoderator Amy Chance of the *Sacramento Bee*, Amy.

AMY CHANCE: Just one quick reminder to everybody. This is not spinning time. We really want to know what happened. This is about history. And, even though this is the primary panel, I want everybody to go back in their minds to the preprimary period and the things you did in the walking-up phase, from choosing a nominee, to raising money, to getting endorsements. Think about that early period. We have an incumbent governor who, for purposes of discussion, has two defining characteristics: he has had his reputation battered by the energy crisis, and he has more than $30 million in the bank, an astounding amount of money, going into the primary campaign. And I'd like to start with Garry South. Why and when did you make the decision to start stockpiling that kind of money?

GARRY SOUTH: Well, we kept a full fundraising staff onboard from the very beginning. And we actually did quite well in 1999. We raised over $12 million; we raised about $13 million in 2000; and about $14 million in 2001. The actual goal of $30 million was set in January of 2001. After the energy crisis had reared its head, we set four goals for 2001, knowing that the energy crisis was going to damage our numbers, that we probably couldn't pull those numbers up in any fashion in 2001, and that we'd have to struggle along with a low job-approval rating. We had four goals. One was a financial goal, which was to have $30 million in the bank by June 30. That was primarily designed to try to ward off primary competition at that point because, as you remember, in early 2001 there were a lot of people being talked about, or talking about themselves as potentially challenging Gray in the primary.

CHANCE: Can you elaborate?

SOUTH: Kathleen Connell was said to be thinking about it. She was term-limited out as controller. Some people thought State Treasurer Phil Angelides might take a shot at it. You even had State Senator Don Perata mentioned in some news reports as someone who may take on the governor, who had been very critical of the governor publicly in the press for several months. So our goal in 2001 was to have $30 million in the bank, socked away by the June 30 FPPC Report. And we hit that target.

BARABAK: But I remember distinctly a conversation that we had just a week after the '98 election where you told me that it was going to be your guy's goal to have $50 million to run for reelection, that running against Al Checchi, a guy with $40 million, you guys were planning to match that and top it with another $10 million. This was a week after the '98 campaign. So deny it.

SOUTH: I said that? I deny it. The figure, $50 million dollars had been bandied around by a lot of people. In fact, both of you asked me many times, "Is your goal $50 million?" I don't recall ever saying, except in that off-the-record lunch I had with you, that we had actually set that goal for ourselves. But that was clearly a ballpark figure.

BARABAK: A lot of us have covered Gray for a number of years and know Gray and the way he thinks and operates. The Checchi thing troubled him, I think, running against a rich guy and facing the prospect of maybe running against another rich guy. Wasn't that in the back of his mind as you were making your . . . ?

SOUTH: No question about it. Remember, there wasn't just Checchi. There was Jane Harman, who spent $16 million, most of it her own. We had nearly $60 million thrown against us in the primary of 1998, which is still, I think, a national record for a primary. And that's an experience you don't forget very quickly.

BARABAK: You were just low-balling me when you said $50 million, you were really aiming for $60–65 million.

DAVID DOAK: Mark, the other thing to remember is we're post dot com crash now. At that point, in the early stages, was in the height of the dot.com run-up, and there were zillionaires everywhere. And I think one of the things that was always in the governor's mind was that one of these guys who had made a huge fortune in the Silicon Valley would get bored and dump $100 million or $150 million to run against him. So not only did he have all these other guys, but he had the prospect of a huge number of people who had just made a zillion bucks.

SOUTH: To add to that, and this is a predicate to the campaign that people tend to forget, in the summer of 2000, when Tim Draper was running the voucher initiative, he chose to go on air over the course of that fall with millions of dollars worth of spots attacking the governor, accusing him of being in the pocket of the Teacher's Union, accusing him of letting down California's kids. So two years out we had a dot.com millionaire running $15 million worth of ads, the bulk of which were negative spots against the governor, when we couldn't contest them. So that was, in this context, a fairly good warning sign that somebody may pop up out of the duck blind, spend $40, $50 million and try to take us out.

CHANCE: We had a terrified incumbent.

SOUTH: We had a prudent incumbent.

CHANCE: What were the other goals you set during that period?

SOUTH: The second goal was to try to avoid primary competition. It was related to the first, obviously. We wanted to make sure that we did not have somebody try to come after us in the primary. We thought we could probably take him out. But we didn't want someone drawing down our reserves in the primary, attacking the governor from the left in the primary, and weakening us for the general. And actually the March primary helped us in this particular case, because the time between the filing of our FPPC Report in mid July of 2001, showing us with $30 million in the bank, and the fact that the primary was on March 5, I think suggested to any potential opponent that the timeline involved here was almost impossible to try to take on the sitting governor in the primary. So the second goal is to avoid a primary challenge, which we ended up doing.

The third goal was to beef up the political staff, starting in early 2001, and go after as many endorsements as possible over the course of the summer, knowing that our numbers were going to be lagging and the picture wasn't going to be particularly good. That was both a prudent move to try to get these groups lined up early, to use their resources, their personnel and all that, but it was related to the second goal, which was to avoid a primary opponent. We wanted to keep these groups—labor, all of those groups that would otherwise, perhaps, coalesce against the governor if there was a primary opponent—to keep them in our camp.

The fourth goal was to make sure that Dick Riordan did not get a cleaned out primary field.

CHANCE: And how did you accomplish that?

SOUTH: Well, I don't know that we accomplished that, although we tried to do some things in that direction. I don't know if Dan Weintraub is here today, but in late 2001, I planted in the *California Insider,* the fact that Gray had given us authority to start producing negative spots against Riordan, if we had to use them, hoping that would send a message to the other two primary candidates that they were not going to be in this alone. Whether they took that to be true or not, I can't tell you.

CHANCE: You were communicating to them indirectly that you would help them out?

SOUTH: Yeah.

CHANCE: Let's, for a moment, move to the Republican side.

BARABAK: Much of the dynamic of the primary was shaped by something that happened back in 2000. Bill Jones had endorsed George W. Bush, but he pulled his endorsement and endorsed John McCain. I'd like to hear your thoughts on how that impacted Bill Jones's campaign for governor.

ROB LAPSLEY: Personally, having served with Bill for 10 years, that was probably the single, greatest impact we faced going into the primary, for two reasons: One is, obviously, the White House will, quote/unquote "never forgive him;" that remains to be seen. But in the primary, without a doubt, they sent the message that based on what happened there was not to be funding. Number two, it was an anomaly for Bill Jones's character and raised a lot of questions, I believe, in donors' minds. Bill is such a rock-solid steady guy that when they saw something like that, it confused them. And while potentially you're able to overcome that, I have found firsthand there is no way to get past the White House when they send the message to the core donor community that Bill Jones is not the guy.

BARABAK: Was there any thought or discussion at the time about, "Gee, if you do this, Bill, this could really hurt you in the future, if not running for governor sometime down the road in Republican politics."

LAPSLEY: Bill Jones was a very practical and realistic guy. There was plenty of discussion about the potential ramifications. From where he stood at that time and from the dynamics that were happening between the candidates in the Republican primary in 2000, he had some very soft feelings about some of the discussions he had had with the Bush campaign in regards to what they were going to do in California, the message they were going to send, and the way some of it was playing out. He felt that it was going in a different direction from what he had discussed with them and what he believed was the best approach in California. That is it in a nutshell. As a result, he took a step that was unusual for him but that he felt strongly about at that point in time. He understood what the ramifications were going to be, particularly in a governor's race, and he made the decision, and the result played out exactly as we had discussed. And the greatest impact was on his fundraising.

CHANCE: But was he really trying, in the year before the primary, to raise money? What I remember is that he hadn't even really decided to run for governor, he was not saying publicly that he would run. Did you have an indecisive candidate, who isn't ready to start raising money?

LAPSLEY: Okay, he made the Bush decision. Now how is that going to impact his fundraising in trying to move forward for the primary? He was trying to constantly access that element. Bill Jones had gone through all the fundamentals in laying a foundation to be able, if he made the decision, to run for governor. He had established the relationships. He had done all the right things. When he made that one decision, it negated years of work that he had done to lay that foundation. So was he indecisive? He was trying to assess what the level of funding was going to be, based on what the Bush response was going to be. It's not as clear cut as you might think. They just didn't come right out and say "Okay, that's it." They quietly filtered out a message that based on what happened, Bill Jones is not the guy. So you're trying to figure out exactly what your funding level is going to be and then figure out if you can get past it and still raise enough money from the base to be able to have a chance. Obviously, it wasn't enough.

CHANCE: But Kevin, you were actively encouraging somebody else to get in the ring.

KEVIN SPILLANE: Bill Jones had always worked his tail off fundraising. In 1994, he would fly into a little central valley town, raise $3,000, $5,000 at a pop. He worked it hard. But even then, he barely won against a basically unfunded Democrat for secretary of state. In 1998, he again barely won reelection against what a lot of people concerned to be a weak candidate for secretary of state on the Democratic side.

So my problem with Bill was never personal. It was that I didn't think he could be elected governor, frankly. I thought Riordan was the strongest Republican potential candidate for governor. His assets were well known. He was the mayor of the most populous city in the state. He was a moderate Republican, who had tremendous support and appeal to Democrats and Independents. He had shown particular strength in the Latino community. He had a record on education, even though it had nothing to do with the mayor's office that positioned him well on an issue that was important to voters, and Republicans often had trouble touting accomplishments or being perceived as having accomplishments in that area. He was very wealthy and that would help him counter the tens of millions of dollars that Gray Davis had raised.

So for all those reasons, it seemed to me and to a number of other people, that Riordan was the best possible candidate for governor on the Republican side. Admittedly, Riordan was a very unconventional Republican candidate for governor simply because of his history in nonpartisan politics in Los Angeles. He had historically been Tom Bradley's number one supporter and had supported a number of Democrats throughout the years. He'd also supported a number of Republicans. So the question was, was the cup half-full or half-empty in terms of Dick Riordan as a good Republican. And I and others decided to believe it was half-full. A number of us were saying, "Well, wouldn't it be great if Riordan ran?" And I heard everyone talking about it, and he seemed to be the consensus establishment choice for a candidate. I don't think that's because we thought, "Screw Bill Jones. We don't want him to be our candidate for governor because he stiffed the President." Sure, there was some of that with some people. But I don't think that was the major reason. Republicans tend to be very hierarchical. We tend to nominate candidates because they've paid their dues and it's their turn. Bob Dole was our nominee for president in 1996, although, most people a year, a year-and-a-half out among the insiders said he had no prayer against Bill Clinton. I remember telling Barabak a year-and-a-half out that Dan Lungren had no prayer for governor. And yet we went ahead and nominated him, and he went down in a disastrous defeat. I think after those two experiences, California Republicans were so traumatized that they were not going to go with the anointed guy because he had been standing in line and it was his turn. They were looking for something different and someone they thought was a winner.

So I began to use my network of personal relationships, clients, former clients—and others were doing this too, independently—but I had Ed Jagles, who is the district attorney of Kern County and an old buddy of mine, a very conservative Republican and a longtime family friend of Dick Riordan, go to Riordan and ask him to run for governor. He had several meetings with Riordan. I had him bring in different people. I asked Roy Ashburn, who is a very conservative assemblyman from Kern County, now a state senator, to go in and meet with him and pledge his support. I had Rod Pacheco, who is now a former state assemblyman from Riverside call Riordan and urge him to run.

And we could see that Riordan was intrigued by it. So we decided to take it the next step. And I asked Buck McKeon, who's a congressman from Santa Clarita to circulate a letter among the congressional delegation asking them to pledge their support to Riordan and urge him to run for governor. I did the same thing in the Assembly with Rod Pacheco, and Roy Ashburn got involved. The response from the congressional delegation exceeded my expectations. We got 16 of the 20 Republicans in the House delegation to sign on the dotted line for Riordan. And we're talking some very conservative Republicans—Dana Rohrabacher, Ed Royce, Duncan Hunter, Duke Cunningham. Frankly, I was surprised at the signatures that were on that piece of paper. We got 13 of the 30 members at the state Assembly to sign on. We got 15 of 30 before the campaign was over. So we exceeded anybody's expectations. How much that factored into Riordan's ultimate decision to run, I can't tell you.

CHANCE: Was Clint Riley involved at that point?

SPILLANE: In the drafting, not at all. It was completely self-generated.

CHANCE: How much were Democrats generating?

SPILLANE: Well, Clinton was urging Riordan to run on his own. The Riordan campaign was a mosaic, and there were a lot of different perspectives. I was not privy to a number of conversations that happened. So there are going to be holes in what I can offer you in terms of information. I'm just going to tell you what I know, or what I have from good sources in the campaign.

SOUTH: I'm curious why you thought Riordan's status as a former mayor of L.A. was a huge political asset. When you go back in the 152-year history of California, we've elected mayors of San Francisco, a mayor of San Diego, even a mayor of Oakland, but never in our entire time have we elected a mayor or even an ex-mayor of L.A. governor of California. And particularly, in the context of a Republican primary where L.A. is going to be suspect to every single Republican outside of the L.A. Basin, why you thought that was a substantial advantage?

SPILLANE: Well, I would argue that we're in an historical age. What happened in the 1998 mid-term elections wasn't supposed to happen. What happened in the 2002 mid-term elections wasn't supposed to happen. When George Bush was elected president as a sitting vice-president in 1988, it hadn't happened for 150 years. So, history may be an indicator, but I didn't necessarily agree. The other thing was that he was, obviously, very popular in the L.A. media market, the most important media market in the state, and one in which Republicans historically did not do well.

SOUTH: But L.A. city only provides six percent of the entire Republican vote in the primary election.

SPILLANE: But it wasn't the city, it was the entire southern California media market. And when you looked at the polling, Riordan's base of support was in southern California. Yes, he was not known outside of L.A., and as we get into what we tried to do to define him later on, we were aware of that. We always knew it would be hairy. Media strategist [Don] Sipple and I always took Simon very seriously. And there were efforts made on our part and on Riordan's part to try and get him to drop out because we considered him very scary.

LAPSLEY: It was a closed Republican primary. If it had been an open Republican primary, you could have gotten away with Riordan being an unconventional candidate. In a closed Republican primary we saw those things as liabilities. And with Garry's help, that played out exactly as we thought it would.

BARABAK: Hang on, before we have Simon dropping out, lets get him into the race. Can you bring Bill Simon, the eventual nominee, into the race for us?

SAL RUSSO: I pretty much agree with Rob. I really thought that the ducks were lined up for Bill Jones to be the nominee. And the endorsement of McCain, I thought was clearly the fatal mistake. I was not aware how fatal it was and it became clear to me when the White House said, "If there's anybody that's for Bill Jones that you need, let us know and we will get them off the Jones campaign."

CHANCE: Who at the White House?

RUSSO: People in the White House Political Office. High-ranking people.

BARABAK: Someone traveling on Mr. Rove's plane?

RUSSO: There's no question they had a very strong animosity to Jones.

CHANCE: Who had a conversation with Karl Rove besides Dick Riordan? Raise your hand. Who here had conversations with Karl Rove at any point in that two-year period—2001, 2002?

JEFF FLINT: I assume everyone on the Republican side did. I'm wondering if any of the Democrats did.

CHANCE: Did everyone here talk to Karl Rove?

SOUTH: I've never met Karl Rove in my life.

CHANCE: Never spoke to him?

SOUTH: I've never had a single conversation with him.

CHANCE: Kevin?

SPILLANE: I don't even know who he is.

CHANCE: Who talked to Karl Rove? Ron, did you?

RON ROGERS: No.

JEFF FLINT: Yes.

CHANCE: Yes. Sal?

RUSSO: Yes.

CHANCE: Sean?

SEAN WALSH: In the primary?

CHANCE: In the primary.

WALSH: No.

CHANCE: No. Okay.

RUSSO: Ron actually met Bill first, I think, in December of 2000 because he had an interest in running. And he ultimately came up to our office, I think it was February 1, February 2, and we had really our first meetings to discuss it, and we spent two or three hours in the office going through what running for public office was about, and what his choices were. It was not really focused on running for governor.

BARABAK: Can I ask, Ron, when you met was it a social thing? Did he approach you at a Christmas party?

ROGERS: It was a dinner that Beth Fong put on for Steve Kinney and myself, and Bill Simon, and we saw Bill as a potential financier of a possible referendum against the Democrat gerrymander we anticipated to come out for reapportionment. So we actually had a plan in hand to discuss with him about getting involved in party politics, because the premise was, Matt said, "Bill wanted to get more involved in Republican Party politics." The latter part of that dinner, he dropped the bombshell of asking the question to the three of us, "What do you think about the possibility of my running for governor?"

BARABAK: What did you say?

ROGERS: I said, "Well, that's an intriguing question." At the time, I didn't think that an outsider would be able to defeat an incumbent governor. But I said, "It's something we ought to discuss and explore." Serendipitously, the next morning when I got back—the dinner had been in Los Angeles—Sal got the call from John Herrington saying, "I want you to meet somebody." John is on the squawk box talking to Sal: "There's this person that someone recommended." And we both said at the same time, "Bill Simon." So that's how Bill came up two days later.

RUSSO: We talked about what his options were. Bill had seen firsthand in Los Angeles a deterioration in California and a lack of leadership. They are very involved in funding projects at schools, and he was always battling with L.A. Unified in his efforts to give them money to do his Sound Mind, Sound Body Program. So he was frustrated with the education bureaucracy. He saw the Los Angeles traffic was getting worse, getting from his house to his office in Westwood. There were a number of things. He was somewhat familiar with the water problems from a friend of his on that board. So he felt like there was an absence of leadership in the state, and he made it a point in his life when he could serve in some capacity. And he wasn't really locked into running for governor or running for any office for being active in the party. As he always said, he wanted to be of service.

And John McGraw, the state party chairman, I think humored him. McGraw went to see him to raise money from him and said, "Gee, why don't you run for governor." I presume he was humoring him. But he put the germ in his mind. Whenever I'm soliciting somebody for money I always say, "You'd be a great governor." So I presume that's what it was, and maybe John really thought he would be a great governor—I don't know.

BARABAK: So he came to you and said, "I want to run for some other office," and you said, "No, run for governor"?

RUSSO: He wanted to hear what we had to say. So we went through the pros and cons for the afternoon, and we went over to my house for dinner. And at the end of the dinner, he said, "Well, I think I'd like to run governor, and I would like to hire you." I was sort of taken aback and I said, "Well, I think you really need to reflect on that. I mean, that's kind of a big jump." And he said, "I have, and I think I'd really like to at least take the first steps forward."

Now, I later found out that Bill is not somebody who does things on the spur of the moment; that he actually does do his homework. And so he knew a lot more when he came into my office than he let on. He's not a rash person. George Skelton has written about Bill's answering questions on policy with, "I don't know; I'll get back to you," which was expressed as a frustration with the press. It was a frustration for me because, in reality, Bill Simon didn't know all the answers. He was, actually, extraordinarily well-prepared and could communicate quite effectively on policy, but he exhibited this overcautiousness, which caused him to give you the impression that he didn't know as much. In reality, he knows a lot more. He's one of these people that knows much more than he lets on.

CHANCE: But once he came to you and you had that discussion, what kind of research did you do on him to find out whether he was somebody you thought you wanted to link your reputation to and somebody you wanted to promote for governor?

RUSSO: At the conclusion of our meeting, I said, "Well, look, let us think about it. And we'll put together what we think the benchmarks would be for good decision-making." And so we did do that. And one of the elements of that, if this is what you're referring to, was a thorough background check on him. And we did retain the services of a former FBI agent, U.S. attorney in New York, who did a relatively extensive background check on him, as one of the elements in getting him ready to run.

At that point in time, I didn't think that he should make the decision to run for governor, per se, I mean, I thought we could look at it. But we kept open all the options as long as we could, and we didn't really make the governor's decision until June or July. And the primary premise was that if you're going to run, it's senseless to run for a constitutional office if we have a weak candidate at the top, because I believed that if there was not a strong Republican candidate at the top of the ticket there was a strong likelihood we would lose the entire ticket.

BARABAK: Well, isn't it ironic that's what happened?

RUSSO: I said, "If some strong candidate emerges, then I would recommend you not run for governor, that you run for one of the other constitutional offices." I didn't think Jones could make it for the reasons we just discussed. I just didn't think he could finance a campaign for governor. And I thought Riordan was his own worst enemy. And I certainly agree with Garry, having done Deukmejian's campaign against Tom Bradley. Mayor of L. A. is the worst thing to be in a Republican primary. In fact, somebody in the press corps, I don't remember who it was, and I went over to the Downtown Plaza when they were announcing the signing of Chris Weber's contract. And there were a couple thousand people in the Downtown Plaza. And spontaneously, everyone started screaming, "Beat L.A.! Beat L.A.!" And I said, "This is why Dick Riordan is going to lose this election." People hate L.A. up and down the state. And one of the things that I found out in Deukmejian's campaign in '82 was that it isn't San Francisco that hates L.A.; Glendale hates L.A.; Alhambra hates L.A.; Long Beach hates L.A.; that L.A. is not the L.A. media market, L.A. is L.A. And there is a lot of negativity with that. But that wasn't Riordan's worst problem in my opinion. Riordan was Riordan's worst problem because Riordan says and does the damnedest things. And there's a charming side to it, but in a political campaign, I would call it stacking the ammunition in a big pile. And that certainly is what happened.

CHANCE: Let me ask one thing to follow up on the research. Going into the primary, did you know about all of his business lawsuits that they were involved in?

RUSSO: Yes.

CHANCE: You knew that he was not a regular voter?

RUSSO: Yes.

CHANCE: Did you know that he had. . . .

RUSSO: He was a more regular voter than you reported.

CHANCE: More regular than the records reflected at the L.A. Registrar's Office?

LAPSLEY: And the secretary of state was accurate.

BARABAK: Did he keep his ballot stubs for all those elections?

RUSSO: There was a hanging chad on his voter registration.

CHANCE: Did you know that at one point he had not been a registered Republican?

RUSSO: Yes.

CHANCE: You knew that? So you knew all of that information going in? There was nothing that he was not disclosing to you?

RUSSO: No. Bill was extraordinarily forthcoming. My concern was never, as I said to him often, "It's not that you're not telling me something, it's something that's just not in your mind that you're not thinking about that has dire consequences." That's what I was more concerned about, that was why we spent a considerable amount of money to have outsiders research his background.

CHANCE: And did he reflect to you at that point how much money he must have been willing to put in on his own, did you have a dollar figure?

RUSSO: I would say that the answer to that is yes with no footprints.

BARABAK: Do you want to clarify that?

RUSSO: Well, he didn't say X dollars, but in the course of the discussion, I pretty much knew the answer.

CHANCE: And what did you believe to be the answer?

RUSSO: I knew he was going to . . . that we had five million bucks in the primary.

CHANCE: Five million dollars in the primary, that's what you knew you had. And wasn't it John Herrington who was saying that he might put $60 million in by the end of. . . .

RUSSO: John can be colorful in his language.

FLINT: And we blame Carla [Marinucci] for it. She got John going and he started talking, and next thing you know, $60 million popped out of his mouth.

RUSSO: We were dumbfounded by the comment, and by the reporting. We lived with it. But that was never a goal ever.

BARABAK: Okay, the Republican field is Jones, it's Simon, and it's Riordan. As the Davis team calibrated and recalibrated, what was your thinking once the Republican field was set?

DOAK: I thought Riordan was the most formidable candidate for the general election. And I thought that given the dynamics of the field that he would probably win.

CHANCE: So the three of you didn't want to run against Riordan?

DOAK: Yeah, I think Riordan would have been the toughest for us in the general election.

CHANCE: Who did you want?

DOAK: You know at one point, we were talking about the possibility of Simon winning, and I joked with the governor, "I'm holding out for Jones." Because at that time Jones had no money. But we didn't really understand that we had a chance to beat Riordan until pretty late in the primary. You know, it was—what, Garry—three or four weeks out? I suspect that all of us in the back of our head thought, you know, it could happen, but it never really crossed our minds.

CHANCE: What were your focus groups saying about Gray Davis? What were voters saying about Gray Davis heading into the primary?

BEN TULCHIN: We knew we were facing a very grumpy electorate. We knew that the economy had turned south; the energy crises had kind of started that up. As always, California started a trend. Unfortunately, it was a negative trend for an incumbent; they were pissed off and we've seen it all before in previous cycles with California voters. Once they get angry, they don't snap out of it very quickly.

So we did a lot of research in the fall of 2001, and we had been doing research throughout the governor's first term. But we saw post-9/11, there was a bump among some incumbents. We didn't really benefit much from that. And we saw that it was going to be an extraordinarily difficult environment to communicate a positive message, because they rejected a lot of the governor's accomplishments. We'd say, "He's done x, y, and z on these issues." And voters would say, "Yeah, you know, schools aren't any better. The environment? No, he hasn't done anything on that." They would just dismiss a lot of our positives. So we knew we were going to be in a difficult environment to communicate a positive message.

DOAK: The environment changed. We focus grouped, not as much as the press thought we did, but we periodically would go out and take a look. And early on, we could go into focus groups and we'd look for information: "Did you know that funding is up for the schools?" We'd go through the things that he'd done. And people would say, "Gee, I didn't know this. It's great." And even at the beginning of the power crises, we'd go and say, "Did you know he's built nine new power plants, more than any other governor in the last 12 years, total?" And people would go, "My God, I didn't know that." And we had a funny thing that happened. We had one focus group, and Phil [Trounstine] came and he was communications director at the time. And one guy in the focus group after we went through the accomplishments goes, "My God, why doesn't he get somebody to do his publicity for him?"

But then the mood began to change. I don't know what it was. There was the length and duration of the energy crisis. It was the fact that—and this is something most people have forgotten now—but remember the energy companies, we still don't know exactly who, dumped a ton of money on the governor in the summer before the primary. And we made the decision not to match them dollar-per-dollar because we thought maybe their strategy was to run us dry, to soften us up. I have no way of proving this, and I hate to make accusations, but I still suspect that was an organized effort on the part of the Republicans to damage us by using the energy companies to try to hang the energy crisis on us.

TOM O'DONNELL: I think the White House was behind that money being spent. If Bush could ever figure out a way to unlock California, he was home free. And I think they felt they had an opportunity here to come after the governor.

SOUTH: And you have to remember one thing that happened, just prior to the American Taxpayers Alliance going on the air with TV and radio against us, and then Americans for Tax Reform following that up—both of them are Republican allied groups totally under the control of the operatives in Washington, and Mark wrote about this in the *Los Angeles Times,* although, the *Times* in its wisdom saw fit to put the story on the inside page of the business section. Ed Gillespie, who's an Enron lobbyist, was the one who actually circulated the memo talking about getting the energy companies to put money into an effort to come out and smack Gray Davis. But prior to that Bush came out here in late May 2001, his first trip to California, and we had him for lunch. He came unprepared; all he wanted to do was lecture us about the evils of price caps, and he made a fool of himself. Even the Republican operatives, here and in Washington, thought that the governor ate his lunch. Bush came out of here with his tail between his legs and, ironically, 16 days after that all of a sudden there are television spots appearing in California all over the place accusing Gray Davis of being the culprit in the energy crises. There's no question this was politically related. There's no question in my mind this was driven directly out of the White House.

DOAK: The question was did the White House begin it, did the energy companies begin it, or were they people who had mutual interests? My theory has always been that Enron had a scheme to nationalize deregulation of energy companies. California was their place to start for obvious reasons—they had control of the White House, they had their people in place in the energy system regulatory agencies. And what they intended to do, in my opinion, was to spook the governor into rate increases. The supply problem would have immediately ended. Then everything would have been honky-dory. It would have made the case for deregulation everywhere, loosening up supply. And suddenly we would have had deregulation and Enron may still be in business.

BARABAK: What did you decide about going on the air to counter those ads?

O'DONNELL: We ended up going on radio.

DOAK: We did a million-and-a-half on radio.

BARABAK: But did you talk about a more extensive buy and decide you were going to husband your resources?

SOUTH: As David indicated, one of our thoughts was that part of the strategy at the national Republican level was to try to get us into a meaningless firefight in the summer of 2001 to draw down our money so they could come in for the kill in the election year. And we decided not to be suckered into that game.

CHANCE: Had Enron disputed or confirmed any of this?

FLINT: No. Somewhere along that conversation, they turned from what their theory was to it was fact, which was interesting.

SOUTH: But it was a fact.

FLINT: That may very well be true, but I'm certainly not aware of it. So I wasn't brought in on the conspiracy.

WALSH: There was no communication among Republicans in the state.

BARABAK: Obviously, the White House cared about who would be the Republican nominee for governor in California. Can any of you tell us what intervention, what conversations took place? To what degree did the White House help shape the dynamics of the Republican primary?

WALSH: Well, as Rob stated, from the Jones side of the equation, Bill Jones was the antidote to Gray Davis. I don't think, based on the energy crises and the budget issues, that the gun and abortion votes that he had cast in the Assembly would have had the same saliency this time out when you match them up to energy and the budget. Jones is quiet; he has a California governor mold in his personality, in his demeanor that you've seen from Deukmejian, to Wilson, to Davis, to Jones. I had a conversation with Gerry Parsky before the primary was over, he said if Bill Jones somehow pulls this thing out, I assure you that all of the Republicans, the Bush White House will be behind you 100 percent and you will be fully funded.

BARABAK: But in the primary, when Bill Jones is setting out to run, did he have people who would say to him, "You know what? Forget it. You screwed the president so I'm not going to give you money."

WALSH: Absolutely. Everywhere. Everywhere. We had to fight a two-or-three-front battle. Number one, some people, had questions about whether they thought Bill Jones was tough enough to take on Gray Davis. Gray Davis is a tough fighter. Bill Jones is a nice, gentlemanly person. And that carried through to his fundraising. He's not mean and hard "You're going to give me the money," and break arms to do it. He's a gentleman who says, "You know, I'd like you to support me because I've got some good ideas," and then he goes off. And if anybody has watched how fundraising actually works and is successful, you've really got to put the arm on people. And I don't think that was in his personality to do that. He had to convince a lot of Republicans that he was tough enough to take on Davis, and I think we eventually did that. And then we had to convince people that we could win, and the way to convince them that we could win was to raise money, and we could just never get over that.

BARABAK: Rob, you're very close to Jones. Did he ever at any point say, "You know what? This just isn't coming together, maybe I shouldn't get in the race?"

LAPSLEY: We've had many discussions to that end. In fact, right before the filing we had discussions with Sean, myself, Ed, and Bill, and Bill's wife, Maureen. We went through the pros and the cons of what we were facing going into filing, believing at that point there was still a question mark whether Bill Simon ultimately was going to file, but believing he was. And, certainly, Riordan was going to file. Based on the money issue, and all the other things that Sean just described, we went through the pros and the cons, and we thought we could overcome those things. We thought we would have the money, ultimately, to overcome Bill Simon's money on TV, or Dick Riordan's money. Bill looked at all the facts. He's very deliberative. But he made the decision, even if we were going to be underfunded that at least it was worth it to move forward and communicate a message no matter how the cards played out. When he was done, he could go back to being a farmer and a rancher, and so there was nothing to lose even if he was underfunded and gave it his best shot.

That was the perspective. The other thing about being tough enough is the office itself. You had to be a statesman, particularly as a Republican, because you're under particular scrutiny to handle things in a judicious manner as secretary of state. That didn't lend itself to being a red meat Republican rhetorical candidate during the ramp-up time before you actually became a candidate. That was always a thing you had to try to balance in Bill's secretary of state responsibilities, message/image, against some things you would like to do to position him to be governor in a Republican primary, to be able to attract some of that hard-core Republican base.

CHANCE: How vulnerable was Gray Davis in your view?

RUSSO: I disagree with the assumptions that the Davis Camp made. I understand why they would conclude that, but I don't think the White House was behind that. I think they did not play a role in that.

BARABAK: Because? Why would you think not?

RUSSO: I agree with Garry's analysis of what happened. I thought the White House, which generally handles things quite ably, poorly handled the energy thing, and the governor was the big winner. Whether it was the president's trip out here or Spencer Abraham's trip out here, I thought Davis won on a consistent basis. It was like "Stop coming. If we have anymore help from Washington, we're going to get killed." Davis won consistently every single time anybody from Washington came here.

FLINT: We agree with your ultimate conclusion that those ads, whether they were coordinated by national Republicans or not, burned in the blame in the voter's mind that Gray Davis was the problem. But I don't agree that Republicans. . . .

SOUTH: Whether? ATA was supposedly run by Scott Reed, who's a former executive director of the Republican National Committee and assistant communications director of the Bush campaign. It's pretty hard to argue "whether," when the evidence is right there. Ed Gillespie, who was Enron's lobbyist and who was also involved in the Bush campaign, was the one who ran this whole thing and came up with a memo that Mark wrote about. There's no question that national Republican operatives were driving this effort.

BARABAK: Do you think the ads were that effective?

SOUTH: I think the fact they were unresponded to, as is often the case in California, meant that yes they were effective. In our focus groups, over the course of this campaign, one of the things that scared us was that people started parroting back to us some of the same charges that were made in those ads, almost as if it was a fact. Because they saw no response, they wanted somebody to blame, they were trying to see a boogie-man. "How did this happen to us? How come Davis let this happen to us?" And then all of a sudden, you've got radio and television ads as well as hundreds of thousands of pieces of mail going out from Americans for Tax Reform, and phone banks. They were doing telemarketing in California, literally clogging the lines at the governor's office in Sacramento, and all the regional governor's offices with people who were automatically transferred to those offices once they got the call, and told to express their outrage and disgust that Gray Davis had not protected California from this energy crisis. This goes on from the sixteenth of June all the way through the end of August.

RUSSO: The energy companies did a good job. I just say it was not directed by Republicans, that's all.

SOUTH: Scott Reed and Ed Gillespie are not Republicans?

RUSSO: They're Republican, but they were working on behalf of the energy companies.

O'DONNELL: No, no, no. You guys know this. There's nobody in Washington who's as close to Rove as Ed Gillespie. We had a memo from Gillespie that laid out the whole plan and talked specifically about Davis. These aren't Republican operatives; this is from the White House.

SPILLANE: It's entertaining that the Davis campaign is blaming the vast right-wing conspiracy for Gray Davis' lack of popularity. During the whole energy crises, he was on television on a daily basis. California is such an apolitical state, even the governor doesn't receive that much television coverage. But during the energy crises, you had in the state capital something that no one has seen since Prop. 13. There were 10, 12, 15 TV cameras there on almost a daily basis during 2001, covering the energy crises. Gray's problem was that voters saw how he handled it; they were actually seeing it on the evening news; and they didn't like what they saw.

BARABAK: I assume that was a rhetorical question, and you will stipulate that Republican ads definitely hurt Gray Davis. Whether the right-wing conspiracy, or Bush, or whoever was behind it, they hurt Gray Davis so we're back to the energy problem.

We're going back to the White House, and their interests, whether they were involved in these ads or not. There is another piece of political lore—the birthday phone call to Dick Riordan, in which Bush either did or did not, depending on who tells you, tell him he should run. What came out of it was that Bush wanted Riordan to run. How much did the Bush White House push Riordan into the race, or at least this putative push?

SPILLANE: The role of the White House in the Riordan campaign has always been exaggerated. Frankly, they've been blamed for a lot of things that they had nothing to do with. I wasn't there for the infamous phone call. Riordan's mayoral staff was leaking that to the press. I heard from a number of people that it was exaggerated; it was a casual comment from the president, joking around with Riordan. And some of his staff decided to run with it and create this image of Riordan as the White House candidate.

RUSSO: The White House story was that Brad Freeman was back at the White House, and he said, "Hey, it's Dick's birthday. Let's get him on the phone and wish him Happy Birthday." Brad got him on the phone, put him on the speaker-phone, and Brad said, "You ought to run for governor." And out of that the

Riordan's staff took that and said the president called and wanted him to run for governor.

SOUTH: Can I add one thing to this? When that call occurred and it was in the *L.A. Times* the next day, I got a call from somebody—and I don't want to give away any confidences here—but from somebody who was actually in the room at Riordan's end when he took the call and heard the whole thing.

FLINT: And everybody knows who it is.

SOUTH: And here was his comment to me. He said, "You probably saw the story today in the *L.A. Times*. Dick did get a call from the president. The president did not broach this with Dick. Dick actually broached it with the president and said, 'Well, you know, Mr. President, some people are saying I should run for governor. What do you think?' 'Oh, yeah, that would be great. That would be great.'"

And he said, "Now, here's my advice to you." He said, "Don't launch on Riordan. Okay? Don't piss him off. Don't insult his pride. This is his way of kind of riding out the end of his term, getting his name back in the paper, becoming a player. I know your style, and you're going to probably come out with your fangs bared on the guy now that he's raised the prospects of running for governor. If you just let this thing play itself out, it will go away. He's not going to run. Ultimately, he'll decide better of this, he'll decide not to run, so just sit tight. Don't castigate him in the press. Just let him have his jollies and it will all work out for the best." And that's what we did for about two-and-a-half months.

BARABAK: This is news—Garry South restrains himself. Let me ask Kevin this. How much convincing did Dick Riordan need? Were people pushing against an open door? Did he really have to be convinced to get into the race?

SPILLANE: He was conflicted about it. He seemed to welcome it to a great extent, but he wasn't necessarily ready to pull the trigger.

BARABAK: So what pushed him into it, ultimately?

SPILLANE: I think, frankly, the fact that Mrs. Riordan was very supportive of him running for governor was a major factor. In 1998, when he had looked at running against Dan Lungren in the primary, she had been a major factor in his decision not to do that. He received a lot of encouragement from family and friends. And he saw that reinforced by political support, by what we were able to generate from the draft Riordan effort and from others going to him and urging him to run.

BARABAK: There was a meeting at Riordan's mansion where, my sense from someone who was there was that Simon might have been talked out of the race at that point if Riordan was really going to run and there was a lot of ambivalence. Can you talk about that?

RUSSO: Well, Dick had encouraged Bill to run all along. They ski together at Sun Valley and Dick was forever taking Bill around and introducing him in L.A. as the next governor of California, so he had always been extraordinarily supportive. Without that, Bill may never have run for governor, but for so much encouragement. But we got a call, maybe from Dick himself, and he wanted Bill to come over to his house and talk about running.

BARABAK: And this was in the summer of '01?

RUSSO: November '01. So Bill and I went over there, and Arnie Steinberg was there with Dick. I later found out there were a number of others in the back room.

RUSSO: In the meeting, it was the four of us, and Dick, without his shoes, of course. And, obviously, we thought that there was going to be a push from Dick to say, "Look, I know I told you to get in the race but I think you need to get out because a, b, and c." And I told Bill, "You can't blink. You've got to go in there confident that you're going to run, you're going to win, and let's see if we can find out where he is."

And Steinberg told me afterwards that Riordan was supposed to try to push Bill out of the race, but he did just about the opposite. It's a typical kind of Riordan thing. He said, "I'm leaving office, and I've got a new life." He was enjoying the speculation. And he certainly gave me the impression that he was enjoying the speculation far more than he was enjoying the thought of actually running.

And Bill said something I wish he hadn't had said, something to the effect that, "Well, should I back off and give you some time?"—something I didn't want him to say. And Dick said, "No, no, no. You keep going. You keep going." And we walked out of there convinced that he wasn't running. Why would he tell Bill Simon, "You keep running. You keep running." He definitely gave us the feeling that he was just enjoying the glory of leaving office on a high, and he was not serious about running, which Arnie told me afterwards was the opposite purpose of the meeting.

CHANCE: Now, there was another thing happening with Riordan during that period. There was a decision to make public the fact that he had cancer. Can you talk about that Kevin?

SPILLANE: Well, the whole cancer episode always really bothered him. He kept his secret from his entire mayoral staff. No one knew about it, except his personal police officer, who drove him to the cancer treatments, and his wife. He started to tell more people about it, because it was so much on his conscience that he had not revealed it. And, ultimately, we knew it was going to get out.

Dan Schnur made the decision that we should make a preemptive effort, and basically ease the mayor's conscience and let it out. It was such a personal issue with Riordan. He was consumed by it, and he wouldn't stop talking about it. So, basically, we knew we needed to do it in our own way, and it ultimately ended up not being a big deal the way that Dan handled it.

BARABAK: But that didn't really serve as a lesson to the campaign. Amy asked earlier about opposition research, that Riordan didn't do any opposition research on himself, and the feeling inside was, "Why bother? Why spend the money? Who needs it? We're going to be the nominee." I know that was not your decision, and you're defending something you were not arguing internally, but can you illuminate for us what the thinking was?

SPILLANE: Well, I started in politics as an opposition researcher, so it was a great irony that we were involved in a campaign that didn't conduct a very extensive opposition research job. Back in December, part of what happened with Jones was that some issues were tested early on and it was clear that Jones was not going to be the nominee because of the Bush flip-flop. The Republican primary voters, according to our polling, viewed that as a huge negative. That and the fact that he voted for the tax increases was part of it. Both those issues, we thought, would destroy Jones if he started to get close to us. So Simon was personally my biggest concern because here's a wealthy guy, he has no public record. I always expected him to be the main rival to Riordan. What in the world do we throw at this guy if he starts to get close? And that was another view that was shared by others in the campaign. We did have a research unit. They were involved with both policy and, theoretically, opposition research. There was talk up until the filing deadline in early December that Simon might drop out. That was giving us a reason to hold off doing any research because he might not even be in the race. Then, once he filed, we thought we have a 30-point lead to a 40-point lead, we've got this in the bag, it's a waste of money. Our staff doesn't have the capability to do it. I argued for bringing in outside people if our staff didn't have the capability to do it; that view was rejected. And I have to admit—that was early December—I pretty much, personally, thought we had lost the race at that point.

SOUTH: Can I ask a follow-up question that's been burning on my mind now for many months? When we did the postmortem after the primary in San Diego at the American Association of Political Consultants meeting, the only person who showed up from Riordan's campaign was the communications director. And when the question came about the "abortion is murder" tape, she explained that when it started to become public that there was this tape out there with Riordan equating abortion to murder, that the thought about it inside the campaign, because Riordan had said this to the staff, was that this was all an urban legend, that there was no tape. "He never said any such things, so don't worry about this." Which was curious to me, because this thing surfaced through the '93 mayoral primary. In fact, we got a spot using a segment of that tape—not as good as the one David produced this time—but we got a spot that we put on the air that I think Riordan, having been involved in that campaign as a candidate, should have remembered.

SPILLANE: You're accurate in that we knew you were talking to people about it, and you weren't shy about bragging about having the tape. And the question was, "Does he really have it?" The sense was that it was an urban legend. That was the sense of the campaign.

BARABAK: Did anybody ask Riordan whether or not he had ever given an interview on tape, where he equated abortion to murder? And did anybody ask Riordan whether he was involved; that this was actually on the air on Los Angeles television stations in the '93 primary?

SPILLANE: And, one of the unusual things about the campaign was that the mayor was dismissive of the tape. He supported the view that it was urban legend, frankly.

SOUTH: Well, that's very interesting.

SPILLANE: My personal view is not that the governor's race was won for Gray Davis when Bill Jones endorsed George Bush, my view is that the governor's race was lost by the Republicans when Bill Wardlaw and Dick Riordan had a falling out over the Jimmy Hahn campaign. I believe that if Wardlaw had been there, a lot of the problems that we had would not have existed.

WALSH: I've got to stop for a second here. Here's a plug for MB & Associates. These guys are fantastic researchers. They did opposition research, and they did a vulnerability study on us. Remember, it is a closed primary. He's the mayor of Los Angeles. He had almost all Democrats working for him—Democrats who were willing to dig up any dirt that was in L.A. and give it to Garry. I mean, hell, his personal staff was giving stuff to Garry. And you look at the issues where Dick Riordan was with Bill Clinton. You look at the issues where he was with the Democrats. You look at the money stuff. If you just analyze all of the issues and all of the things that Riordan was involved in, in a Republican primary, if that could get out to a broad based public, he was in real trouble.

BARABAK: Well, you guys were the ones who were digging up all this opposition research and putting out all this stuff about Riordan and his record. Can you guys talk a bit about that? And Sal, you guys basically stood back and let Jones beat up Riordan. You guys were sort of the clean, genial candidate of ideas the whole time. Can you talk about that?

WALSH: Our strategy was that we had to kill off Dick Riordan to have any chance at all. And there was not much communication, except spinning in the hallway. It's like he'd say something, and I'd say basically the same thing in front of reporters. But the issue was we had to kill off Riordan and then we thought with Simon's voting record and the fact that he's a newcomer, and wealthy candidates, you know, didn't have a great track record, that people would go on Jones's experience, etc., and that would carry us forward, and we would have enough money to put that out when it got close. But on the Riordan side, we always thought that once we got that stuff out—and you could get that out through a media perspective—Republican activists and conservatives would look at this stuff, and a newspaper story has far more salience to them than a TV ad. What really made it for us is conservative Republicans kept putting up with Riordan. They held their nose. The conventional wisdom was he was the most likely guy to beat Gray Davis. But as Kevin indicated, and I got this from Wilson people in the campaign, the mayor would go out on weekends and talk to a bunch of Democrats on the Westside, and they'd say "Ata boy, man, you went out there and really kicked those right-wing conservative Republicans in the ass today. Ata boy, we're going to be with you in the end of the general election." And it seemed like this stoked this guy's fire to keep going out and kicking conservative Republicans.

He goes out and says, "You're a bunch of dinosaurs, you're going to ruin the party." And these people would only take it so much. And then when we ran into that convention in San Jose, the *Chronicle* wrote a story about Riordan giving money to Willie Brown, costing Curt Pringle an election. And then Deukmejian comes out and says, "Not only will I not support this guy, but I won't vote for him." Three Republican chairmen come out and say, "I won't support this guy," which was I think very devastating to the Republican masses. And then the killer, the straw that broke the camel's back, was in the debate when he opened up and, trying to be funny, attacked Deukmejian, and it just literally snapped the Republicans. They hemorrhaged, and they never came back.

BARABAK: So what happened in the Republican primary? The virile, hairy-chested Jones is showing that he can beat up on Gray Davis, and Bill Simon is willing to stand back and let him do it and be Mr. Genial ideas candidate.

RUSSO: Well, there were two dynamics. One is that, for reasons that Sean has articulated, we didn't really think Dick Riordan was going to be a serious candidate. Bill Simon is one of these guys that ask you everyday, "What are my chances of winning?" He always wanted a percentage. And from the very beginning, I said that I thought there was an 80 percent chance. This was back in March of 2001, and all through 2001, I said, "Eighty percent was your chance of winning the primary." I said 30 percent is his chance of winning the general. Those are the numbers that I gave him consistently through 2001 and into 2002. For all the reasons that Sean just said, Dick Riordan was a horrible Republican primary candidate. It was hard to come up with a scenario in which Dick Riordan could win the primary. I struggled figuring out if I had Riordan's campaign, how I could win it for him.

SPILLANE: He almost did win the primary.

RUSSO: The second thing Riordan was saying that had a nefarious effect for Republicans the entire cycle was that Republicans were totally despondent about their prospects in California. The Lungren campaign left a bad taste in people's mouths, not to mention the Dole campaign in California. Then everybody got pretty enthusiastic about George W. Bush. Everybody believed the polls that existed or didn't exist that said Bush was going to win in California, at least everybody in the donor community thought that Bush was really going to do well in California. Then we get our clock cleaned. The fact that Bush got killed in California, with Gore spending no money, made Republicans think that we couldn't win. I'm going to give Garry credit—whether he deserves it or not, I don't know—but I think the Davis campaign did an outstanding job of perpetuating that myth that Gray Davis was unbeatable. And that was a burden that we could never get over. When someone says, "I'll forgive Dick Riordan for being as quirky as he is and for taking some of the oddball positions he's taken over the years," that comes about when a party wants to win at all costs. But when the party thinks it can't win, they get picky and choosy. And that helped Simon because we ran as the conservative in a very conservative primary election.

CHANCE: Now, how much were you counting on the Davis campaign to help you in the primary? In the 80 percent calculation, did you expect that they would hit Riordan?

RUSSO: Well, we had a little bit of communication with the Davis camp, and we didn't really think that they were going to do it. In fact, I think they were going trying to goad us into doing it, and we didn't do it because I thought we could win without it until we had to do it at the end. I think the only thing we did against Riordan in the entire campaign was to show him jogging with Bill Clinton. What that showed us in the focus groups was that he wasn't just a liberal himself, but he actually liked liberals. He would jog with them. That was kind of the final thing for Republican primary voters.

CHANCE: Well, Garry's alluded to it, but I think now we really need to get the Davis side to tell the story of the tape.

SOUTH: But before we do that can I go back to a question you asked several questions ago, and give you a summation of our evaluation of Riordan as a general election candidate, and why we went after him in the primary? I still believe, given the fact that Riordan didn't hold up very well over a four-month primary, that we would have beat him in a general election because he clearly wouldn't hold up all that well over an eight-month general election period either. But with him as a nominee, our calculation was—and I think we had pretty much agreement on all these three points—it would have complicated our lives in three different very specific ways. One is financial, because our donor bases, Gray's donor base and Riordan's donor base, are both very heavily in southern

California, and they substantially overlapped. During the campaign, in the primary, we were holding Monday morning meetings in Ron Burkle's office over on Sunset Boulevard, with all of our big donors to try to keep them in the fold because Riordan was going after them unmercifully, not because he was trying to screw us, but because these are his friends. Then we would show up on Monday mornings with people who had been at dinner parties with the guy and his wife at his house in Pacific Palisades the Saturday night before.

We could have kept them away from Riordan, but it would have taken a fair amount of effort to do so. Financially, it would have complicated our lives keeping our own donor base from giving him the $50,000 he wanted or the $100,000 he wanted because, "Hey, you know, you've been my friend for 23 years, and Dick and Nancy and I love you, and you've been there." So that would have complicated a lot of this.

The second way it would have complicated our lives is that if Riordan had been the nominee, we all concluded there would have been some substantial Democratic defections right off the bat for Riordan. Now, we didn't know who they all were. We were gaming this out all the way back to November of 2001, trying to put a master list together. You remember meeting with people saying, "Okay, who out there—former legislators, former county supervisors, maybe former mayors—who dislike Gray, who thinks he's abandoned the Democratic base, who thinks Riordan, even though he may be a little goofy, is acceptable from a philosophical standpoint, and they want to teach Gray Davis a lesson? Who could Riordan go after?" I had the experience in the '93 Primary, in L.A., of seeing him do exactly that in the run-off, with a Republican against the Democrat.

Despite the fact Riordan had NRA operatives working in his campaign office, despite the fact he had the state chairman of the Christian Coalition in California as a paid staffer, despite the fact he's trundling around Reagan's endorsement and that of a bunch of other right-wing conservatives, he's out there literally getting Democrat after Democrat after Democrat to stand up with him and endorse him. Black Democrats, Asian Democrats, Jewish Democrats, Westside Democratic women, and I knew that that was his experience from the Non-Partisan Municipal Primary, and that's exactly what they would try to do, and they would get some high-profile defectors. And that would have given a signal to our base voters, who weren't all that happy with Gray anyway, that it was okay in this particular instance to go to the other side.

The third way it would have complicated our lives is that in the L.A. media market—and we found this out clear back in 2001—the perception exists of Riordan as a fairly successful mayor of L.A., and a fairly popular mayor of L.A. And not just in the city of L.A., but in places like Torrance, in places like San Bernardino, in places like Costa Mesa, where we focus grouped. And to try to tell these people that he was a gigantic screw-up as mayor and to talk about Belmont and Rampart, and all the other multiple problems and disasters that occurred on his watch, was simply not very credible to people, and they would fight it, they would fight it tooth and nail. One example was where he put the spot up in the primary about him rebuilding the freeways after the Northridge quake, which was total garbage. The freeways don't belong to the city. He had nothing to do with it. It was Pete Wilson using his emergency powers and FEMA shipping in millions of dollars.

People accepted that at face value. And when we would try to run a spot on the same focus group saying Gray Davis had built 12 power plants to get us through the power crises, they resisted that to the last atom of their bodies.

So our challenge was how do we run a campaign against this guy on the air, in the L.A. media market, the biggest and most important media market in California? What will be our message lines against this guy, if you can't take apart his stewardship of the city of L.A.? So those three very substantial problems we foresaw if Riordan was the nominee. Although, ultimately, I think we could have beat him. I actually thought we needed more help from the Simon people to knock him off in the primary. But I thought we could knock him off if. He was inept as a campaigner, and I saw that in 1993.

CHANCE: When did you make that decision to go on the air again?

SOUTH: Oh, clear back in November.

O'DONNELL: Let me back up. The bottom line is the last quarter of '01, we were in a tight general election with Riordan. He was the one we had to defeat; he was the formidable one. Before anybody went on TV, that's where the general was at that point in time. And Riordan had a 40-point lead in the primary.

TULCHIN: Seeing the benchmark in October, and after doing a series of focus groups, we found what Garry is talking about. With a low single-digit lead over Riordan, we saw the structural problems in the race. The L.A. market is the most expensive, the biggest market in the state, and it would cost us a lot of money to try to damage him. The best case scenario for us to win against Riordan—even if he imploded, he still had some appeal to swing voters and Democrats—was to draw in the L.A. market, be competitive in the Central Valley, and win by 30 points in the Bay Area. We knew we could probably do that, especially in the Bay Area where he wasn't as well known and the "beat L.A." phenomenon was very strong. But it made our lives much more difficult compared to Simon or Jones. It would have been much more of a partisan race against those two.

DOAK: In addition to that, we feared that, because of Riordan's base in L.A., which cut into our base, both in votes and money, if we sat back and let Riordan win the primary, and it was a coronation, Riordan stood the chance of coming out of the primary with a lead on the governor, which would have affected the governor's fundraising and his ability to be competitive with the money. It could become a self-fulfilling prophecy.

SOUTH: We're told by people close to Riordan that he had taken out a $10 million line of credit by putting up property he owns as collateral, and that his first act, if he had snared the nomination, was to come after us unmercifully on the air. So there was a financial fear about what would happen right after the primary, because we knew from pretty good sources that he was ready to dump his own money in against us right after the primary.

BARABAK: You said you would go and meet with your donors in Ron Burkle's office, and they had just come back from a lovely brunch with Dick and Nancy over the weekend. What did you say to them to keep them on board?

SOUTH: Well, there were two factors that played into that. One was that even though a lot of these people are social friends of Dick and Nancy Riordan because they're in the Westside social swirl in L.A., many of them knowing Riordan as well as they did, were pretty dismissive of his prospects to run for governor. They thought he was a good mayor only in a limited sense that they had access to him, and that he'd done a couple of good things, but they didn't kid themselves for the most part about this guy's set of political skills. Some of them would laugh and make fun of him during these meetings.

The second thing was we were very firm with these people that it was an unfriendly act to the governor of California to give this guy a dime. And Gray would say, "Look, I have this job. I fought like hell to get this job. This guy wants to take my job away from me." And one of the things that was galling to the governor about Riordan's decision to run was that if you go back to 1998, Riordan endorsed Lungren right at the end of the campaign. We got wind of the fact he was going to do that, so we pulled out the stops to try to get our mutual friends, some of whom I've mentioned here today, as well as the vice president of the United States and a lot of others to call Riordan and say, "This is a mistake. Lungren is going down in flames. Why do you want to put yourself on the other side of the guy who is going to be governor of California, when L.A. needs state support? You're constantly running to the state to bail you out of this and bail you out of that. Why do you want to alienate the obvious next governor of California by endorsing a guy who's run an incompetent campaign and who's going down in flames?"

But he would hear none of it. Even Bill Wardlaw, I'm told, said to Dick Riordan, "That is a mistake to do that." But he went ahead and did it anyway, which ticked us off. And then, to add insult to injury, he had the nerve to show up at our inauguration and seat himself in the governor's box at the Arco Center for the gala, three seats down from Sharon Davis with a big, shit-eating grin on his face. When I turned around and saw that, I wanted to go up and strangle him, and he forced his way into the governor's office the day of the inauguration after we took control of the office, and waited in the cabinet room to have a private meeting with the governor, and asked if a photographer can come in and take pictures of him with the governor. And during the entire governorship, every time Dick Riordan asked the governor for anything for L.A., within reason, he got it, whether it was money for the Disney Performing Arts Center, whether it was money for security at the Democratic National Convention, whether it was Nancy Riordan asking for Foster Care money for the Foster Care Assistance. . . . Everything he asked for, within reason, he got.

So there was no policy reason for this whatsoever. This was, basically, Dick Riordan, a bored guy, who had just left the mayorship, deciding for reasons of ego, in my view and I think in the governor's view, to go "Hey, what the hell. Let's just run for governor."

BARABAK: You put out a memo that was seen as very threatening to people who were going to give money to Dick Riordan. Was that a threat? Was that a legitimate political tactic or did that cross the line? Was it intended as a threat?

SOUTH: It was intended to do what it did. This memo was not put out to the press, it was not air-dropped with helicopters across the state of California, it was put out to our list of donors of $5,000 and more. Okay? And it was very clear what the memo said, if you go back and read it. A lot of these people did not know that under Prop 34, and under Senate Bill 34 that the governor had signed a year previous, there were new reporting requirements that meant that you could not hide money anymore by giving money strategically timed to avoid the next FPPC Report, and then three months would go by before anybody found out that you're giving the money.

As I said in the memo—and the Riordan people dispute this, but some of the folks in the meetings at Burkle's told us this, which is how I found out about it—one of the arguments that was being made by people on Riordan's behalf was that if you timed the money right, it wouldn't be reported for several months, or several weeks. Our message to our donors was, "Look, if you want to run around and call yourself a good close personal friend of the governor of California, that's your prerogative. Close, personal friends of the governor of California do not give money to somebody who's out there to take his job away."

BARABAK: So Garry was just being thoughtful and considerate? Was that a legitimate tactic?

WALSH: It was a bold tactic that worked. Do I think it was over the line? Yeah, but he got away with it. And it worked. Let's be honest, we know how fundraising works. It may have gone to your list, but all your fundraising friends are the same people as the Chamber and all these other business people, and they share that memo. So, if somebody has smallpox and they're sitting next to you, you're going to catch the disease.

CHANCE: We have to get to the ads, because that was an important component. Riordan went on the air in January?

SPILLANE: Middle of January.

CHANCE: And you actually took a little shot at the governor.

SPILLANE: I think that was exaggerated. It was used as the whole excuse for Davis to come in, "Oh, he said something implicitly bad about the direction of California and so, we're just. . . ."

DOAK: Something about gross mismanagement. It was a personal attack on the governor.

SPILLANE: Yeah, I know. It was a vicious personal attack.

SOUTH: Let me remind you for purposes of clarity and truthfulness, that over the course of the primary, your candidate, among other things, equated the governor to Mussolini, equated him to a mass murderer, and equated him to somebody who killed his parents.

FLINT: If the shoe fits. . . .

DOAK: In all seriousness, and I think you guys probably have to agree, Riordan's strategy was to run a general election campaign, to ignore the primary and to focus on Davis, run against Davis, and run as the person who could beat Davis. It's a common strategy for front-runners in primaries. And when you're sitting there with a 40-point lead, it looks like a very palatable strategy.

BARABAK: Okay, so you get him in the race not thinking, "Gee, we're going to take Dick Riordan out at this point." That comes later, and we'll get to that. You got in the race thinking, "We're getting beat up. We need to respond."

SOUTH: And that we could not allow him to come out of the primary unscathed with a lead on us, which we thought and the governor thought would unleash more money than God has on us. If he pumped in his own dough, which we knew he was preparing to do, and if the national Republican forces thought they had the best candidate, and they would turn the spigots on for him.

DOAK: It was not a tactical move generated by Riordan's attack on us. That was the cover that we used to do it. We were employing a strategic move against Riordan, not necessarily at that point. Although, I think all of us sort of thought that there was a small chance we might beat him. But I don't think everybody really thought that.

BARABAK: How did you choose the line of attack that you pursued?

DOAK: It went around a while. For those who've done media, you know you usually get in two or three things. One of the first things we tried to do was to go at his competence because he was undefined outside of L.A. And we made a group of ads about Belmont, and crime, and so forth. We focus grouped those in the outlying areas of L.A., and, frankly, they were marginally successful. In L.A. city, they weren't any more successful than some of the stuff we did outside of the city of L.A. We wanted to test them there because once they worked there they'd work everywhere. But we didn't think that was a way to go after him.

We had always assumed the abortion thing was something we would use as a flip-flop in the general. And I was on the phone one day with Ace Smith, and Ace said, "You know, we could kick him on abortion," because we were thinking about just snapping the numbers back. And that caused me to start thinking about using the abortion thing. And the more I thought about it, the more I thought it was a perfect trap, you know, because he can't get out of it. If he publicly says he's pro-choice, it puts him at odds with the Republican base. If he sits back and lets this go and the painting is right to life, which would help in the Republican primary, it will kill him for the general. We thought remember when you were a kid and you had these Chinese handcuffs you put on your fingers and the harder you pull, the tighter it got? That's sort of the way I thought it was.

But the second piece of it, which was very important, was not using the tape first. Our strategy was to lay out the first attack, which was to accuse him of being pro-life, and then to save the tape as the counter-punch. We thought he'd come back with an ad that would say, 'No, no, no, I'm pro-choice.'

BARABAK: I want to ask Kevin, who is in the position of defending decisions he may not have agreed with or been privy to, but there was a decision in the Riordan camp to go up with a negative spot, and rather than respond they put up an ad that had been in the can, sort of a generic, "Oh, gee, he's attacking me, and he's such a bad guy." Why wasn't there a direct response to the abortion attack?

SPILLANE: As David was saying, there were other ads that went before the abortion ad. And the polling showed that the other ads weren't having a huge impact. It was the abortion ad that had the most dramatic impact. If you look at the primary results, you'll see that Riordan not only lost badly throughout the state, he really lost badly in the Bay Area. So we clearly lost not only pro-life voters, we lost pro-choice voters. And a lot of moderate Republicans didn't end up supporting Riordan as well.

They wanted us to go out and say, "I'm pro-choice." And the argument was not to play into their hands, but basically ignore it. In fact, saying he was pro-life was actually helping us in certain segments of the primary electorate.

WALSH: Wait. Hold on a second. This was a Republican primary. They already knew he was pro-choice, and they held their nose and were willing to tolerate it. What hurt the campaign so badly is how they responded to it. First, there was the canned ad, then Riordan said some things, and then the campaign said things. He already had trouble with the Democrat stuff anyway, and when Republicans looked at that they thought, "This guy doesn't have his act together. He's not the guy to go to."

CHANCE: How did you get the tape?

SOUTH: Well, in 1993, in the runoff between Mike Woo and Dick Riordan, a friend of ours in Beverly Hills called and said, "You know, I just saw a TV show, where Dick Riordan equated abortion to murder." This half-hour program with him had been taped in 1991, before he had ever gotten into the mayor's race. It was a local access cable channel program on the Beverly Hills cable system, whatever that is, where this woman would try to get celebrities, or semi-celebrities, or would-be celebrities to come on the show, and she would interview them for half-an-hour. And because Riordan was a philanthropist and all that, she had him on the show. And the cable system decided to re-air this thing in 1993, when he got into the primary. And one of our supporters, a woman in Beverly Hills, saw it, and called and said, "I just saw this amazing thing where Richard Riordan is talking about abortion being murder."

So we went to the cable system, we found out who the woman was who had this show, and I contacted her. Now, she was a young woman probably not more than 30 or 32, very nonpolitical, was very suspicious about our motivation, but she eventually agreed to go have lunch with me in Beverly Hills. I had to have lunch with her three times to try to get her to cough up a simple VHS copy of this program. Now, at that time, I had never seen the program, and neither had anyone else in the campaign. All we were going on was the word of the woman who called us in Beverly Hills, saying, "I just saw this show."

Ultimately, we bought this simple VHS copy of a half-hour local access cable channel show for $10,000, and in order to use the tape, we made her sign the rights away to the tape, so she didn't have any legal standing to say, "You can't use this tape." She had no animus against Riordan whatsoever. She thought he was kind of a nice guy, and she was very concerned that if we used this tape, that we would get her involved in it, and people would come to her and ask questions, and she didn't want any of that. So she was very, very leery about this whole thing, and it took a lot of sweet-talking to get this tape out of her.

In retrospect, it was worth the $10,000 because the Mike Woo campaign had to pay it.

TULCHIN: That $10,000 was money well spent. We were tracking during the general election, we kept an eye on the Republican primary, as well, for obvious reasons. In mid-January, I don't know when Riordan first went on the air, but in the head-to-head with Riordan, we were actually a few points behind. In the primary, Riordan was at 41 percent, Jones was at 12 percent, Simon was at 6 percent. We put the first spot on the air, followed by the second ad over three weeks. Riordan was at 41, and after we pulled that ad off the air, it was 33 to 28. In other words, we made this a race because of those two ads. The power of those two ads hurt him in the general electorate, it hurt him with the primary voters, it hurt him everywhere. Sean alluded to some events that happened, but the reason those numbers changed so dramatically was because we put 2,400 points in 85 percent of the state.

CHANCE: Did anybody go to the mayor and say, "Mayor, we don't think this is an urban myth?"

SPILLANE: Well, when it was on the air, we learned it wasn't.

CHANCE: So what was that conversation about?

SPILLANE: The conversation was, "Holy shit!"

LAPSLEY: Directly after that ad went up they went fetal, literally. Riordan went down for a couple days. They didn't know how to respond. They didn't know what to do.

DOAK: We always assumed that Riordan knew we had the second ad. We were hoping that the campaign didn't know that we had the second ad, or thought it was an urban myth and you'd go up and respond.

SPILLANE: The campaign didn't know about the second ad. Whether Mayor Riordan knew or not, only Mayor Riordan can answer for himself. Now, the impression of the campaign was we had no reason to believe that it existed.

DOAK: There were two important decisions to be made about how to roll this issue out. One was the timing of it—to roll the first ad, the second ad, I think it made it much more effective. In fact, I believe, and correct me if I'm wrong, that when we put the first installment on which said Riordan was a right to lifer, his numbers went up in the Republican primary for a few days. And then we hit him. But we had focus grouped this, and we knew how devastating it was; the one-two punch was just a killer.

SOUTH: We knew it would be relatively fatal, but the damaging thing when we played out this one-two punch in focus groups was that when we were focus grouping swing voters, both right-to-lifers and pro-choicers in the same focus group, and we showed them the two spots. . . .

WALSH: All Republicans? General election?

TULCHIN: General election swing voters.

SOUTH: The right-to-lifers thought this guy truly was right to life, he truly was against abortion as a very strong Roman Catholic, but then he just cravenly and crassly changed his position to run for mayor in 1993. As a matter of fact, that's kind of what he said, when you ask him about it—"Well, that was before I ran for mayor." So their view was that this was a fundamental shift for crass political reasons against the most strongly held belief in his heart that abortion was, in fact, murder. And the pro-choicers thought the guy was just a liar, that he was out there saying to everybody, "I'm pro-choice, I can win because I'm pro-choice. I can bring women flooding back to the Republican party because I'm pro-choice. I can beat Gray Davis because I'm pro-choice." And he was just lying about it. It was a classic two-edged sword.

DOAK: The thought was not to run this as a "Dick Riordan is going to take away your right to abortion" issue, we decided to run it as a character issue instead, which was critical.

SOUTH: He did it to win the election, that's what he said.

DOAK: "A record you can trust," was his tagline. We thought about a lot of taglines we wanted to put it on, put it on the character, the trust, the integrity. You know, it's much more devastating and broad, and gave you other avenues to go down as we did later. We went down the death penalty avenue, we went down taxes, we went down when the Deukmejian thing. We crafted the ad, which I still think was probably the most effective ad we did, we called it the Deukmejian ad.

LAPSLEY: That's an important point. When all that mix was going forward, when we moved forward with our strategy to nail Riordan at the convention using Deukmejian to say, "He's a man I couldn't vote for," that literally changed the numbers in a huge way, because that's when Simon literally took off.

SOUTH: There's no question that that was a seminal event in the campaign.

LAPSLEY: Absolutely.

BARABAK: I want to ask you guys here if the Davis campaign had restrained itself throughout the entire primary, never run any advertising, would the outcome of the Republican primary been different?

FLINT: I think it changed things on the margin. I think Simon still would have won, because Riordan would have found he was a flawed candidate just because he wasn't good at it, and so he would have found something else to screw up. The Deukmejian stuff, our state party chairman, losing the straw poll, and all of those other things would have happened. It would have been a lot closer, but I think Simon would have still won.

BARABAK: Kevin?

SPILLANE: I disagree totally. There's a lot of revisionist history here. You've got 10 guys up here telling you that Dick Riordan never had a chance, and what a stupid idea it was for him to run for governor, and the reality is these guys spent $10 million to keep him from being the nominee, and both of these campaigns came very close to dropping out. So if Dick Riordan was so damn beatable, why did they both almost switch to other races or consider not running altogether. Jones didn't have enough money to be effective on an attack. And Simon was not attacking; in fact, Simon did not attack us on television until we started to attack him when the numbers were going south dramatically. It was a last desperate move, and he turned around and attacked us.

I was one of the people arguing to hold off doing anything to piss Simon off. I didn't want him to go negative on Riordan because he did have the money to carry the message. The point is Riordan's less than pure Republican credentials, and if the voters didn't know about that and these guys didn't have the money or the inclination to carry the message, then he could have survived the primary. I knew it wasn't going to be pretty, but I thought he could survive the primary.

WALSH: With the Republicans he probably could have.

FLINT: But that's my point, Riordan chose to do that on his own. He went out to piss off the only people who could vote for him.

SPILLANE: But he would have won the primary if they had not put on the abortion ad. The abortion ad was critical, because you've got it coming and going, and it was a character ad, and it became more than just about abortion. And, we didn't just lose the conservative counties; we lost the moderate counties badly as well in the primary.

BARABAK: Just to close the circle, why did it go from, "We can muss this fellow up," to "We can take him out and knock him out of the primary, and eliminate the guy we don't want to face in November?"

SOUTH: I think it was late February that we agreed we were essentially going to go positive for the rest of the primary campaign, because the governor believed that we probably couldn't take out Riordan, and that we might as well put the final gloss on him, the governor, in the last 10 days of the campaign. But Paul and Ben came back with some numbers the very next day literally showing that not only had the margin closed between Riordan and Simon, but that the margin between Riordan and Davis had closed substantially from the beginning of the primary. I was actually on my way to Montana because my mother was ill, and we convened a conference call while I was at LAX, and we decided to go back on the air with the negative, and try to take the guy out. And that was the first time the governor ever believed in his heart of hearts that we could actually do this.

DOAK: We'd say, "Governor, I think we have a chance to take this guy out." And he'd go, "This is a pipe dream, you guys are just smoking. . . ."

O'DONNELL: This was with about three weeks to go.

DOAK: It was almost as if he thought we might be able to, but he didn't want to admit to himself that there was a chance.

O'DONNELL: But we made the decision with three weeks to go, to try to take him out. We thought we had a shot at it then.

DOAK: Mark, you asked when the decision was made. You were on the doorstep of having the story, because you called right in the middle of the meeting. We're sitting in the governor's house, making these decisions to go on the air, and my cell phone rings. I pick it up, and it's Barabak.

BARABAK: What were the flight days of the abortion ads?

TULCHIN: January 21 to February 3 was the first one; and then the second was the February 4 to February 11.

BARABAK: And the Republican convention was at the tail end of that, right?

TULCHIN: February 13 was when he poked Deukmejian in the eye.

BARABAK: The convention was February 8 through the 10th.

TULCHIN: Right, but the debates were the 22nd and the 9th, and then the Deukmejian quote was the 13th.

FLINT: The Deukmejian quote was at the debate.

TULCHIN: The third debate was February 13th.

FLINT: Right, but he insulted Governor Deukmejian on the 9th.

BARABAK: But Dan Borenstein had the story a couple days leading into the convention, where Deukmejian said he wouldn't endorse him, and then there was a press conference at the convention where Deukmejian said it again. And then the next day Riordan insulted the. . . .

FLINT: Since Rollins isn't here I'll take the liberty of making the boxing analogy. It was like taking the body blows where you don't see the damage, but it's being done under there, and then it's easy to push the person over. And that's how I came to view it; he was beating the crap out of Riordan. And we didn't see a lot of movement in our polling; you say you saw it in yours. We didn't see a lot in ours, we saw some Simon going up because we were on the air with the Giuliani ads, and obviously, Giuliani was an effective spokesman and all that. But at that convention, it became okay for Republicans not to like Dick Riordan. Up until then, it was Gray Davis hitting him, and they were disturbed by what they saw about Riordan, but it was Gray Davis saying it, and "We're just not all that sure that we can trust what Gray Davis says about Dick Riordan." And then Republicans started saying it's okay to be against Dick Riordan. Governor Deukmejian did, our party chairman did, most of the papers in the state the Monday after the state party convention had screamer headlines, "Republicans

Reject Riordan Candidacy" because of the straw poll and other things. That all coalesced at the same time.

CHANCE: And then the Jones campaign sealed that image in people's minds with your ad. And can you talk a little bit about that final ad that you did, including Deukmejian?

LAPSLEY: We had to go after Riordan. We set it up at the convention to set the stage. We knew we had just a couple hundred thousand dollars that we were really going to put up on TV. We had a former governor who is literally venerated in the state of California, who goes out, sends a message directly, "I will not vote for Dick Riordan." So we do it in the convention, 40 minutes before the debate. Who was the reporter that you set up? I'm giving you credit here. It was the reporter who took that question right into the first debate, right into the first question, and then we were in. Then Larry McCarthy had to do an ad that tried to do everything for the whole campaign in one 30-second ad. He had to do a negative on Riordan, a negative on Simon, and a positive on Jones in 30 seconds, which is, obviously, impossible, especially when you don't have the point totals behind it in any of the markets, particularly L.A., and southern California, to be able to even begin to drive it home. We wanted to close the door on Riordan, regardless using Deukmejian. That was the sole goal at that point, just to take Riordan out.

BARABAK: When did you learn of Deukmejian's antipathy toward Riordan? Was it early on, or did he say one day, "Boy, I just can't stand that guy," and a light bulb went off?

LAPSLEY: I had the most discussions with the governor, because I was in direct communication with him. He had given it to Dan Borenstein. Dan got to him and he jumped the gun, because we wanted to take it one day closer. He was supposed to hold. But Dan got to him. He gets the credit. My discussion was probably 10 days before that. I said, "Governor, how do you feel about Riordan at this point?" And he said, "Well, you know, I just can't vote for this guy." So we were talking about where can we utilize it. We didn't think we were going to do it publicly, so we were just kind of kicking it around, but we didn't at that point think we would really try to push him, because the governor, with his integrity, is not a person that you push. But Dan got to him. So I went back to him as soon as I saw the quotes, and I said, "Well, Governor, you know, will you say it publicly, in a press conference? I won't vote for Dick Riordan. I can't vote for Dick Riordan." And he thought about it, and said, yes. So I passed it on to Sean, and away it went. That's what it all boiled down to. We didn't think he would do it publicly, we didn't want to push him, but that article set the stage for it.

BARABAK: Can I ask a quick question about the convention? It seems to me that Simon very wisely sort of spun something out of the straw poll. I know that people in high places in the Republican party were working on Riordan's behalf to kill the straw poll. Talk about the straw poll, and how you turned basically nothing into a big something in the Monday headlines.

RUSSO: We had two big surges in the beginning. One was the Giuliani surge, when we put Giuliani on the air to talk about Bill Simon. That was credibility building for somebody who was an unknown, and we definitely got a big bump out of that.

FLINT: And we should say since we're doing this for history that we underestimated what the bump we would get out of Giuliani. We thought that it would raise his name ID, raise his positive, get people to think about Bill Simon, but not actually move us from 5 to 20 in the polls, just on, "I know Bill Simon, I think he will be a good governor." We underestimated that.

SPILLANE: We were, frankly, startled by the growth that Simon had. We knew he was going to grow, and he had the potential to grow rapidly. But you guys didn't even put all that much money on Giuliani initially, did you?

RUSSO: We were on radio for the first two weeks and then. . . .

SPILLANE: We were surprised how quickly Simon moved up. He was in the 20s before we knew it, and it was not even that heavy a Giuliani buy.

RUSSO: The second thing was to establish ourselves as the economic conservative in the race, partially for offensive reasons, and some defensive to get away from the social issues. So we embraced the Jarvis initiative, and we had the taxpayer groups at the first debate. And we put Bill on TV talking about taxes and the budget, to coincide with the appearance with the tax groups at the debate, and the party straw poll. Winning the straw poll was really important with Riordan being the anti-Republican, and the perception in the media that Jones was the establishment Republican. We had to take over that establishment Republican role. So we did put a lot of energy into our organization, which Ron spearheaded, so we could win that straw poll. That combined with taxes and Giuliani, in the poll we did right after the convention, we were ahead of Riordan with voters that had heard of Bill Simon. We were behind with all voters so it was clear that as the campaign unfolded, that would get replicated as voters paid attention. So we were pretty convinced by the 13th of February that it was done. I raised my number to Simon from an 80 percent chance to win to 100 percent.

CHANCE: Did the Jones ad help you?

FLINT: It helped some.

RUSSO: Deukmejian was key because Deukmejian gave the credibility to, "That's right, Riordan's not really one of us." That was key.

FLINT: And Rob knew when we saw the ad that they were trying to do three messages in one ad, which is hard to do. But the message that was going to penetrate from that was Governor Deukmejian saying, "I can't vote for Dick Riordan, and you shouldn't either."

RUSSO: As Rob said, they didn't have any money to put him on TV, and yet it was still very powerful.

O'DONNELL: We were using Deukmejian in our ad at the same time.

RUSSO: And the Davis people were questioning Riordan's credibility as a Republican, so it just all came together, and Riordan's numbers collapsed.

CHANCE: And you had a nominee.

III. The General Election Campaign

CHAPTER 7

The General Election Campaign—
An Unhappy Electorate Opts for Davis

Introduction
by Carla Marinucci, *The San Francisco Chronicle*

It was the morning after the March 2002 primary, and Bill Simon, Jr.—
surfer, scion of a Republican political family, and millionaire businessman—had
just pulled off a miracle. He had won his first political race.

As he looked out over the assembled audience at a GOP "unity breakfast,''
Simon prepared to address his party for the first time as the Republican gubernatorial nominee in crucial California. Then came the call: a public pat on the back
from the president of the United States.

"I've got a lot of friends out there, including the folks you defeated,"
George W. Bush told Simon, before a listening audience of Republicans—many
who had hoped Simon would fall to the White House's pick, former Los Angeles mayor Richard Riordan, or to veteran state GOP insider Secretary of State
Bill Jones. "You deserve to be congratulated. I know you can beat Gray Davis,
and I want to help in any way I can," Bush said. Simon beamed.

Across town, the team of Democratic governor Gray Davis was equally
buoyant. The increasingly unpopular Davis, a 30-year veteran of state politics,
had been unopposed in his own party's primary. But it took a $10 million adver-
tising barrage against the moderate pro-choice Riordan to eliminate what was
seen as the biggest GOP threat to a second term by Davis. As Simon celebrated
his win, Democrats did too, believing that the neophyte would be no contest for
the veteran insider.

That morning—the official starting gun of the general election contest of 2002—may have been the political high water mark for both newcomer Simon and the battle-scarred Davis.

What awaited in the months ahead—a brutal, expensive campaign demolition derby, the likes of which most Californians had never seen—would have lasting effects on the state's weary voters, and become the genesis of a shocking voter revolution that would shake the country's political landscape.

Republican attacks would portray the struggling Democratic governor as the slave to pay-to-play politics and special interests, heading an administration rife with corruption and extortion, crippled by indecisiveness over critical issues like energy and the budget deficit, which loomed in the billions.

Democratic operatives would paint the GOP businessman as a right-wing extremist, a spineless incompetent, doing business with drug dealers, and hiding his own financial mismanagement. And they got some help from Simon himself, who many GOPers said bungled the ripe chance for Republican defeat of poll-battered Davis with a campaign full of flip-flops and embarrassing missteps.

From that March morning until the November election, the Republican self-described "candidate of ideas" and the Democrat who touted "leadership Californians can trust" not only demolished each other—but also managed to destroy millions of voters' will to be involved in the political process.

The 2002 California general election would become a story of how two political machines burned nearly $80 million dollars on a contest so utterly negative that, in record numbers, millions of voters—even the most regular and conscientious of them—turned off and stayed home in disgust.

With an election that Davis's own chief strategist, Garry South, described jokingly as a choice between "damaged goods versus defective product," many voters wondered if California politics had finally hit rock bottom.

When the stage was set for the 21st century's first gubernatorial election, there was reason for hope, and high expectations in the nation's most populous state, where demographic changes were continuing to shift the political landscape—and provide surprises.

In 1998, Davis had sailed into office, ending an 18-year Democratic drought in the top office in Sacramento. His first election was a triumph for both the underestimated politician described as the state's "best trained governor in waiting" and his party—and capped a disastrous GOP defeat by former Attorney General Dan Lungren, whipped by a painful 58-38 margin points.

Davis's first term began on a high note: he headed a dominant party flush with new power, a 26-14 margin in the state Senate and a 50-30 majority in the Assembly. He assumed control in a state with an economy so robust that Joel Kotkin described it "something like the Internet, with a bunch of random connections and poles that are always recreating themselves."

With two U.S. Democratic senators, and a Democratic majority in the congressional delegation, it looked as though the party's winning streak would only continue: polls showed Californians, and its increasingly influential Latino voters, were more sympathetic to Democratic positions on the issues: pro-choice, anti-gun, anti-tobacco, pro-environment and pro-education.

Davis would preside over a redistricting plan that assured his party would face few contested races in the years ahead, and allowed Republicans the gain of just one seat in the GOP-controlled U.S. House of Representatives.

From the minute he entered the governor's office, Davis sought to solidify his position. He hit up labor unions, lobbyists, and trial lawyers, stockpiling an astounding $26 million in contributions—a full two years before he would face his opponent.

But he couldn't control an energy crisis that battered California, kicking off blackouts and brownouts statewide, reminding irritated consumers of the fragility of their comfortable life and finite power supply. Republicans complained Davis failed to act decisively to forestall that crisis, even as another hit: the economic downturn.

High tech, the engine of California's money machine—an industry where instant millionaires, innovators, and venture capitalists had captured the world's imagination—sputtered to a halt. A ripple effect meant jobs lost and revenues gone, but legislative spending dominated by Democrats went unabated. The once healthy surplus turned into a black hole of budget deficit.

By the time he prepared to square off in the 2002 general election against Simon, Davis's approval ratings had sunk 30 points. And the former prosecutor under Rudy Giuliani was promising to bring his business expertise to help California from its malaise. The fresh-faced conservative, whose vocabulary was peppered with words like "golly" and "gee," had never run for school board, had only irregularly voted, and until recently, and had limited his public life to a few carefully orchestrated speeches.

But the Pacific Palisades mega-millionaire, a "true conservative," defied the odds when he won the GOP nomination over Riordan and Jones in a bitter, unexpectedly lively contest—sneaking to victory by an unbelievable 20 points. His win was seen as a message from conservative grassroots GOP loyalists, slapping back moderates hoping for a more centrist course.

So the general election was cast as an unusually rare opportunity to draw contrasts for the voters over issues and ideology, style and substance.

It was a tax-and-spend liberal against a fiscally conservative Republican. A Catholic pro-choice champion against a Catholic pro-life advocate. An unpopular lifelong politician with 30 years experience against an "outsider" with fresh ideas and real business credentials. An uptight, buttoned down personality against a family guy with four kids. A man of modest financial means versus a man who had inherited his daddy's name and bucks.

Simon's own political team was well aware of the odds of beating Davis, the Democrat in control of California, the nation's biggest political theater.

"There was complete, total pessimism that Gray Davis could be defeated," recalled Simon's chief political consultant Sal Russo at the Institute of Governmental Studies seminar, who told his client he had "a 30 percent chance" of **being** the 30-year political veteran in the general election.

Still, Republicans believed Davis to be petulant, personality-deficient, and vulnerable—a man whose single-minded concentration on fundraising and political partisanship fired up the ire of GOP loyalists, while turning off Democrats and swing voters alike.

Newspapers coverage chronicled the "pay to play" accusations being leveled almost daily at Davis—and they were shocking. The president of the California Teachers Association groused Davis hit the union up for a $1 million donation while in his Capitol office. UC Berkeley students reported getting fundraising letters offering a chance to meet with Davis for "a mere $100." Pipe fitters, prison guards, law enforcement, high speed rail advocates—it seemed that Davis's circle of friends included just about anyone who could write a campaign check.

The Oracle fiasco came next: a no-bid $95 million contract, a $25,000 campaign donation passed in a bar, a fired aide, accusations of document-shredding—and a governor who claimed he didn't know what went on.

Russo called Davis's fundraising the "heroin of our campaign, because it really felt good, we got a lot of press coverage, the press was infatuated with it."

Then Davis was dogged by the criticism of his energy policies, and the suggestion that he had fiddled while California's fuses blew. A frustrated Davis blew a fuse himself, bitter and combative when questioned at the *San Diego Union Tribune* editorial board on the matter.

"I kept the lights on. . . . I think I should get a round of applause. I don't get squat," he groused. "I saved this friggin' paper. I kept the lights on in this state. Do you understand that? I kept the lights on."

Energy combined with economy; repeatedly asked about his plans to trim the burgeoning state deficit, the governor deferred on details—handing ammunition to critics who claimed he couldn't steer the state ship out of troubled waters. Davis polls sunk further.

Still, newcomer Simon couldn't take advantage, demonstrating he still had his learner's permit when it came to hardball California politics.

In his first postprimary press conference, Simon was asked by reporters if he would explore important social issues like guns, gay rights, and abortion in the election. He appeared to blithely dismiss the question. "I think 'change the topic' might be an accurate characterization," he laughed.

No delicate dancer who could waltz easily from right to center in the general election contest, Simon's troubles were just beginning.

On the business front, campaign insiders were shell-shocked when headlines erupted about a legal case involving a former drug dealer who was awarded a $76 million judgment, saying he was defrauded by Simon's firm in a pay-phone company partnership. The story made national news, embarrassing Bush as he prepared to come to California—and Enron corporate scandals erupted. Even with a later legal reversal, Simon couldn't recoup the damage.

On the financial side, Simon couldn't—or wouldn't—tell reporters if he paid his income taxes, then balked at releasing his records. Stories followed that the government was inquiring about his tax shelters and investments.

On the professional front, former prosecutor Simon, who boasted the endorsement of Giuliani, faced questions about whether he had really—as his campaign claimed—taken out "the heads of all five New York area Mafia families."

New York defense attorney Gerald Shargel, whose clients had included such Mob stalwarts as "Dapper Don" John Gotti and Sammy "the Bull" Gravano, put that to rest. "I don't even remember hearing of him," he scoffed.

On the ideological front, Simon executed an embarrassing flip flop on gay rights issues—at first, appearing to support some domestic partnerships and a Gay Pride Day, then backing down.

The missteps prompted the GOP circular firing squad to lock and load. Former Simon adviser Lyn Nofziger called the candidate "inept, weak, not very bright" and "too dumb to win." National Republican Congressional Committee head Rep. Thomas Davis of Virginia piled on, calling Simon's "the worst-run race in the country."

And then came the *coup de grace:* Simon triumphantly announced at a debate that he had the evidence nabbing Davis in the act of illegal fundraising. But the photo from the hapless California Organization of Police and Sheriffs was bogus—and so were the charges.

Ouch.

In the final days, Simon pumped $10 million of his own money into attacks on Davis, and Davis exhausted his store of campaign funds in a TV political barrage that devoured Simon like an Uzi set on automatic. The airwaves were crowded with gunk, and the voters sank into despair.

By election day, roughly half of state voters said they believed California was heading in the wrong direction. Record numbers of Californians said they wouldn't even bother to vote. They were true to their word.

Jay Hanson, a city planner in Chico, expressed the mood. "I threw out my ballot as a protest to our lack of choice," he said. Hanson wondered why "the great state of California (can't) find at least two honest politicians worthy of running."

When it was over, in a Democratically leaning state, disgusted Democrats abandoned Davis in droves. There was little to celebrate as the battered governor crawled to an embarrassing four-point victory over the stumbling Simon—hardly the 20 points he had so confidently predicted.

Davis had won the war.

But the embers were still burning in California's battle-scarred political landscape.

Less than a month after the Democrat's re-election, two GOP consultants would begin the talks about a recall. Eight months later, the unthinkable happened: 1.7 million Californians signed petitions and put a recall measure on the ballot.

Davis would battle again with a political newcomer—this time, one of almost mythical proportions, an action hero, a "Terminator" who promised to end partisan politics. Actor Arnold Schwarzenegger promised "action, action," the brawn—and literally, the broom—to "clean up Sacramento," end partisan battling, and bring Republicans and Democrats together.

Little more than a year after his brutal victory over Bill Simon, Davis would turn his hard-won office over to the man who promised "action, action, action."

On his way out the door, Davis said he understood that voters, apathetic and too disgusted to vote months before, had had enough of rock bottom politics.

"The people of this state," he said, "want change."

The General Election Campaign Panel

CARLA MARINUCCI: If you saw the McLaughlin Report recently, John McLaughlin said, "The best politician in 2002 was by far California Governor Gray Davis. What a comeback from a political graveyard. The worst politician, panelists Eleanor Cliff and Tony Blankley agreed, was Bill Simon, the Republican candidate for governor in California. Even Democrats were interested in giving Gray Davis a second term. Simon blew it." That was the pundit's look at the 2002 California governor's race. Today, we're going to take a closer, chronological look at what happened.

RANDY SHANDOBIL: But before we go chronologically, those remarks lead to one obvious question: given that the perception was that Governor Davis was so vulnerable, that pretty much anyone could have beaten him in this race, what happened?

SAL RUSSO: Well, first of all, that's revisionist history, which is why those talk shows on Sunday morning are not worth watching anymore. One of the more pronounced problems Republicans had in California was complete and total pessimism. Everyone thought there was no chance for Republicans to win the governor's race. I don't think there was a reporter in this state that, in any discussion I ever had with him, would say anything other than, "You don't have a snowball's chance in hell of beating Gray Davis." There was complete, total pessimism that Gray Davis could be defeated. And that permeated our campaign from beginning to end. It affected the quality of the press coverage because we were seen as not having a chance to win. And it certainly affected our fundraising. It affected the confidence that the White House had in playing in a big way in California. At the end of the campaign everybody said, "Well, any idiot could have beaten Gray Davis." Well, certainly nobody said that in March, in April, in May, in June, July, and August, and September. So I think there's a great deal of revisionism in that view.

MARINUCCI: We're going to do the introductions, but, first, one more general question to Democrats; we're not going to give all the tough questions to the Simon guys. A lot of Republicans said, "Hey, this was the moment. We could have taken down Gray Davis," and "You're the guys that spent $67 million and still came in with a squeaker." If it were a level playing field and you didn't have that kind of money, which was more than Al Gore raised in his presidential race, would Gray Davis be sitting in the governor's seat today?

GARRY SOUTH: Remember all the press inquiries saying, "Why do you guys need all this money?" Well, now you know. I've heard all the Republican post-election spin about $67 million and five percent election victory, but that's a little disingenuous. We had a full-bore political operation in '99, 2000, 2001 all during the governor's first term. We did raise $67 million over that four-year period, but $13 million of it was already spent by the time we ever got into the

2000 election year just on our political activities. And, if you want to be fair about it, you've probably got to move $10 million of that off our side of the ledger and over to the Simon side of the ledger, based on what we did to Riordan in the primary. So it's not true that we spent $67 million against Bill Simon and got a five percent victory. That's simply not statistically true.

MARINUCCI: Let me introduce our panelists. Jeff Flint was a key strategist for the Simon campaign, and Rob Lapsley was the general election campaign manager for Simon. Sean Walsh was one of the key spokesmen for Simon, and Sal Russo was a senior strategist for the Simon campaign. Garry South . . . guru for Governor Davis. David Doak and Tom O'Donnell did the Davis media, and Ben Tulchin was the pollster.

SHANDOBIL: Let's start with the morning after the primary. Bill Simon wins. He's riding a wave of momentum. You had to expect that the morning after, Gray Davis is going to attack him on his positions on abortion and gun control. When reporters asked him at the hotel, the obvious question, he seemed very ill prepared. He said he was going to change the topic, didn't want to talk about it, didn't think that those things were important. Was that the planned response?

JEFF FLINT: He was asked a question that had the phrase, "change the topic" in it. And he said yes to that, "Yes, change the topic sounds about right." And I think if you were there you could count that as a joke as much as anything. Now maybe he shouldn't have made the joke. But somebody asked, "What are you going to do when they come after you on abortion and guns, and gays, and everything else, are you just going to change the topic? And he laughed and said, 'Yes, change the topic . . .' or 'change the subject.'"

SHANDOBIL: But, he did change the topic. He never did answer the question.

FLINT: That's what I'm saying. The Davis campaign spent a lot of time trying to convince people he had done a good job on energy, and finally gave up on it because it was not a successful argument.

SAL RUSSO: Jeff is right; you're mixing apples and oranges in your question. There are three things that had to happen for us to have a viable campaign. One is that the energy problem had to turn into a full crisis. That was one thing that had to happen. On the budget, I had praised Gray substantially in the press his first year as governor. I ran into Gray in December after his first year, and he thanked me profusely for all the good things I had said about his first year in office. But the second thing that had to happen was the budget had to get out of control. He had to succumb to the Democrats wanting to base-build the budget, and we had to have bad economic times to create a budget crisis. And the third thing is his successful fundraising had to become a two-edged sword. It had to not just be a positive, they had all this money to spend, but there had to be a negative, and that was the emergence of pay for play. Those three things, I thought, were conditions precedent to even making this thing a race. That's why I said to Simon, I thought his chances of winning the primary were 80 percent and winning the general were 30 percent because we had to have those three things just to get to the starting gate.

Now the energy thing, I think pretty much worked out, even though, as Garry pointed out, they out-maneuvered the White House at critical times. But at the end of the day, Gray definitely took the bullet for the energy crisis in a substantial way. He did something with the budget, but I didn't think it was possible to dodge responsibility for increasing spending 37 percent and exacerbating our budget crisis. So that one didn't completely happen. And, certainly, pay for play came and was a material factor.

So I thought those three things were conditions precedent to our having a viable campaign. Once we got through the primary, two other things had to happen. In California, the Democratic base vote is too big in this day and age. We had to do something about that. And we tried to do two things to either dissuade Democrats from voting or give them a reason not to vote for Gray Davis or to vote for a third-party candidate. And that was how pay to play emerged, to get liberals to be disgusted that Gray Davis was selling out liberal principles for big corporate interests. That was why that was an important issue for us.

And Sean did a really good job, particularly in those early months, to take some of the liberal issues—the environment, offshore oil drilling—we came out against offshore drilling in the primary, but Sean took that issue to a new level with dioxin. And he did the same thing on the environment, because we really had to drive liberals away from Davis. So that was one thing that we had to do.

The second thing that we had to do—you know I have referred lately to pay for play as the heroin of our campaign, because it felt really good, we got a lot of press coverage, the press was infatuated with it. But it was sort of a dud issue with the public, because the public thinks everybody is a crook in politics. And so it had limited value—it had value, but limited value. We had to get to another level, which was that Gray Davis was a failed governor. We got so hooked on the heroin of pay to play, we never quite got as far as I thought we needed to get.

MARINUCCI: Your campaign was almost like a scene from the movie, *The Candidate,* where you all looked at each other after you won the primary and said, "What do we do now?" I want to hear from Garry on this side. This guy is being held up as a political giant killer; it was a big surprise. He was a wealthy guy. What were you expecting from the Simon campaign after the primary?

SOUTH: You ask the question in the context of the day after the election, but in my view you have to go back to the night of the election. Our question was whether or not the Simon people, as I sort of indelicately put it at the time, believed their own bullshit. Because as you remember, on election night what happened was I think Jeff and Sal showed up at a press conference with a memo that laid out the brilliant, flawless, ingenious strategy that they had used to win the primary all on their own, and that the Davis effort had had no impact whatsoever. It was all like spitting in the wind, and everything they did was perfect, it was perfectly timed, the media was perfect, everything was perfect, everything worked according to Hoyle. And they did this all by themselves with no outside influence. The Davis impact was nil. I saw the memo that night and I said to myself, "Boy, far be it from me to criticize somebody for spinning, but I hope to God for their sake that they're spinning here, and they don't really believe their own B.S. Because if this is, in fact, the way they think they won this thing, they're in serious trouble in the general, because they don't get it."

SHANDOBIL: In the primary, there was speculation that your campaign might be making the same mistake that Pat Brown made in 1966, trying to knock out a popular, moderate Republican mayor to get in a more right-wing, first-time politician, and, that politician obviously ended up to be Ronald Reagan. Was there ever a point in March that you were afraid that might happen? What were you fears about Bill Simon?

SOUTH: Well, our initial fear was that some of the same outside groups, these 527 committees or 501C4 committees, would come in after the primary in the absence of the candidate having enough money to do so, and try to do to us what they did in the summer of 2001 on energy. One of the reasons we sued Americans Taxpayers Alliance, which cost us a lot of money—we won in Superior Court, lost at the Court of Appeal and the Supreme Court turned down our appeal—one of the reasons we sued them with a great deal of fanfare was to send a message to these out-of-state groups from that point forward that if you come in here and try to mess with us, we're going to go after you legally. We're going to go after you with every resource and every available tool that we have.

We never had any plans to go on the air the day after the election to try and take out Simon. We never had any spots in the can; that was never our intent. I know people speculated about that, including many in the press. That was never, never our plan. What we did fear would happen is that in March after the primary, in April, and in May, there would be these outside forces coming in here trying to soften up Davis like they did in the summer of 2001, with unaccounted-for sources of money to soften us up for the kill. And every single day, we thought it may drop today; it may break today; they may come in tomorrow. Every single day that didn't happen, we thought if we can get to June without that occurring, we'd win this race.

TOM O'DONNELL: The other thing that happened the morning after was we got on our regular conference call, and the governor got on all of us. He chewed us out.

MARINUCCI: What was his concern?

DAVID DOAK: He said, "You guys spend all your time slapping yourselves on the back." He was sending a message to us, "I don't want you going on vacation on me."

MARINUCCI: Was he worried about Simon?

DOAK: He was more worried about our attitude.

SOUTH: I know the governor pretty well. He's the kind of person who does not allow himself to exult very much, and doesn't particularly like it when people around him do. But what is true is that—and we had an internal disagreement about this, as all these guys know—the governor was convinced that Simon had far more in resources than we thought he had available. And he was telling us that on the phone, hollering at us saying, "You guys don't get it. You know the guy is going to dump $10 million, $15 million right off the bat. He's going to try to go after me on energy, go after me on the budget, go after me on the sleaze, and everything else." And my view from day one was that the guy didn't have that much money to put into this thing. I don't know how much he had. I don't think anybody really ever knew how much he was worth, even at the end of the campaign. But I'd been told by very close sources to Simon clear back in February or March of 2001, "Look, I know his financial situation. He doesn't have $25 to $30 million to put into this race." But the governor never believed that was the case, and he was arguing clear up until the end that somehow there was going to be this huge, huge dump truck show up, dumping $15 million, $20 million out of Simon's own personal resources at the end to try to take us out.

BEN TULCHIN: In terms of the structure of the race and how he felt about Simon, we didn't see how Simon could win, even when people were saying the governor was vulnerable. Simon was the conservative Republican, he called himself that in the primary. He's antichoice; he's against gun control. He'd taken all these very conservative positions. And then the business record, in the year we had Enron collapse, and WorldCom, and all these other scandals. And some of the stuff that happened over the campaign wasn't even in our research, like the fraud verdict. So we had a huge arsenal against this guy.

DOAK: But we didn't know how big an arsenal we had.

TULCHIN: That's true. But we knew he had huge vulnerabilities. In terms of the governor's vulnerability, everyone knew about them already—the budget, the energy crises. There's nothing new and, ultimately, voters are going to have to make the decision, "All right, stick with this guy. Maybe I question his handling of the energy crises and the budget, but he seems like a decent guy." Simon was a guy they were going to learn a lot about.

MARINUCCI: What about it, Sal? The iron was hot right after the primary. It seemed like the time to dump $10 million to $15 million into the race. Did you have a conversation with Simon, "Yes, you've given us $5 million for the primary, now what can we expect for the general?"

RUSSO: I knew at the beginning, back in February of 2001, the parameters of what he was prepared to do. I said before that I think self-financed campaigns have a real problem. I told Simon that first night that if he wanted to self-finance then I didn't want to do the campaign; that I didn't think he could be successful. It's very difficult to finance your own campaign and be successful. Now, would it have been helpful at that point in time for him to put some money in? It would have been, but given the dynamics of our fundraising, if he had put the money in that he put in at the end at that point in time, I think it would have killed our fundraising. I think that would have been the end our fundraising.

SHANDOBIL: What was your fundraising like at that point? I've heard some people grouse that the campaign wasn't aggressive enough in reaching out to Republicans in the early days after the primary victory to get funds coming in.

RUSSO: Well, the one bad thing about Riordan being in the primary was that he definitely owned the donor community. Our finance committee was extraordinarily weak. And it never, ever really got to be as good as Wilson's or Lungren's. We never got to that level. There was all the negativity that existed over the course of time and Bush's poor performance in California. Combine that with a little bit of hope springing in the donor community with Riordan; and after that gets quashed, they just closed their checkbooks. So the president came out graciously and did three events, and we really struggled to raise money. But we were greatly under where we wanted to be in terms of those events. It was not so much that we should have raised more money, which we should have, but we did not get the commitment of the donor community to the campaign at that time when we needed it. Like Garry, we had heard all the stories about all the groups that were going to do the same thing the energy companies did. And we got names and organizations that were supposedly going to do this any day now, any day. So we, in fact, expected to get carried for a period of time by third parties going out and beating up on Gray Davis on the issues. To my knowledge, none of that happened; I don't think any of them did.

DOAK: Could I ask a question? When Ken Lay came out and had the meeting with Riordan and Schwarzenegger, did he promise to do anything, or was this just a meet and greet?

RUSSO: Bill got invited to the meeting, and we chose not to go. So I don't know what happened.

MARINUCCI: Five million dollars in the primary—was that all he intended to ever put in?

RUSSO: Yes.

MARINUCCI: No, going through to the general?

FLINT: Russo had more conversations with Bill about money and how much he was able to put in than I ever did. But, Sal always told me he had the impression that Bill had in the neighborhood of $10 million to put in the race. And it ended up being five in the primary and five in the general—a little more than five in the general at the end of the day. But that was always our assumption; at the end of the day, it was going to be around 10.

MARINUCCI: Russo, was that the figure you had discussed?

RUSSO: He made it clear to me what he was thinking without any fingerprints.

SHANDOBIL: Obviously, you are hoping for President Bush to help you with fundraising, and leading up to that, Mr. Simon went back to the White House for a meeting with the president. You guys shared the fact he was going to do that with media; we went back there. But no cameras were allowed, and a lot of the stories seemed to be coming out that the White House really wasn't embracing him as warmly as advertised. Can you share some of the stories on the negotiations with the White House, and what you had hoped for out of that meeting, and what you actually got?

RUSSO: The press coverage of the trip was certainly negative. The meetings were not negative. In fact, we got quite a bit promised, and the meetings were relatively constructive. We were promised more visits by the president than anybody other than Jeb; they came through on that promise. Mrs. Bush was not going to do any political events. They said they would see about that. And the president ended up telling us on Air Force One that he would lobby her on our behalf, and he did, and got her. So I thought they were pretty helpful. There was a great deal of skepticism for the reasons that I said earlier about whether or not California was winnable. They believed that they had done everything right in California, and they were convinced they were going to beat Gore in California. They spent $12 million, or so to Gore's zero. And then they got their clock cleaned. So there was tremendous pessimism that California was a liberal state, and Republicans can't win here. That definitely crippled a lot of what we tried to do.

SHANDOBIL: Had you been hoping for some kind of symbolic embrace in that visit? What ended up happening is staffers started coming out and quietly, off the record, off camera, kind of muttered that, "We don't really think he has a chance. We're doing this because we're supposed to do it."

RUSSO: Right. Well, the conversations on money in those meetings were in the neighborhood of $10 million to $15 million is what we would expect to get from Washington. We ended up getting about a million.

ROB LAPSLEY: How do you define "getting money from Washington?" Is it when the president is fundraising?

RUSSO: I'm talking about just not the president coming out here but checks coming. It was about a million.

SOUTH: Well, let me make a point about the money. One of the reasons you do not run a neophyte candidate at a race at this level is because they make assumptions that range from naïve to foolish. If Bill Simon, in his own mind and in his own meetings with his accountants, could not come up with $25 million to $30 million of his own dollars that he had available to put in this, he was a fool to run. We raised $67 million over four years with a sitting governor, who's been raising money since 1973. Our database goes all the way back to the Bradley campaign in 1973. He's a legendary fundraiser. We had a full-bore staff, several consultants on contract. We had for some period of that time the sitting president of the United States helping us raise money, and we raised over that four-year period $67 million, which is nothing to sneeze at. But for somebody to come into this thinking that you could win a primary on March 5, and then, having never run before, having never raised a dime, with no donor base, no existing contact network out there, to think you could raise what it takes to be competitive at a governor's race, is foolhardy, pure and simple. If he didn't have that much of a commitment monetarily, it's one thing to say, "You know, self-funded campaigns don't work." But what about unfunded campaigns? They don't work either.

LAPSLEY: Let me clarify a couple of points. These are just facts, as I know them. Number one, Lungren spent $32 million in 1998, when he basically went head-to-head with Garry and Gray. Two, the Simon campaign raised in the general election, about $25 million, and then Bill put in an additional five. So he had just under 30, roughly, for the campaign as a whole. From the Washington side, from the Bush money that was raised, from the RNC money, from the Laura Bush money that was raised, that total came to probably just under half of the $25 million that we raised. So those are the facts.

SHANDOBIL: How much of that did you spend on media? Where did that money go?

MARINUCCI: I think that was an issue Dan Weintraub raised in a story suggesting that an inordinate proportion of the Simon funds went to consulting. And had they spent the same proportion as the Davis campaign, the outcome could have been quite different. How do you answer that, Sal?

RUSSO: Well, we made a decision early on in the campaign that we were going to run and win a guerrilla campaign. And there are certain aspects of the campaign that were going to be bigger than what you would expect because of the uniqueness of the circumstances. One of them was our policy people; we had a huge policy staff. But there were a lot of reasons why we did, which I won't go into, but we did. We had a big advance and candidate support staff.

LAPSLEY: You're asking the wrong questions. You're asking where that money went. You should be asking how much additional money would you have needed in order to truly prevail given the environment? They spent $67 million; that's all we've been talking about. While Lungren had that much money in a head-to-head, where they were comparable, they outspent us three to one. So, come on, this is really what the question should be. The question should be, how much more would we have needed? We barely lost in the two key markets. We underperformed in the L.A. media market by five points. We needed to spend another $10, $15, $20 million with a little better defined message, and, with energy and a couple of things, we would have taken the L.A. media market and we would have won the campaign. So I think some of the questions are wrong here today for where we were in the funding levels.

MARINUCCI: We're going to get back to the media in a moment. You talked about the policy staff that you had, which was huge. And you announced a series of summits that he was going to do, and early in April you hit the first big wall in the campaign, which was Simon's refusal to release his taxes. What discussions went on on this? What did you advise him to do?

RUSSO: The tax issue was not really an issue. The press likes the issue but the public isn't as keen on the issue as the press is. The tax issue became a problem when the IRS KPMG thing came out, because then it raised the question, and then we had to release the taxes. But it was not an issue until that happened. Was that July 2?

MARINUCCI: I'm talking about on tax day in Sacramento. April 15, he was surrounded by reporters, many of them here, who said, "Mr. Simon, did you pay your taxes?" And he said, "I'll have to check on this."

RUSSO: That was a source of some frustration for the campaign, because Bill Simon was extraordinarily knowledgeable and had a great deal of information. I think part of it was his training as a lawyer. If he does not have everything together, he tends to not answer the question when he has the answers. And the one that got written about the most, thanks to George Skelton who keeps writing about it, was at Brulte's fundraiser when George was being George, and Bill became convinced that George had some trick question. George asked him a simple question, "Are you for the death penalty?' And Bill said, 'I'll have to get back to you on it." Now if anybody else had asked the question, he would have said, "Of course." But because Skelton asked the question, he was thinking, "What trick is in this question?" Bill suffers from an overabundance of caution.

MARINUCCI: To clear all the doubts about his tax returns, why didn't he just say, "Okay, we'll release them. We'll show you." The governor already had done it. Why not just get rid of the question?

RUSSO: Two reasons. One, because of the nature in which the family runs the business, Bill Simon disclosing his tax returns reveals a lot of information about his brother and his sisters. He felt he was intruding enough on the family and that was a further intrusion. He wasn't against releasing them. It was actually a close call whether to do it or not. We did take advantage of some polling data and saw that the press cared about it a great deal, but the public didn't. It was one of those things that we just take the little bump in the road and get through it. When KPMG happened, there was no longer a bump in the road, because then it was a question as to whether he paid taxes. All the issues that then become a problem come to the fore, and we had no choice but to release the taxes.

SOUTH: We were astonished watching this, day after day, how the campaign would send this candidate out to make a statement or to make a charge and, clearly, had not prepared him for the absolutely totally inevitably obvious questions that would be asked of him as he was making the same charge against the governor. Example: tax day, April 15, he goes out there making some comment about taxes. The governor had publicly filed his taxes, publicly released his taxes. And nobody prepared the candidate to answer the inevitable questions, "Did you pay your taxes? Are you willing to release your taxes?"

Case study number two, he shows up at the Reagan Building to demand that the governor release his fundraising schedule. "It's imperative he release his fundraising schedule." The candidate wasn't prepared for the obvious question, "Okay, are you going to release your fundraising schedule?" And when asked that, he said, "Well, no, not mine, of course." He shows up to criticize the governor for taking money from Metabolite, which is the creator of Ephedra, right? And is asked at the same time, "Well, did you take money from Metabolite?" "Well, yeah, but that's different." He shows up to criticize us for taking money from Tosco and then helping them dump dioxin in San Francisco Bay, and then has to admit he's taken money from the same company that owns the Tosco Refinery. I don't know how you can send your candidate out into the wilderness like that, time after time after time and not prepare him for the obvious questions that are going to be asked when he's making an attack against his opponent.

SHANDOBIL: Garry is raising some issues with some barbs attached, but he raises some fair questions.

RUSSO: Well, let me distinguish between the two examples. In the first couple of examples, Bill was prepared. But as I said, he tends to be overly cautious. He generally knew the answers to the question. He was well prepared, but he's very cautious, very lawyer-like. And it was a frustration, I think the Ag Summit was maybe the worst.

MARINUCCI: I was at the Ag Summit, and he was asked maybe eight questions following the Ag Summit about agriculture.

RUSSO: Well, there were three questions that he had been briefed on thoroughly, and he got asked questions that Bill Jones spent the whole day going over with him and the staff had gone through. He knew all the answers, but for some reason unless he's completely comfortable and confident he knows every last detail he's so cautious, he tends to say, "I'll get back to you." He could give very good answers if he just did it. And we had to continually push him to give the answers. He had them. He knows the answers. He's very bright. He's very capable.

SEAN WALSH: We're all around the press all the time. We're used to having eight reporters come in and fire questions back and forth. And I think, 'So what?" He'd never done this before. The reporters really didn't give him a lot of scrutiny and a lot of real hard stuff during the primary, not until it got late in the process. And so you go through this process. You get people yelling at you. You get all sorts of questions. And instead of going out and saying the wrong thing, the caution mechanism kicked in.

SHANDOBIL: Given that problem, if another inexperienced candidate comes to you with a lot of money, thinking about running for some higher office, do you back away?

RUSSO: Every candidate has their own idiosyncrasies and a way that they work, and a way that you can get the most out of them. Bill does better when there's a more deliberate process. He does things in a lawyer-like way. And when way he gets prepared in a lawyer-like way, he does better.

In the campaign, sometimes, we didn't have to do it in a lawyer-like way. Something would happen and Sean would call him on the phone in the car, and he didn't have a brief in front of him, and so he would tend to react with, "I'll get back to you." Sean had told him what the answer was, and he knew what the answer was. Maybe we could have done a better job, but he was a much better candidate and much more knowledgeable than came across.

Now, the second thing that Garry said, which I always thought was unfair, is we didn't say there was anything wrong with taking money from Metabolite. We said there was a problem with taking their money and then doing political favors for them. Bill Simon, as a candidate, couldn't do anything for them. Gray Davis was doing something for them in public office. That was the distinction.

SOUTH: Didn't he aspire to be governor? Wasn't he planning on being in a position to do something for them?

RUSSO: Well, when he's governor, then you can judge him. In Gray's case, there was a pattern in which he received money and policy changed.

SOUTH: Sal, when you send your candidate out to demand that the sitting governor release his fundraising schedule and do it now and do it in detail, and your candidate is not prepared to stand there at the same press conference and say,

"And to prove this is important, I'm going to release my fundraising schedule, as I'm asking my opponent to do." And, in fact, start to split hairs on the issue about, "It's important for the governor to do it for the following reasons, but hey, I'm not in office yet; I'm still a private citizen."

RUSSO: I thought we did do that.

SOUTH: You didn't.

FLINT: Bill misspoke and talked himself into a corner and couldn't get out. We did release the fundraising calendar for the rest of his campaign, but that was just one where he misspoke. He said he misunderstood the question. I was not at the press conference, but he made a mistake in that one instance and talked himself into a corner.

SOUTH: What you released was "He's got a fundraising event tonight in San Luis Obispo." You didn't say where. You didn't say how much. You wouldn't release the guest list or anything else. So it's a little disingenuous to say, "You guys fully disclosed, and we didn't."

FLINT: The point we made was that the governor was neglecting his duties because he cared more about fundraising. So our point was always to try to drive the issue of how much time. Because you were always trying to respond, "What are you talking about? We're going to release our fundraising report that says who gave money." We weren't quarreling with that. It's like saying, "We'll comply with the law. Congratulations."

MARINUCCI: If I may play devil's advocate, you can criticize him for not releasing a "schedule." You released nothing to us.

SOUTH: We did not stand up and demand that Bill Simon release his fundraising schedule. The onus is on the person making the attack. If you want to make an attack, you better be clean as Caesar's wife.

MARINUCCI: Steve is rolling his eyes. Was releasing his fundraising schedule ever discussed with the governor? Because we're getting into the period now where Oracle starts hitting, pipe fitters, stories about $100 fundraisers with Berkeley students, and as all of you know, there's almost a month of stories on Gray Davis fundraising. What kind of conversations went on with the governor over this? There were some reports that the governor was almost comatose as the Oracle story started hitting and there was a lot of discussion going on in the campaign on how to deal with them.

DOAK: I don't recall that we ever seriously discussed releasing the fundraising list.

SOUTH: Never.

DOAK: My God, no one's going to show up to give money if there's going to be 45 reporters standing there taking pictures of them.

O'DONNELL: The general public didn't care about this. We saw this in the research and the focus groups. Politicians raise money. They go to fundraising events, and they raise money. I doubt we got any letters to the campaign demanding that we release our fundraising schedule.

SOUTH: This was largely a press phenomenon, with all due respect. Come on, Carla. You can always go down the street in San Jose and find some Democrat who criticizes Gray Davis for raising money. That is totally illegitimate. The fact is we had a candidate trying to accuse us of being unethical and being guilty of sleaze and hitting up contributors for money and doing favors for them. And the fact is the last three PPIC polls of the campaign, when they asked, "Which of these two candidates is the most ethical?" We won all three of those by a double-digit margin. The last two Field polls when asked, "Who would bring integrity and ethics to the office of the governor?" We beat bill Simon on those. And we tracked on those questions every night and we won this question every single night. This was largely a figment of the press's imagination.

WALSH: It really isn't, and it really wasn't. The issue is not solely to go at fundraising, fundraising calendars, politicians raising money. The issue was to go at Democrats try and suppress them from coming out, to get them to dislike Gray, and to create problems with liberal Democrats and feed on the Burton issues that the press would write about, and to really hold them down. And I think it did hold them down. I think the turnout really, really came down and people would say, "Well, you know, he raises doubt. Maybe it is the Tosco stuff on the Bay. He doesn't live up to my ideal standards. It's not what I want for healthcare or whatever, and I don't like this stuff." I think it did work. I think our problem was we got defined with Enron and all this business stuff, and then the lawsuit and everything else. And that's what hurt our ethics issue. I saw polling from private companies that said business people in America rated lower than they did right after the 1929 stock crash. So that hurt our ethics issue. But the strategy really was to keep the Democrats down.

SOUTH: I thought Ed Rollins would be here to discuss your voter suppression program.

WALSH: Our goal is not to get maximum voter turnout, our goal is to try and get enough voters to get our guy elected.

DOAK: But we never saw any indications of any erosion in the base. If there was any lack of turnout, it probably contributed to the size of the margin. We were only running a comparative question, "Who's going to win the election?"

MARINUCCI: But you had a historically low Latino turnout, a historically low African-American. . .

TULCHIN: Let's talk about turnout. Maybe they contributed to that to some degree. They were attacking the governor, and it hurt. But these weren't new negatives. The governor was carrying negatives from the beginning of the energy crisis, starting with Tim Draper when he attacked the governor in the fall on education. That hurt his favorables then. And over the summer, the energy companies came along, and they had the last word, because if you remember, they finished in mid-August, boom 9/11 happened, the energy crisis got wiped off the page. And then in the primary we took a toll by spending a lot of money on negative ads, there's no doubt about that. But, at the end of the day, in terms of turnout and what happened and the margin being five, there were two factors that made a difference. One, nationally, the trend was Republican. Look at all the close races in the country; they broke overwhelmingly Republican. These are races that were tied up going into the last week of the polls. Just go down the list, in terms of the trend going Republican. California is more Democratic, but we're not impervious to that national trend. Two, you have a tough year for incumbents—19 of 36 states had a change in party. Three out of five incumbent Democratic governors lost. Only one other Democrat won, besides Davis. It was not a good year for an incumbent governor, particularly a Democrat.

And in California, this race could have been closer throughout. Who knows? After the May revise, Oracle was breaking, and in early June, this race was within the margin. Then we broke it open because of our strategy. We went on the air in June, in parts of the state, July, parts of the state, and we broke it open in August. And by Labor Day, we're up. . . . The pollsters talked about it yesterday. It was pretty static from Labor Day to election day. We saw closing in the last few days.

Why? In March, when we asked, "Who will win the election?" We had an 11-point advantage. At the end of October, it was 66 to 19. Two-thirds of the electorate said, "This election . . . the race is not close. It doesn't matter." So that gave Democrats a pass to say, "It doesn't really matter I don't have to turn out." Minorities felt, "It doesn't really matter; I don't have to vote." Enough Republicans showed up so Simon got his base, but he did nothing beyond that.

MARINUCCI: Okay, so let's talk June. That's when the most negative TV campaign in history began. And you all started positive, as a matter of fact.

DOAK: We always do.

MARINUCCI: But you started out with ads immediately going after Simon on his business practices, instead of social issues. Why did that happen?

DOAK: It was quite a discussion. We'd gone after Lungren on the social issues, and that had been a tried and true record, and I think that's what everyone expected. And frankly, I think that's where the governor probably wanted to go first. Tom and I argued pretty strongly that the governor's vulnerability was competence-related issues because of the energy crisis and the budget stuff that was going to cut. So I thought it was important for us to take Simon's competence away first, to take him away as an alternative competence-wise, and after we did that, step two, would be to come back and do the social issues. As it turned out, when we started the confidence attack on business, we didn't have all the elements. It was very hard to get Simon's record. We did the negative research on him, but because a lot of his holdings were private you weren't able to get them. So I think we had four or five failed businesses. And we started with the S&L and the four or five failed businesses. And then the break came with the AP, which found four or five more failed businesses. And then the KPGM story broke in *The Wall Street Journal,* and then the lawsuit broke, which we had no idea about. And I assume you guys didn't have any idea about. No one seemed to know.

O'DONNELL: Before we get to what we did substantively, we also made a decision when we saw Simon's money report that we had a window of opportunity. He only had a certain amount of money on hand at the time. We made some guesstimates about how much we thought he'd have. We saw June and July as a window of opportunity for us to start defining this fellow. When Simon came out of the primary; he wasn't that well-defined. The Republican electorate knew him, but certainly the broader, general electorate really didn't. And so we saw that even before we got into the substantive discussion about what we're going to run, we saw that, given his money situation, we had a period to define the fellow.

SHANDOBIL: So you were concerned about the budget last year. What sort of conversations were you having with the governor on his thinking on last year's budget?

SOUTH: Basically, the budget is put together by the Department of Finance.

RUSSO: The campaign Department of Finance.

SOUTH: Let me address the budget question this way. Our concern was—and I think there was considerable evidence to suggest this as a fear—that the Republicans were going to gum-up the works on the budget and allow this thing to go on forever. In fact, they were talking about coming back after the November election for a special session to try to get the budget passed. And we knew that the summer before, there had been RNC operatives out here telling individual legislators, Republicans, not to vote for the budget because they wanted to put Davis over a barrel. This was something that, to some degree, came out of Washington. The more you can muck-up the budget, the more you can muck-up the fiscal affairs of the state. The Republicans were willing to sit there and let the state go into fiscal meltdown, basically, in order to make a cheap, political point about the governor. Our fear was that if this thing dragged on through the general election campaign, and we didn't have a budget as of election day, and the state was out of money, we had to issue IOU's again, programs were shutting down, employees were being let off, schools weren't getting their money, that it would be a disaster for us.

SHANDOBIL: I think we could all agree that there were some Republicans who openly talked about doing just that. On the other hand, isn't it fair to say that there's at least a suspicion that the governor would create wallpaper solutions, and that's part of the problem this year?

SOUTH: Well, let's be fair. When the governor presented the May revise, included in that May revise was about $7.2 billion in legitimate spending cuts, and about $5 billion in increased revenues, including increasing the car tax, which is not popular, and increasing the cigarette tax. Right? When it came out of the legislature, to some degree because of the problems with our own side of the aisle, on the spending cut side, we couldn't get either of those two aspects of the budget passed. So what finally emerged—although the governor was polite about it, as he tends to be and says, "Well, this follows the general configuration of what I propose," we were painfully aware of the fact that we didn't get either the spending cut or the revenue increases that he had proposed in May. And that put us in a bigger mess.

O'DONNELL: The other thing about the budget, I'm not sure in terms of the saliency of that issue with the voters. People weren't talking about the budget at this point. So I'm not sure it was really out there, that it really mattered all that much.

SHANDOBIL: If he talked about the budget last year the way he was talking about it this year, it would have been an issue. And a lot of the same concerns existed last year. And so my question is did you suppress it becoming an issue?

DOAK: No one could predict what happened. This has been the longest bear market in history. Everyone kept thinking that the recovery was right around the corner. And, generally speaking, California's budget woes are primarily because nobody's paying cap gains taxes anymore, among other things, but that's a big factor in it. So, everybody thought the recovery was going to be a lot quicker. But Garry, I don't think any of us political people had a very big hand in designing it. Hell, none of us know state budgets. I think it's unfair to say that that was designed politically, it just wasn't.

SOUTH: Our specialty is closing vote deficits, not budget deficits, but one other point about the budget. One of the reasons we decided not to go and pound heavily on the social issues over the course of the summer was because we had a collective view that if we did that, that if we went after him on abortion and guns, that if the budget process wore on, and got very messy and very ugly and it was a stalemate, and the governor's competence came into question, that even voters who agreed with some issues of abortion and guns and the other palliative social issues, would view that on our part as kind of a diversionary tactic to get their mind off of what we knew was developing in there, which was, "Can this governor manage the state of California?'

And so one of the reasons we went was because the business environment was not a very good one for somebody running as a businessman; we had all this specific stuff on him. But, in addition to that, we thought that a really strong play on the social issues over that period of time, although it may help us with our base, would be devalued to some degree, because people would view it as a diversionary tactic to get away from the notion that was developing that the governor couldn't manage the state.

DOAK: I agree with that. I used the argument that I was worried that the public and the press would think we were a one-trick pony, that we had taken Lungren out on abortion, taken Riordan out on abortion, now we're coming back. And I thought that that argument could be devalued. I thought we ought to go with the competence stuff and come back with that.

MARINUCCI: In the end you were handed the issue that made national news, the Los Angeles Jury finding Simon liable for civil fraud, a $78 million judgment. Sal, how many people in the campaign knew about that case? And what went on within the campaign the day that broke?

RUSSO: Well, I knew. Jeff knew. Did you know the trial was going on?

LAPSLEY: I knew that there was a trial. It was structured so that there were specific communication channels, because it was something that had been paid attention to in the primary. The natural evolution of that is that Sal and Jeff had leads on it.

MARINUCCI: Did Ed Rollins know? Did any of the White House people know?

WALSH: No. We were in a meeting in Sacramento, a strategy-planning meeting at the Hyatt, and their cell phones went off.

RUSSO: I did, when we had one of our White House meetings, run through the issues. And this was one of the ones that I mentioned. But I could tell you why it's easy to forget, because of the way I presented it. The lawyers said there's a 90 percent chance the judge is not going to even send this to the jury. It's an open and shut case. There's a 99.99999 percent chance we're going to win. There's really no chance we're going to lose. He wants a lot of money. We're not going to give that drug dealer crook a lot of money.

SOUTH: Your drug dealer slash business partner.

RUSSO: Right. That guy. Obviously, given what happened they had a bad jury.

MARINUCCI: How much was he asking for the case to go away, several million dollars?

RUSSO: I don't remember; it was a lot of money, though. The fraud thing bothered the donors. But with the public, they think all politicians engage in fraud everyday, so there was no news there. The fact that Bill was in business with a drug dealer was far more damaging with the public than that there was a fraud.

MARINUCCI: There was no way of delaying this case, or putting it off?

RUSSO: No, we tried to delay it, and they wouldn't. The judge said, "No more delays."

SHANDOBIL: So you're saying it's more damaging with the public that Bill Simon, a former prosecutor, didn't vet his business partner?

RUSSO: Yes, that's correct. I don't even know if I'm at liberty to disclose the whole story. Because there are other legal issues that are involved about other material nondisclosures that happened, which is why there was a reason the due diligence did not uncover this. It was not sloppy due diligence, it was worse than that. There was more to it than that. And so it's one of those things that was more damaging from the standpoint that it stopped our fundraising on July 30, and we couldn't raise any money. But I don't know what you do when the lawyer says there's a 99.999 percent chance you're going to win this thing. I don't know what you do about it.

WALSH: It fit into all the stories that were going around with the whole energy stuff and all the accounting and everything else. It glommed, in my view unfairly, but it glommed all the national crap right onto us. It prevented us from having an upbeat message, and it cemented our path to be much more negative as we go on with the campaign. You try telling the story about the good business stuff, and you just have this fraud thing slapped right back at you every time.

SHANDOBIL: I think one thing that Carla and I were trying to get at was, were your troops aware ahead of time? Was the White House aware that this was a possibility? It seemed that part of the problem was everyone being caught so off guard, that there was going to be other secrets out there, there were going to be other shoes to drop.

RUSSO: Obviously, by the way that I just told you, the lawyers that had gone through the case with us, and the way that I would have reported that, it would not have made red flags go up, because this did not seem like something that was a problem. We did not believe it to be a problem. Lawyers never tell you it's 99.99. Well, in this case, they said, "99.999 percent." The other three law firms looking at this all came to the same conclusion.

DOAK: Sal, if we'd known you were on trial accused of fraud, we could have done the same thing that we ultimately did to you just for being on trial for fraud. The nature of the accusation is so great that it's almost catastrophic.

O'DONNELL: We got a spot up on this decision quickly. We weren't going to wait for your appeal. You were saying people were much more worried you had business dealings with a former drug dealer. Our research showed the fraud decision being much more problematic to you than that issue. As a matter of fact, we almost had too much. We didn't know what to do. So we decided not to do anything with it at that point-in-time.

SOUTH: We actually did produce a spot about going into business with a convicted drug dealer, and we focused grouped that spot. I wanted to use it, just because that's the way I am, but we decided not to because it drew a decidedly mixed reception from focus groups. One of the problems we had in the ad was trying to explain to people that he didn't go into the drug business with a drug dealer. And that's what people took out of it. It was too complicated to explain. That spot never went on the air. It was too complicated.

WALSH: Fair or unfair, you had a harmonic conversion of an earned media thing that was engulfing the world, and it worked right with your paid media stuff, and it was free.

LAPSLEY: And that was the biggest break of the campaign. Let's be clear. You were talking about seminal events earlier, and there were two: You had the KPMG thing that resonated with the tax charge that you guys already had up, and then you had right behind it the fraud verdict. That is a one-two punch that was just absolutely devastating.

Prior to that, Gray is getting his ass kicked on Oracle, just getting his ass kicked. And you guys were kind of dead in the water going into May and June, because you had to deal with Oracle, and he was getting his ass kicked all over the legislature. Unfortunately, the legislature didn't do anything they could have done, or should have done *vis-à-vis* a Quackenbush-type investigation to be able to truly drive either that issue or some of the other ones that they could have that were out there that would have had a greater impact. But that whole thing changed. We were actually up in one poll, a survey USA poll in July, and we were fighting back. We were actually looking a little better. And then we got our ass kicked with the harmonic convergence on those two things. And you guys defined us during that whole period.

SOUTH: But you're forgetting the predicate to all of that, which is when Simon first reared his head in February of 2001, 1 was quoted in some places saying, after we found out about the Western Federal Savings and Loan debacle, that if he got into this thing, we would make him a poster boy for the S&L scandals. There's a reason why we went up with that spot. As opposed to the problem in explaining drug dealer business connection, the failure of the S&L was a simple, open-and-shut case that resonated in everybody's mind because they got it, they understood what happened. These rich guys came in, took over these things, milked them, drove them into the ground, and the taxpayers had to bail them out. Of all the focus groups we did, that was the single thing that people most often brought up of their own volition about Simon, was that he ran a bank into the ground, he's asking the taxpayers to pay for it, he's a typical shyster. And that was the predicate to all the other stuff breaking.

WALSH: When those two things hit, it was like a napalm bomb going off. It sucked all of the money. It just put everything on hold. They go on with paid media, and we don't have any money at that juncture to go on with paid media to counter, or do anything else for a month.

TULCHIN: This is building from our perspective, because we were on the air starting June 1, so the fraud verdict, from Simon and from the voter standpoint didn't come from left field. We had built the case against this guy as an incompetent and, basically, a crook as a businessman. And this came, and we put three more weeks of that on the air, and we expanded our lead; we didn't get the lead from that.

SHANDOBIL: Topic change. In June, the Simon campaign touts an endorsement that I think, in retrospect, you wished perhaps you never got, from the COPS organization. And you did indeed pay for that endorsement as the governor had once before. One, how much money was given to the COPS organization? And how tethered was the money given to the COPS organization to knowing they had this photo that turned out to backfire later on in the campaign?

RUSSO: COPS endorsed Simon on January 17.

SOUTH: And if we'd paid the money, he would have endorsed us in the Democratic primary.

RUSSO: Yeah, you cheap bastard, I don't know why you didn't.

SOUTH: It was money well worth not spending on our part.

SHANDOBIL: How much did you spend? And, is it correct that the slate mailer that you were buying didn't get to the voters until November 18.

RUSSO: No. That's not true. I happened to be at Bill's house when it came to him. And it showed up at his mailbox sometime in the middle of October.

WALSH: That's when mine came in, too.

SHANDOBIL: How much money was given to COPS? And how tethered was the money to the photo?

RUSSO: It wasn't tethered at all because we didn't even know about the photo. There was the *L.A. Times* story about Wayne Johnson being solicited by the governor for the million dollars during his meeting or alleged solicitation. And what Kelly Moran from COPS said was he was cleaning up some old boxes, you know, having just read that article, and going through the boxes ran across the picture and said, "Oh, my God, I guess we got asked for money, and Engle gave him the money." And he later said to us that the board had decided not to give the check. And there was some internal bickering that went on—I don't understand what it was. And so the board members that were unhappy about it, they believed that the reason that Engle went against what they thought the board had directed him to do was because Davis had put the squeeze on him in the office. That's what their belief was. But we didn't even hear that story until after the *L.A. Times* ran Dan Morain's story.

FLINT: It was early May, because we went back and checked. We signed our contract with Kelly and with COPS, and wrote them checks, and bought the slate, and bought the endorsement, if you want to say that, and all the other things in late March, early April. And Morain's story ran in early May.

RUSSO: They didn't discover the photo until after that. And then it was about a month after that before they called Jeff and said, "We've got some blockbuster news, but I can't tell you about it on the phone."

FLINT: It was actually earlier. It was within days of Dan's story about the teacher solicitation in the capitol, where Kelly in the course of ongoing conversation I had with him, he would ask me all these cryptic questions, and he would never tell me what it was about. He would say, "Do you know if the governor has ever been asked on the record whether he's taken a check in a state office building?" I said, "I don't know if he's been asked that." He said, "Well, do you think you can get a reporter to ask him that question?" And I said, "I don't know." I wasn't paying that much attention to it in the initial conversation. And I don't remember the exact date. Somewhere along the line they let us know that they had a photo that they believed was the governor taking a check in the lieutenant governor's office.

RUSSO: Sometime early June was the first time we found out that a photo existed. They did not want to show it to us because Engle was up for confirmation in the Senate, and they had internal board issues. They weren't sure what they wanted to do, or whether they wanted to use it or not. They wanted to keep it under wraps and not share it. So we never saw it.

MARINUCCI: When did you finally see the photo?

RUSSO: On the Thursday before the Monday debate, Rob and Ed and I met with Kelly. Now, in previous meetings, we had met with board members of COPS, and we inquired as to its validity. And it wasn't just Kelly, we had six board members swearing that the photo was taken in the lieutenant governor's office. And their attorney, who was the counsel for the Republican party, said it was in the lieutenant governor's office.

MARINUCCI: Did you ever send anyone to check?

RUSSO: Well, first of all, we hadn't seen the photo. We didn't have the photo. And so we were relying on not only their attorney who happens to be the Republican party's attorney, as the third-party verifier, but on board members as well as their staff. So we had like 10 people telling us that the picture was genuine.

MARINUCCI: But that they could have just gone down and walked into the lieutenant governor's office.

RUSSO: We hadn't seen the picture until the Thursday before the debate when Kelly said he had the picture with him, and did we want to see the picture. And Rob said, "Well, we've never seen it as this point. This is your deal, not our deal. No, I don't want to see the picture." And he looked over at me, and I said, "No, we've gone this long. This is your deal." And Ed said the same. And then he looked at Ed, and Ed said, "No, I don't want to see it." And Kelly said, "Okay," and he whips the picture out.

FLINT: Let me just go back one step, because eventually we found out what they were talking about from Kelly's cryptic questions to me. I had a conversation with Dan Schnur and Rob Stutsman about this. And I said, "I've got this group that's telling me they've got a photo of the governor taking a check in the State Capitol. What do you think?" And then we had internal campaign conversations about it. And the plan always was we would try to get them to give the photo to a news organization and let them do the verifying. And that's one of the things, you know, frankly we just talk it out right here. Because what I don't recall is where, along the process, we got away from the plan that we knew was the right thing to do.

RUSSO: I do.

FINT: I remember Sean and I beating each other up afterwards.

WALSH: Rob joined the campaign in what, mid May? And I guess I joined about June. And before I'd even joined the campaign and talked with you guys about that picture, something along those lines had been raised, as far as I was aware. But I wasn't onboard. Things went along. And then, periodically, something would come up about this item. And so as some people occasionally do, they visit their favorite reporter friends and say, "Hey, I might have something that may be of interest to you later on." And I had done that over a long time period, putting ticklers in, occasionally, to a couple of reporters about this issue. But the picture never came, and it never came.

And, again, we have crack opposition research staff, who could have and would have done the scrutiny. They kept pushing very, very hard that we should see this; we need to verify it. And for whatever reason—the reason that I was told was that the COPS organization was filing a complaint with the FPPC. There was a legal ramification that was going to come with that legal filing, they didn't want to for legal purposes have any collusion from the Simon campaign. They were going to do it all on their own, blah, blah, blah, blah. I mean, it went on.

So we never really got the picture. And we got to the point, the opposition research folks that this thing was never going to pan out. And then we got closer to the debate, and all of a sudden, for whatever reason, the COPS organization figured out what they had to figure out with the FPPC, and they were going to cough this picture up. And at that juncture, we had a lot of problems with regards to other issues around the campaign and we needed a big blast to make it go. And so the conclusion was instead of flipping it to a reporter, if it's really good, if they're going in front of the FPPC, if there's going to be legal action, and, maybe we wanted to believe, we decided to go forward with it in the debate. But the plan always was just to flip it to a newspaper until we got jammed right up until the debate, and all those other factors came. And that's basically how it came forward.

But the issue was not for Simon to embrace it. The COPS organization was making this allegation. Let the COPS organization do it. We'd actually written up some remarks for Mr. Simon to give in the press availability—it's like freelancing with Riordan in the primary—if he read those remarks, it would have been COPS. If the COPS thing panned out, it's fine. If it doesn't pan out, it's a COPS problem. We'd get a little bit of blowback, but it was their deal.

SHANDOBIL: There's something really ironic in what you're saying, in that, Sal, you were saying one of the frustrations you had with Bill Simon was that he was trained as a lawyer, and he's always so cautious and never said anything. And then here was a time where he answered a question.

WALSH: Remember, we go back to why he said on the campaign trail, "Well, I'll have to get back to you," etc. This was huge. The amount of press in that *L.A. Times* room was absolutely huge. Their team is there; our team is there. I mean, this is big. This is the Super Bowl of having press around you. And then Dan's yelling at him, and everybody's yelling at him. When they went to Sal—I don't know if it was Sal or Ed—to say yes, it wasn't to say, "Yes, I have proof"; it was to say, "Yes, the COPS organization is filing a letter with the FPPC. Go check it out." Even then we tried to build in a safety valve.

RUSSO: I called Bill at home that morning, and I said to him on the phone, "Remember, you're a former federal prosecutor, you're going to be held to a higher standard. Whatever you do, don't make any accusations, because we don't know whether this photo is valid or not." Now, I actually didn't question its location. But they said that Garry South had taken the picture; that he was the photographer. One of Garry's close friends told me, when I told him the story, he says, "Well, you know Garry will cop a plea."

SOUTH: But let me ask you a little basic question, because this has been on my mind since this occurred. One of the classic examples of Bill Simon kind of making a fool of himself was when he was peppered with questions about why he would stand up and make this charge and not even verify it. The former federal prosecutor, which he was touting as one of his major qualifications for office, running Giuliani out here every 15 minutes, why he didn't take the time to ascertain that the facts were correct before accusing the sitting governor of committing a felony. And he said, "Well, I had no reason to doubt the word of this reputable law enforcement organization, the California Organization of Police and Sheriffs." I mean, come on guys, you know COPS. You may have bought their support. This is the scummiest, most venal bunch of political whores in western civilization. And you took their word for this? I mean, my God!

FLINT: Gray said, "No endorsement makes me prouder than the California Organization of Police and Sheriffs'."

WALSH: Anyway, the bottom line was it wasn't supposed to be that way. And it ended up that way. You know, that line in *Animal House* where they bring back the crashed car, 'Hey, you trusted us."

SOUTH: By the way, I missed the answer to your question about how much money you actually gave to COPS? Wasn't that your question?

SHANDOBIL: Yeah, we did ask that and it wasn't answered.

FLINT: I don't know how much the exact dollar amount was. It was. . . .

SOUTH: Was it six hundred grand?

FLINT: I don't remember the exact amount. There was an amount for the slate, and then there was an amount for them to try to set up a grassroots organization.

SOUTH: And then you're subsidizing Kelly Moran on the side, too.

RUSSO: There are two things that we did from the primary on that we felt were important. One is to keep Bill's credentials in law enforcement and to keep his credentials on the tax issue, which is why we did the Jarvis Initiative, the homeowners' exemption. We thought we had to be on the tax issue, and we had to take advantage of his prosecutor experience and the Giuliani thing. And so we needed COPS. Generically, it ended up being COPS because they also were very good at going out and getting these little rinky-dink law enforcement groups to endorse us, which we must have got about 25 of them that ultimately endorsed us in the course of the campaign. So that was the reason why the only two places we put money were into the tax groups and in the law enforcement.

MARINUCCI: The next month wasn't so easy for Governor Davis either because the high-speed fundraiser stories began to hit. That was that the governor signed the High-Speed Rail Bill a day before a major fundraiser was planned, or the day after . . . e-mails went out to high-speed rail advocates causing yet another fundraising issue that caused him to actually cancel two fundraisers. Was there ever any discussion in the campaign that, "Hey, we've got $60 million at this point. We've got the danger of a lot of negative stories. Let's cool it. Do we need any more money?" Did anyone ever suggest laying off the fundraisers?

SOUTH: Carla, let me put it to you this way. I challenge you to go to a candidate running for public office and tell him to cut off his fundraising. That's not realistic. You have things booked. You have things calendared. You have a full-bore fundraising operation. Just like the Simon people, just like everyone in the primary, just like anyone in every campaign I've ever been involved with, you try to raise as much money as you possibly can. And you take the lumps for it sometimes even when you're very successful, probably even because you're very successful.

You've heard me say this before—you disagree with this—but I will tell you that on the fundraising stuff, we made some mistakes. There's no question about it. We shot ourselves in the foot a couple of times, and we should have been more careful about some of the things we did. And there were internal discussions about that. But the fact of the matter is reporters in general and editors of newspapers in general believe that fundraising is basically scummy. And that the better you are at it, the more scummy it actually is. So the more successful you are, you're a victim of your own success because the more money you raise, the more you're going to get inquired about by reporters saying, "Well, my God, there's got to be something wrong with this. There's got to be something scummy going on here. There's got to be some quid pro quo. There's got to be payoffs involved here." And, frankly, as we said before, this was not something that was on the voter's mind. It just was not. And it was a feeding frenzy by the press. I actually went to the Sacramento Press Club in June and took the press to task, who were essentially looking at our fundraising with a microscope while letting Simon off the hook by flipping you off and saying, "I'm not going to tell you how I make my money, how much I'm worth, how much I'm going to put into the campaign, or anything else." And you all say, "Okay, fine, let's go back to Davis."

MARINUCCI: Well, at anytime, Garry, did anyone in any session say to the governor, "I think politically maybe we ought to cool our jets. We've got enough money right now." Did anyone say that? Or is the governor the one who suggested that every fundraiser matters.

SOUTH: How much is enough money for the Hearst Corporation to make in a year? Is that my prerogative to determine that? It's not a newspaper's prerogative to determine how much a candidate needs to run his campaign.

TULCHIN: Well, there's another context, too, where Simon's campaign is attacking the governor on ethics, on a wide range of charges, so you can't tell the governor, "Stop raising money, so you won't be able to respond to these attacks."

LAPSLEY: Yeah, but the reason it looks scummy is because it is scummy. Let's be clear, there's a clear, clear connection between policy and fundraising.

SOUTH: Prove it. Prove it, Rob. Prove it, prove it.

LAPSLEY: Garry, all you have to do is. . . .

SOUTH: That's a felony offense. You go prove it, my friend.

FLINT: Hold on, Garry, earlier today, you said that because Bush came out here and 16 days later somebody ran a TV ad, that's a terrible coincidence.

SOUTH: It's not a felony offense.

FLINT: I didn't say it is, but, clearly, there's something about the governor's fundraising operation, whether or not he crosses illegal lines, that caused everybody that's involved in politics and public policy in the state to believe they do. It's not impressive that you know where the line is and you kind of dabble your toe near it. That's not good for public policy in the state; the fact that he may or may not have crossed a legal line is a different question.

WALSH: We weren't just going after core competency, we were going after the fact that even if you want to give him the benefit of the doubt, he's paying too much time and attention to fundraising, and not enough time and attention to the energy crisis, and not enough time and attention the budget crisis, etc. We were trying to weave in those issues using fundraising as a vehicle.

The problem that really hurt Governor Davis very, very badly is you may have had overzealous staff people doing things and saying things that they had no business doing or saying. You get the High-Speed Rail e-mail. Whether there's impropriety going on or not, there's the appearance of impropriety, and that went on for a very long period of time. And then you would have these things periodically pop up on a fairly regular basis, because the opposition research team is very good at what they do. And then you would get elements of the Oracle issue. And fair or unfair, whether you did everything right or whether it was wrong, the appearance of that pay-to-play attitude would then carry on and be renewed in the media over a two-and-a-half-year period. And that does go, in our view, to the heart of why a lot of Democrats got very disheartened with regard to Gray Davis, and selling out things, or not caring about their issues, and why the numbers went down. I'm not saying it's fundraising. Fundraising is a nexus for issues on energy and the budget. It's not paying attention.

SOUTH: When we focus grouped the whole fundraising stuff, which we did constantly, people didn't like the fact Gray Davis was raising money. When we put the question to them, "Would Simon be any better?" "No." "Would he take money and do favors for people?" "Yes." This is a generic issue that applies to every politician, whether you raise one cent or a trillion dollars. If you're in for a dime in the public mind, you're in for a dollar.

WALSH: But you're asking one question, and it's not the deteriorating effect that it has across the board in the spectrum. I still say it's part of Gray's problem with this stuff

DOAK: I want to say something. And I want to say this to the press. You must be careful in your obligation to the political system if you're going to have states like California, where it takes so much money to run. You know, $67 million sounds like a ton of money. We didn't have all the money we wanted. We had to lay off on Simon early because we didn't have the money to run a campaign all the way through. Now, it's a lot of money, granted. But if you're going to design systems like we have, and then you're going to attack people for raising the kind of money it takes in these huge states, while the TV stations keep jacking their rates up all the time. I'm not without sin here, because we make a lot of money off of it too, but you have to really be careful about the process, and you've got to understand what it takes to run in these big states. If this were Missouri, or if it were West Virginia, or even Virginia, it's not as much as money. But you get to Florida, California, Texas, it takes $40-, $50-, $60 million to run nowadays. And you guys have got a looming problem. In four years, you're going to come back. I think you've got a system designed now where only rich people can play. I don't think average politicians can run in this state anymore.

MARINUCCI: One last question on that whole issue, and then we've got to move on. Was it a Pyrrhic victory? That he raised all that money, but he so damaged his image in the public eye by doing it?

DOAK: No. Gray Davis never gives anybody what they want.

SOUTH: That is not why the governor's numbers were down. It had to do with the energy crisis and a few related things that had nothing to do with fundraising. I said that in the campaign. We tested that. Every time we polled. PPIC tested it. The *LA Times'* poll tested it. This was largely a figment of people in the media, who have an ingrained belief that there's something basically sleazy about political fundraising and going out there to find every little tidbit of information that they can concoct into some case that somehow there's something sleazy about fundraising. That's what it amounted to. And then you guys would say, "Oh, the governor must have been dragged down by his incompetence on the energy crisis, and because of his excessive zeal for fundraising." There was no evidence to make that case. It was all in your own mind.

FLINT: But, there's the question, "If you had never gone through a single Oracle, High-Speed Rail, etc., etc., etc., would you have won by more or less votes?" Would it have still been a five-point win?

TULCHIN: The reason it closed had nothing to do with fundraising.

FLINT: I'm not saying fundraising caused the closing at the end. I'm saying if there had never been a single fundraising scandal, do you think he would have won by more?

DOAK: I don't know if he would have won by more. I don't think there's any evidence that this played a great role in the campaign. I don't think it was helpful; don't get me wrong. That's why I question how you cover it. But we didn't see anywhere in any of the research that this was a burning issue with the public, not because it's not damaging to Gray and everybody. It's damaging systemically because they think every politician is a crook.

SHANDOBIL: I want to ask the Simon campaign about the Log Cabin questionnaires and the confusion about that. No one answered; someone answered; who answered? How did it happen?

RUSSO: Well, Bill is somebody who felt that there were some important issues in California that we needed to address as a state. And he wanted his campaign to focus on where he thought, as a governor, he could make a difference, issues where he thought Gray Davis was failing—energy and the budget, schools, water—issues that he talked about on the stump all the time. He felt that there are a lot of issues like abortion and gay rights and guns that are extraordinarily contentious that are irreconcilable and nothing's going to really happen. You can tweak it here, and tweak it there, but nothing is going to happen one way or the other. And to have protracted prolonged discussions and debates on issues that don't matter when the state is facing serious problems is a waste of time. But he learned in the process that a lot of people want to talk about issues that are not very relevant to what governors do on a day-to-day basis. And so he really endeavored, which is consistent with his personality and his demeanor, to try to be open to people with differing views on these contentious issues, listening to them, hearing them, and kind of moving on from, "Okay, well I understand where you're coming from and we have people that have different views. But now that we've discussed all that, let's move on to what we can do about the energy crises and the budget, and we'll try to work together and find common ground, but it's going to be hard to really do much on these other issues." That was his kind of overall approach.

So we met, as we did, all during the campaign with different people. We had all of our policy task forces everybody was aware of. These task forces not only had Simon supporters on them, they had Davis supporters on them, which is one reason we didn't release all their names, because some people were active Davis supporters. They were legitimate and honest efforts on Simon's behalf to have the best people come up with ideas. And so in keeping with that, we met with a group of 50/50 Democrats and Republicans, and gay leaders in Los Angeles, not because it was a political thing per se, but because it was part of our policy to understand some people's perspective.

In the course of that meeting, a lot of people offered a lot of advice and a lot of suggestions on how to approach the issue and how to deal with the issue and how we, as Republicans, can make this an issue that doesn't divide us because it's not an issue that you can reconcile very easily. And so in the course of that, a lot of people produced a lot of documents, and a lot of drafts. It's like our abortion statement. It was like draft 28 or something that was the final draft that we used. It just had gone through so much massaging and so many people kibitzed on it.

We deliberately didn't meet with the Log Cabin Club because we were trying to make it a policy issue and not a political issue. So we tried to not meet overtly with political organizations on the issue, but met with people that had a legitimate concern with the underlying issues. And that's why we met with this bipartisan group rather than with an organized political group, which, of course, made them unhappy. And so they wanted us to fill out this questionnaire, and it was something that got done hastily. In hindsight, we should never have filled it out. A lot of the material that different people had prepared and suggestions got incorporated into it. And it just went out hastily.

SHANDOBIL: Who filled it out? Did Bill Simon fill it out?

RUSSO: No, Bill did not. We made a decision early on in the campaign because Bill knew that despite the fact that we're barraged with thousands of questionnaires, that we were going to tend to fill them out, rather than not fill them out. Unless there was a group that was really just out to play games, if somebody sent us a questionnaire, we filled it out. And so they routinely would go out based on materials that were prepared. If there was a question that we had to run by Bill in asking me what he thought about something, we would, but on a normal course of events, he wouldn't see them. They would be taken from things that he's written, because we did prepare extensive documents that he approved in terms of what he believed and what he thought. And, sometimes things got in there that he hadn't approved.

MARINUCCI: Did you fill them out?

RUSSO: No. I didn't personally fill them out, no. The policy people worked on it, and I am the one who finally had a stack of them and I just signed off on them all, and I did not read it very carefully.

SHANDOBIL: So he did not read it before it went out?

RUSSO: No.

SHANDOBIL: And had he read it, would he have changed some of the answers?

RUSSO: Yes, I think that's safe to say, yes.

SHANDOBIL: And how did that happen that it was filled out with answers that he didn't agree with?

RUSSO: Usually when we have our policy meetings, people who participate or people on the staff would prepare drafts of statements of what Bill thinks, and suggestions on how to answer questions, and that gets incorporated into our policy stuff. And it was just at a period of time when we were expanding and changing our system around a little bit, and I had been out of town, and it was due at 5 o'clock. And I got into the office like at 5:30 and I had a stack of these things of different ones to approve, and I just rattled off and approved them all. And it was my mistake. I should have looked at it more carefully. No big mystery there.

SOUTH: Well, the humorous thing about this episode from our perspective was you had Bill Simon running around for about three-and-a-half months, accusing the governor of personally executing the Oracle contract, probably negotiated out all of its terms, personally signed it, and sold off a $98 million state contract for a $25,000 contribution from Oracle. And as the governor of a state of 35 million people, trillion-dollar economy, $100 billion budget, he had to know about this one specific contract. And then a few weeks later, this same candidate is hit with a questionnaire that went out of his office—of course, he had no knowledge of that whatsoever. He never saw it; didn't even know it went out. It was signed with an autopen. From our perspective, you have to admit that was pretty funny.

RUSSO: Well, I think there's a big difference in the seriousness with which you take a thousand questionnaires and the biggest software contract. . . .

SOUTH: Do you know how many state contracts we have going out?

RUSSO: Yes, I do know. And I. . . .

SOUTH: And by the way, Sean was the one, when Wilson was hit with the allegation that a Lockheed contract had gone out because he took $10,000 from Lockheed, Sean Walsh, as his spokesman, came out and publicly said, "This is ridiculous." The governor of California has no involvement, personally, in the state procurement contract.

WALSH: Except there's never been in the history of California a GAR, which in government bureaucratese is basically a Godlike document to get five cabinet secretaries and the cabinet secretary for the governor all to sign it and date it all on one day. So, again, was there anything done wrong here? Maybe not. But it sure looks funny.

SOUTH: Well, you know what, if there was, we had a very hostile committee chairman, who is trying to make a name for himself for a statewide office, who was totally off the reservation. He had total control of that committee. And he had almost unlimited time to go after this. It was exactly as the governor said to begin with. He had no knowledge of the Oracle Contract, didn't know it had ever gone forward, had no knowledge of the Oracle contribution, and, in fact, when all the hullabaloo was over with, that's exactly the conclusion that was reached.

RUSSO: And he didn't return Larry Ellison's call, and we all believed him.

SOUTH: He did not return Larry Ellison's call. That's another fact.

RUSSO: Nobody believes that.

SOUTH: I can go on the rest of the day giving you a list of people that are pissed off because the governor didn't return their phone calls.

IV. The Recall

An Antipolitician, Anti-establishment Groundswell Elected the Candidate of Change

Introduction
by Susan Rasky, UC Berkeley School of Journalism

On October 7, 2003, for the first time in California's history and only the second time in the country's, voters recalled a sitting governor. On the same ballot, they elected in very convincing numbers a successor known worldwide as a hero of Hollywood action films whose previous political experience consisted of serving on a presidential commission, sponsoring a successful statewide initiative for after-school programs, and marrying a member of the Kennedy clan.

To describe the events leading up to that election as merely historic or unprecedented, or silly or circus-like, all of which they were, is to understate the extraordinary and profound nature of what happened in California in the summer and early fall of 2003. Gray Davis had been elected to a second term less than a year earlier. While widely disliked by colleagues as well as the public, and particularly unpopular because of his voracious fundraising, Davis was not accused of any illegality or malfeasance that would rise to the level of impeachment. Indeed, had he been convicted of a crime or impeachable offense and forced to resign, he would have been succeeded by Lieutenant Governor Cruz Bustamante.

What the recall mechanism offered, apart from the opportunity for opponents to remove him without having to assert misconduct, was an electoral short-cut for replacement candidates. It is a fair bet that not one of the major contenders to replace Davis, including Schwarzenegger, could have made it to the governor's office in a conventional race.

In the 77 days between the certification of signatures demanding a recall and the actual election, Californians accustomed to the vapid, disembodied cam-

169

paigns waged in paid television commercials, experienced something akin to the suspense and intensity of a New Hampshire primary. The lightening campaign drove the presidential race off the front pages and airwaves, attracted hordes of reporters from around the world, and tested the nerves of a California press corps that had to elbow its way through Academy Awards style crowds to get to the candidates. While much of the nation looked on bemused or horrified at the latest display of California's extreme civics, politicians across the country worried that the recall fever might spread.

Officially, the recall story begins on February 5, the day Ted Costa, head of the taxpayer organization People's Advocate and veteran of a dozen initiative campaigns, fulfilled the almost quaint ritual of notifying the governor in writing that he was about to be a recall target. Costa's associate, Mark Abernathy, who actually drafted the letter, recalled the first line with relish: "It said we're recalling the governor because of gross mismanagement of state finances by overspending the people's money."

The real beginning goes back nearly a year earlier to Gray Davis's successful intervention in the 2002 Republican primary. Davis poured millions of dollars into television ads to demolish the candidacy of Los Angeles Mayor Richard Riordan and assure himself an easier general election opponent in the far more conservative, and politically inexperienced, Bill Simon. It may not have been the first time a politician had played across the lines—although no California gubernatorial candidate had ever done it in so overtly heavy-handed a fashion—and it is at least arguable that Riordan might have self destructed anyway in a general election campaign.

But it was a bare-knuckled move, even for California, and infuriated Republicans well to right of Riordan who had swallowed their ideology to back him. Having finally accepted a moderate candidate as the ticket to victory, they were denied their chance. As GOP political strategists would discover in focus groups months later, anger about what happened in 2002 would come back to haunt Davis in 2003.

The November 5 general election played out against the backdrop of a spiraling budget deficit, a lackluster economy, and a legislature in gridlock. Dispirited Californians stayed away from the polls in droves, and Davis squeaked by Simon with a mere five points. For Republicans, that was almost worse than having been trounced.

In a telephone conversation two weeks later, Costa and Abernathy began talking about recall. They were especially exercised about the increasing budget deficit, and their first thought, according to Abernathy, was a tighter spending limit. "We discussed that, but we also discussed Gray Davis, and how we felt that he was probably the worst manager we'd ever had, and that people would probably agree with that," he said. "So Ted said, 'you know, maybe we ought to recall him.'"

Although it would take several weeks for the two men to fully research the constitutional provision on recall, their initial conversation already encompassed the key points in its favor. They were required to gather only 900,000 signatures —12 percent of the voters in the previous gubernatorial election to qualify the recall. They would need to gather more, of course, as a cushion, but the depressed turnout on November 5 was a plus. Maybe they could do it with volunteers.

There would be no primary and only one ballot, with everybody on the same ballot. They figured on 20 to 30 candidates, and probably two or three strong ones, which meant it would be possible to win with 33 to 35 percent of the vote. And, they already had a particular candidate in mind.

"Well, on that call we mentioned Arnold Schwarzenegger—that it's the kind of thing that would be tailor-made for somebody like Schwarzenegger," Abernathy said. "And we were quite excited that somebody outside of the mainstream political sphere could win, an outsider, because we felt strongly an outsider had to come in. I remember saying to Ted, 'This is a thing of beauty, a thing of beauty,' which I continued to repeat throughout the process as it continued to unfold."

Separately, GOP political consultant Sal Russo, who had managed Simon's 2002 campaign, began putting together a recall effort of his own. Russo said his first discussion on the subject came at a January 24 meeting with "a number of Democrats." Russo repeatedly declined to disclose whom the Democrats were or to say whom they represented. He described them as "highly sophisticated politically" and well versed in polling numbers.

"They shared some information they had and said that Gray Davis was recallable," he said, adding that the Democrats "had some help they could give" but that the effort would have to be broad based to appeal to liberals and separate from any driven by a "right-wing Republican taxpayer group." They warned against any involvement by Simon in particular.

Abernathy and Costa's basic plan of action was set by December 17. They had $200,000 in the bank and estimated they would need at least another $800,000 to qualify the petition. By the end of December and into January, Costa started making the rounds of talk radio shows to discuss the need for a recall. Conservative talk show hosts in San Diego, Los Angeles, the Central Valley and San Francisco had begun to spread the word to their listeners, but it was a slow process. Even with two recall efforts, Costa's and Russo's, which was headed by former Republican Assemblyman Howard Kaloogian, neither the Davis administration, nor Republican elected officials appeared to take either effort very seriously.

California political reporters, meanwhile, were busy watching the state budget implode and the possibility of a recall was so far off the official radar that the Fair Political Practices Commission did not decide until March to update its recall fact sheet in response to press calls. It would be June before the commission began work on updating the regulations covering spending in a recall campaign.

By the end of April, only 65,000 signatures had been gathered and funding was short. Enter Republican Congressman Daryl Issa of San Diego, with ambitions to be governor and a checkbook big enough to underwrite a major signature gathering effort. Issa called Dave Gilliard and signed him on to run the drive. But Gilliard found the state's traditional signature gathering firms mysteriously unavailable. Moving quickly to cut off a well-funded, professional signature-gathering effort, Davis's antirecall forces had hired every firm in the state and deployed them on "other projects."

Gilliard figured the volunteer effort eventually might produce enough signatures to place the recall on some ballot. But Issa needed a fall ballot in order to avoid giving up his congressional seat. Gilliard put together a $1.8 million budget, gave Issa a strict schedule for when each cash infusion would be required and hired an organizer to begin training paid signature gatherers as quickly as possible.

If the timing, logistics, and issues of a recall were tailor made for a Schwarzenegger candidacy, they were also tailor made for talk radio—although not quite as Costa and Abernathy first envisioned when they designed a signature petition that could be downloaded to a home computer and printed on a single page.

According to Russo, 45 radio talk show hosts up and down the state were taking campaign material from the recall backers and using it daily on the air. With paid signature gatherers on the streets, listeners angry with Davis over the budget, the economy, the last election, or merely his cool, distant demeanor now had a convenient way to translate what they were hearing into action.

The governor's camp, for months in some strange combination of denial and paralysis, began to stir. At the end of May, Steve Smith, a long-time Davis ally took leave from his state job to head the antirecall campaign effort that Don Terry and the fire fighters union had been fronting for months.

The immediate goals were to dry up Issa's money and halt or at least slow down the signature gathering drive. Discrediting Issa would prove easy enough. As the congressman's own advisers had warned, combining a run for governor with the funding of the recall drive would automatically taint him in voters' eyes. But stopping the signature drive became increasingly a moot point. Through all the negative press, Issa never missed a scheduled payment to the recall effort.

By mid-June it was clear to the Davis forces the recall would qualify. The problem was what to do about it. Publicly, there was a show of unity. Senator Dianne Feinstein, the most popular politician in the state and herself the target of unsuccessful recall as mayor of San Francisco, succeeded in convincing fellow Democrats with aspirations for the governor's job in 2006 to oppose the recall and stay off the 2003 ballot. Privately, the Democrats were in turmoil as relentless internal polling and focus grouping showed Davis in more trouble than even the dismal public polls suggested.

Arnold Schwarzenegger's advisers did a little June polling of their own. Schwarzenegger's political ambitions were hardly a secret; a team of aides to former governor Pete Wilson, had been grooming the Austrian born bodybuilder turned actor for at least two years.

Under the direction of long-time Wilson adviser Bob White, the team had guided Schwarzenegger through a successful initiative campaign, and in April, the actor had discussed his 2006 gubernatorial aspirations with White House political adviser Karl Rove. The June polling, as political strategist George Gorton would later describe it, was as much a test of Schwarzenegger's own desire to run as it was of voter reaction to him. According to Gorton, the findings showed that Schwarzenegger did well even among very conservative Republicans, and that while Feinstein did well against Schwarzenegger in northern California, "in southern California, she didn't do that strongly at all."

By July 7 the recall groups halted their efforts, believing they had more than enough signatures to qualify for a fall ballot. Desperate for anything to buy time, Davis and the labor groups supporting him unleashed a blizzard of lawsuits aimed at slowing down certification because of alleged irregularities in signature gathering. If the recall election could be pushed to March 2004, a hot Democratic presidential primary might boost turnout and improve the governor's prospects for keeping his job.

But the suits, like all of the legal challenges to the recall, ultimately would prove unsuccessful. On July 23 Secretary of State Kevin Shelley certified a recall election, and Bustamante, fulfilling the role prescribed for him in the state constitution, set the date for October 7.

As July moved into August, even the outward show of Democratic unity crumbled. Each day another congressional Democrat came forward to plead that the party run a Democratic candidate to replace Davis. Among the prominent voices publicly breaking with the earlier strategy was Senator Barbara Boxer, up for reelection herself in 2004.

San Francisco Mayor Willie Brown tried several times to broker a peace among the Democratic factions, but the situation had become impossible. With a ruling by a federal court judge that voters who left the recall question blank might still vote for a Davis replacement on the second part of the ballot, the pressure to do something about a Democratic candidate only grew. There was a brief move to draft former Congressman and Clinton administration budget director Leon Panetta and continued talk that Senator Feinstein herself might enter the race.

Davis petitioned the state supreme court for permission to place his name on part two of the ballot, but his lawyers knew it was at a long shot at best. After Feinstein made clear in a statement on August 5 that she had no intention of running, things began to happen rather quickly.

The following day, Schwarzenegger, apparently surprising his own political consultants as well as his good friend Dick Riordan, appeared on the Tonight Show and announced he would run. For months he and Riordan had carried on an elaborate Alfonse-Gaston routine, each professing to reporters that he would stand aside if the other chose to enter the race.

On same day, August 6, Bustamante let the other Democratic shoe drop, announcing that he would be a candidate and that he would urge Californians to vote No on the recall and Yes on Bustamante. It was a textbook example of the "mixed message" campaigns are supposed to avoid giving voters, but by the end of the month, the California Labor Federation and the United Farm Workers would endorse it as a strategy.

On August 7, the state supreme court denied five separate challenges to the recall, and a superior court judge rejected a suit alleging fraud in signature gathering. With tears in his eyes, Congressman Darrell Issa, the man whose money breathed life into the recall, dropped out of the race.

By the August 9 filing deadline, there would be 135 names, including Bustamante, Schwarzenegger, Simon, State Senator Tom McClintock, a Ventura Republican; columnist Arianna Huffington, who over the years had migrated from the conservative right to the liberal left and was running as an independent, Peter Camejo of the Green Party, who had also run for governor in 2002, and former baseball commissioner and southern California businessman, Peter Uberroth. Uberroth and Simon, neither of whom ever made strong showings in the polls, ultimately dropped out before the election to clear the way for Schwarzenegger.

Although *Hustler Magazine* publisher Larry Flynt and assorted other porn stars, eccentrics, and self promoters received most of the attention and provided endless fodder for TV's late night comics, the vast majority of the candidates were middle class, college educated white males.

Three weeks before the election, a panel of three federal appeals court judges ordered a delay until six counties could replace their punch-card voting machines. But a week later a larger panel of the 9th Circuit overturned that ruling, clearing the way for the recall vote.

By their nature campaign postmortems suggest inevitability to the election outcome. Every decision the winners made becomes, in hindsight, a step to victory, and every decision on the losing side is a miscalculation that helped seal defeat. In this election, the most important and the most revealing campaign decisions were the assumptions the candidates and their strategists made at the outset.

For Green Party candidate Peter Camejo, the race was never about winning; it was about tapping into voter anger at the two main parties and advancing a clearly defined alternative party platform. But as Tyler Snortum-Phelps of the Camejo campaign explained, Schwarzenegger's presence shifted Camejo's focus entirely. "One of the only ways we tend to get attention is through the spoiler factor," he said. "And when you had Arnold out there so strong, that issue was no longer there. So then we had to actually ask the people to just pay attention to Peter, based on what he was saying, which doesn't always work with reporters."

Simon's campaign strategist Wayne Johnson positioned his candidate to run a primary style race in the early going and assumed the race would then turn into a general election when one of the Republicans broke out of the pack. "I think there was an assumption that somebody would take Arnold down," he said, adding that he had expected the Democrats to lead the attack. "As it turns out, the way we read it, they simply weren't on the same page. The Democrats were fighting an internal battle over whether to oppose the recall or support Cruz." Simon withdrew from the race on August 23.

Tom McClintock, who remained in the race despite strong pressure from Republican colleagues to withdraw, also believed Democrats would take on Schwarzenegger early in the campaign and weaken him. "I made the wrong assumption that this was going to be a mediocre turnout election," said John Feliz,

McClintock's manager. "If that were so, we figured we had about a million and half identified voters throughout the state of California and that would get us about 26 to 28 percent of the vote which I thought would be enough to win. . . . If Dianne Feinstein had decided to enter the race, we probably would not have run," Feliz said.

Richie Ross, the strategist for Cruz Bustamante, was also looking for a fractured electorate. In Ross's polling about whether voters preferred a Democrat, Republican, or Independent in the governor's office, the word Democrat never got above 36 percent. "That was stunning to us," Ross said, adding that the hope to keep a Bustamante candidacy alive rested on McClintock capturing 20 percent of the vote and Peter Uberroth staying in the race to splinter Republican votes further. "Our calculation was always about the way the Democratic primary electorate was split," he said. "Could we just be in the right place, kind of at the right time, play the splits, appeal to the Democratic base, hope there wasn't massive drop off or work to control the drop off between question 1 and question 2."

For the Davis strategists, the problem was always the math. "How do you get 50 percent plus one of the voters to vote for somebody with a 26 percent job approval rating?" said Garry South, a long-time Davis political adviser. "In our tracking, there were only two occasions where we got yes on the recall below 50." One was in early September, when the yes polling dipped to 49 percent and the other was on the Saturday night before the election in the wake of a *Los Angeles Times* story about women who said they had been groped and sexually harassed by Schwarzenegger. South noted that by Sunday night, the internal polling moved back to where it had been for most of the campaign, with 53 percent of the voters favoring recall and 44 percent opposed.

Don Sipple, media strategist for Arnold Schwarzenegger, said that both the candidate and his advisers understood from the outset that the unconventional recall process favored an outsider. "Given the environment, which is distinctly antipolitician, anti-establishment, he's the embodiment of change," Sipple said. "It wasn't about eight-point plans, because there wasn't time for it to be about eight-point plans. It was about symbolism, messages, and messengers."

The Recall Panel

AMY CHANCE: Welcome. I'm going to introduce our panel here, and get you oriented. At this table, we have the "Oust Gray Davis" team: Dave Gilliard from Rescue California, Mark Abernathy from Davis Recall.com, and Sal Russo of Recall Gray Davis.com.

On this side, we have the Gray Davis defense squad: Steve Smith from Californians Against the Costly Recall, and Carroll Wills from Taxpayers Against the Recall.

And for those of you who are new to this format these sessions are about saying what really happened for historical purposes, not about trying to make your side look smart.

DAN BORENSTEIN: This is the time to put the spin aside.

CHANCE: That's exactly what we hope to do, and we're going to try to follow a chronology to draw out some of the events in the course of the recall campaign. We ought to start around February 4, shortly after we last met here, when just three months after the 2002 gubernatorial election, taxpayer activist, Ted Costa, announced his intention to launch a recall campaign against Gray Davis. It was an effort that was going to need 900,000 valid signatures to put the matter before voters, and there weren't a lot of people giving it a lot of credibility at that point. And perhaps, we can start with Mark, to give us an idea of what led up to that. What was the original germ that became the recall. Where did it start?

MARK ABERNATHY: A successful student has many teachers. And there were a few good people thinking about it and working on it during January and February when this started. The first I heard of the idea was on November 17, when Ted Costa and I talked as we usually do. Ted and I have been buddies for 25 years and political comrades, and we worked on many, many campaigns, the People's Advocate Organization originated by Paul Gann, and going back to Proposition 13 in 1978. Ted's organization has qualified 12 ballot initiatives, and he's never failed to qualify one. This recall will be number 13. So we've worked on many on those. The last one that we worked on together was Proposition 24 in 2000, the redistricting initiative. It was qualified and then it was thrown off the ballot by the courts. But it was November 17 when we first mentioned the recall as a possibility.

BORENSTEIN: What exactly did he say to you?

ABERNATHY: We were talking about what to do about this, in our view, terrible election that happened in November; when there was a very small turnout, and people didn't feel like they had a legitimate choice. Gray Davis had overspent the budget by $21 billion a year before, and $24 billion this year, and looked like even more according to Elizabeth Hill for the next year. So what could we do about it? And Ted said, "You know, maybe we ought to come back with a Paul Gann Spending Initiative, and redo that one, tighten that up the spending limits because they're getting around that." And we discussed that, but we also discussed Gray Davis, and how we felt that he was probably the worst manager we'd ever had, and that the people would probably agree with that.

So Ted said, "You know, maybe we ought to recall him." And we said, "Well, yeah. What does that take?" So we went to the Constitution and started reading back the Constitution. And it was rather dusty since 1911, and no governor had ever been recalled, but obviously there had been attempts, feeble attempts that had gotten nowhere. So over the next couple of days we went through the Constitution, and we deciphered what it said, and said, "Okay, this is something that could be done. You know, the people can do this by themselves. They don't need politicians to participate in this. And it's the one act that can focus on the problems the state is having." And we looked at the dates and said, "Okay, we got to get 12 percent of the signatures." Figured that up: it's about 900,000. We thought, "Well, we'll have to get 1.2 million, because we have to have a cushion." And we looked at, "Okay, it's one ballot, everybody on the same ballot. No primary. Somebody could win probably with 33 to 35 percent of the vote. It might be 20 or 30 candidates. There will probably be two or three strong ones, and the winner will probably get 35 percent of the vote; somebody else at 25 and down. So we could win.'

CHANCE: Did you have a candidate in mind?

ABERNATHY: Well, on that call we mentioned Arnold Schwarzenegger—that it's the kind of the thing that would be tailor-made for somebody like Schwarzenegger. He doesn't have to go through the primary, and all that very partisan battle. He could go out to the general public and utilize the attributes that he has. So we definitely thought Schwarzenegger would be the kind of candidate, possibly the candidate, but the kind of candidate who could win in this case. And we were quite excited that somebody outside of the regular mainstream political sphere could win, an outsider, because we felt strongly an outsider had to come in. I remember saying to Ted, "This is a thing of beauty," a thing of beauty, which I continued to repeat throughout the process as it continued to unfold.

BORENSTEIN: Mark, how much did you know about the budget for the current fiscal year at that point?

ABERNATHY: Well, I knew that the '02/'03 budget, which Elizabeth Hill said was going to be $17 billion in debt back in January '02, when Davis said it would only be $5 billion in debt. And it ended up $21 billion. Then the '03/'04 budget, which was worked on from June to September, which in mid to late November, Elizabeth Hill said it looks like it's $21 billion in debt, and Davis pooh-poohed that. But then right after the election, Davis said, "Well, it looks like it's . . " I believe at the time he said it looks like it's $21 billion in debt, and others said it might go up from that. Well, eventually, of course, in December, he said it was $28 billion, and then it was 32 and 35.

December 18 is when Ted and I decided we were going to push the recall. There were other things we were discussing possibly doing, like the spending limit, but we decided that we would do the recall. We had $200,000 in the bank, the Political Action Committee, that we could start with. We figured we would need about a million dollars; we might be able to do it with less. Certainly, we talked about what the Internet would do. It could be something quite different from what we had before because you got all the little old ladies now, and everybody that's got a computer at home on the kitchen counter, and they've got a printer right there, and they can go on the Internet. So when we started making the petition, we made it very specific that it would be downloadable on one page, and printable on one page. That's why we put five signatures—we messed with it a lot to see if we could get as many as 10. We'd like to get more room for signatures on the sheet, but this had to go one page, and we had to go around and around with the secretary of state quite a bit on that. But we finally settled for one that was five, on one page, and downloadable. We thought we might really have something, a different dynamic, because so many people had access to the Internet and had the home printer.

CHANCE: We didn't hear much from Davis about this until about mid February, and at that point he was denouncing this as a right-wing effort to overturn his election, sour grapes, that kind of idea. What was going through the governor's mind and the governor's team's mind as Costa came forward?

STEVE SMITH: I don't think we took it at all seriously until Darrell Issa put in money, bottom line. Frankly, it wasn't serious until Darrell Issa put in money. At that point, we took it seriously. So back in February, yes, you had to make public responses to it, it was the beginning race, but it just wasn't taken all that seriously.

BORENSTEIN: Weren't you worried at all about being able to just put out this little brush fire before it turned into a conflagration? Was there any discussion about that?

SMITH: There has not been a California governor since recall was around that there hasn't been at least one recall filed. There's something like 30 of them. It's an incredible number. They aren't serious without money. So until significant dollars were put in, there were discussions, there was nervousness, but it was nothing significant.

BORENSTEIN: Gray Davis has just come out of an election in which there is record low turnout. In an election he should have by most predictions stomped his opponent, he barely squeaks by. He promises that he's learned his lesson, and tips his hat to that. And then it seems like it's business as usual. It seems he was leaving the door wide open for these guys.

SMITH: Well, it was business as usual to the degree that we didn't respond to their efforts until much later.

CHANCE: Issa didn't get involved until April.

ABERNATHY: I take a little bit of exception to that because when we served notice on Governor Davis, I think it was February 5, I remember the first line of it because I wrote it. It said we're recalling the governor because of "gross mismanagement of state finances by overspending the people's money." That was the first line. And that's the reason, in my estimation, from beginning to end throughout this, that the governor recall went so good and that the governor was recalled—"gross mismanagement of state finances by overspending the people's money." Now, when we went to serve that on the governor there was quite some discussion among the governor's political folks. Steve, you were probably in on that discussion whether the governor should respond or not, because the governor had the opportunity to put his response in there. He was getting advice from someone, and maybe you could tell us who was advising yes and who was advising no. But it was decided then that he would make a response, and some folks were quite surprised. That was in early February that he decided to make that response, because maybe he did take it more seriously than others. Later, we'll talk about the timeline of where the signatures were coming in and why you probably should have been worried a lot more a lot earlier.

CHANCE: Why did they decide to respond? How did that happen?

SMITH: It was essentially a decision that there is a process here just in case we should respond. We don't think this will ever be necessary, but just in case, we will respond. It was not the kind of thing where, as is normal in a ballot measure or something else like this, you go through polling, focus groups, all that stuff, to decide. We didn't do that. It had just not gone to that level. It was using some of brains around the operation. It was a response draft.

CHANCE: The Republican Party wasn't getting behind this, was it? Sal, maybe you can address that point. At the convention there was not a lot of institutional support from the politicians and the Party structure.

BORENSTEIN: It's the February convention we're talking about.

SAL RUSSO: We did the first rally at the Capitol that day, and it was noticeable that of all the people at the rally, very few of them were from the convention, which proved something to us, that there was a grassroots movement afoot that had nothing to do with the organized parties. The party people literally didn't come across the street. These were all people in the community. And that's probably the biggest mistake that Gray Davis made in not, as Mark made an illusion to a second ago, recognizing that this was serious from the beginning.

As I said in the January conference when we were here last, the one element that was always missing from the 2002 campaign was voters were never angry at Gray Davis. Every reporter in here heard me say that multiple times, that while they thought it was a failed governor, they didn't think he did a very good job, there was no anger. There was no "we got to throw the rascal out" sentiment, and it never came. I thought that ultimately the final budget problem would be tipping point on the anger. But it never came.

After the election in November, Gray Davis—and you can play with words all you want—but he basically admitted that he had not been all that candid. I'd like to say he lied, but he was deceptive. Clearly, he gave people the idea that things were okay with the budget, that he really had it managed. And when they found out three weeks after the election that we had a budget debacle, that suddenly fueled the anger that I kept waiting for in 2002. And I've likened that to pulling threads on a sweater. The thread they were pulling on was anger over the budget. And as they pulled on that thread, then they started to think about the electricity crisis, and how Gray Davis had failed on electricity. And then they started thinking about roads, and how our roads were ranked the worst in the nation. They started thinking about all the other elements that led Mark to put that line in his petition about failed leadership. And we really had anger.

A newspaper column in December was the first time it had ever been in print; Melanie Morgan jumped on it pretty early on KSFO, and that's where we got the talk radio thing launched. But I had I had my first discussion on the recall at a meeting with a number of Democrats on January 24, in which they said, "Gray Davis is recallable, but we don't think that it can be done if it's a right-wing Republican taxpayer. . . ."

BORENSTEIN: A number of Democrats. . . .

CHANCE: Yeah, which Democrats? Now, it's time to name names.

RUSSO: This is one I can't be candid on. . . .

CHANCE: Candidates or strategists?

RUSSO: Neither one. Unfortunately I can't be candid on this. . . .

CHANCE: Legislators?

RUSSO: I can't say.

CHANCE: You can't categorize?

RUSSO: They shared some information they had and said that it was very doable. If it were not taxpayer-driven, and it were broad-based, it would appeal to liberals as well as conservatives. They had some help that they could give if we got this thing started, and stayed independent of the taxpayer group. So I called

Mark that day, and I told him about my meeting, and I said why I thought we needed to work on parallel tracks, but we had to be in close contact, use the same petition. I encouraged him not to turn the petition in on February 5, I said, "because I don't think we're ready yet." I had a great deal of skepticism. I had worked on what we call the "Brown-Out" campaign in the '70s, on behalf of our ad clients, when we were looking at recalling Jerry Brown. In the course of that we discovered that people didn't take kindly to recalls, that recalls were an extraordinary remedy, that people didn't think they were appropriate. Because you wouldn't spray Malathion to kill the medfly was not a reason to recall a governor. It took more than that.

So even though this chatter was going in December and January, I was highly skeptical. And even in the meeting with the Democrats on the 24, I said, 'I'm not sure that this is doable. But" I said, "if it is doable, it's going to be doable because we do have anger," which I could see that we did have, "and, second, is that we have tools available to us that we've never had before, and that is, the marriage of the Internet with talk radio," which still I don't think people really grasp how important that is.

BORENSTEIN: Wasn't your involvement? Wasn't the very nature of having you involved potentially dangerous? Here you've just managed what many people considered one of the most failed gubernatorial campaigns. Wasn't there a real danger it was going to look like sour grapes?

RUSSO: One of the things they shared in that meeting was that if there was a protagonist in the recall that person was going to be negatively viewed. And in the instance of this meeting they were saying that they thought it was very important that Bill Simon not have anything to do with this thing, which I happened to agree. When we did our focus groups and polling shortly thereafter we found that whoever led this thing was going to be negatively viewed, that he would have done good deeds, but it would hurt him personally. Which is what Issa found out. While he rallied the faithful in a positive way, he took on such negatives and the Democrats piled on.

CHANCE: To what extent did this get fueled, maybe not initially, but ultimately, by the dynamic of just a lot of political consultants, generally, casting about for some business and casting about for some activity in an off year? Steve, would you like to speak to that?

SMITH: No, I think the other side needs to talk to that first, because that comes about from their side of the table.

BORENSTEIN: Well, that brings us appropriately to April 23. And it was a slow year for you, wasn't it, Dave, until that moment?

DAVE GILLIARD: I was planning my summer vacation, as a matter of fact, right about the time I got the call from Congressman Issa.

BORENSTEIN: Did he call you or you call him?

GILLIARD: He called me. And he asked me: 'Is this recall thing real? Can it really be done? Do you feel that it has a chance?" And, in his case, the more important question is, "Can it be a fall election?" And, he said, "I'll give you 24 hours to let me know what you think about that."

CHANCE: Why did he want it to be a fall election?

GILLIARD: Well, I think it's obvious, he was interested in running for governor.

CHANCE: And that would have conflicted with his congressional. . . .

GILLIARD: Not legally, but, yeah. So, I called some friends around the state, I did as quick an inventory as I could. I called Ted Costa to see how things looked on the petition. The next day I called Issa back and I said that I felt it was real, but that it wasn't to the point now where it would happen unless somebody stepped in with a large amount of money very quickly.

BORENSTEIN: And he suggested he might in your first conversation?

GILLIARD: He said, "Well, if you formed an organization, I think you would probably find yourself with the resources to do it." Having dealt with him in the past, I understood what that language meant, and I formed the organization the next day. We decided to choose a name that put a little positive spin on what we were doing, so we chose "Rescue California." He initially was hoping that others in the Republican establishment would step forward and he wouldn't have to fund this, but I warned him early on that it didn't look that way; I suspected that he would have to put up the bulk of the money.

We put a budget together of about $1.8 million. I was not a believer in the Internet as a vehicle to qualify a measure that needed this many signatures. I do think an initiative where we're down in the 300,000 range of valid signatures is possible now, but this had to happen fast, and it was a large number of signatures. And we had some big obstacles. I found out very quickly that the major paid signature firms in the state that I had dealt with in the past were all, curiously, not available to us. So a guy named Tom Bader, who had been in California earlier, and had come back out at the invitation of Ted Costa, was available. And he had to start an organization from scratch to get paid signatures.

CHANCE: Steve, why weren't those firms available?

SMITH: Because they were otherwise engaged.

CHANCE: Did you look for businesses that might be available to them, and make those connections?

SMITH: I can't speak for prior to about May 15, because I literally wasn't part of this discussion. And, just for the record, the group I'm supposed to be representing didn't exist at this phase of the campaign. It showed up several months later. But Taxpayers got formed in the last week of May, probably. I think that's about right. And, basically, it was Carroll's boss, Dan Perry, who came knocking on my door saying, "You need to take a leave, we want you over here."

BORENSTEIN: It wasn't Garry or Greg?

SMITH: No, it was Dan, and some of the labor leaders, frankly, who came knocking, because I've done initiative campaigns for unions before a number of times on both sides. So they came knocking. I, of course, checked. You know, you don't sort of take a leave willy-nilly, and so I called and said, "Do you all mind if I do this?" And they said, "Go forth."

CHANCE: So there really wasn't any leadership coming out of the governor's office?

SMITH: In terms of forming Taxpayers, that really came from outside of the governor's operation.

CARROLL WILLS: And I can actually speak to that a little bit because when Steve was talking about the nervousness factor in response to what Mark was saying about whether or not the governor's folks were actually taking it seriously, I can tell you that organized labor, in general, and my boss, in particular, were very nervous. The firefighters had been with Gray Davis since the earth cooled, when the Gray Davis for Governor Committee was formed. At the start it was Dan Perry, Garry South, and Gray Davis, sitting at a table working it out. So the firefighters had been involved with the governor from the beginning for reasons that have been ably documented by the *Sacramento Bee*. And so he was nervous, he was genuinely concerned about this. I'm the communications director for the firefighters, and he kept coming to me because he knew I had been a journalist under another name, and he said, "Is this thing for real? I mean, is this thing really, really going to happen?"

BORENSTEIN: And what was your answer at that point?

WILLS: Well, my answer was it's real if there's money.

BORENSTEIN: Does everybody here agree on that point: If not for Darrell Issa's money, we would not be here today.

GILLIARD: No, I don't agree.

ABERNATHY: No, not at all.

RUSSO: We wouldn't be here today; we'd be here in March.

ABERNATHY: We might be here later. But the recall would have qualified. I may have been as close to figuring whether the signatures were going to come as anybody. But the chart that I have here, and I'll give this to the record-keeper here so they can utilize this, but the chart here that we had made back in January shows how it was going to be. This blue line shows what we had to do in order to qualify by our target date, which was July 4.

BORENSTEIN: So you were assuming that your signature-gathering would not be linear, but would be parabolic in nature.

ABERNATHY: Right, as it grew, more and more people would get interested, and it would go faster and faster. That's the way we set it out when we drew this chart in January when we first said, "What are we going to do?" This red line shows where we would have to be in order to qualify by the first week in September, which would have been the deadline to qualify. That would have put the thing on the March ballot. So you can see that for the most part, we were ahead of the July 4 projection, and we were far above the September all the way. March 25 was when we finally got to circulate. And by the second week in April we had hit 100,000, and by the fourth week in April we were at 200,000 signatures.

BORENSTEIN: Did you do that chart before or after the fact?

ABERNATHY: This chart has been kept since the beginning on the website. Some reporters went to the website and found it. It's been there all the time.

BORENSTEIN: Then, Dave, why do you disagree?

GILLIARD: Well, in late April, I knew how many petitions were out there in the stream, but my problem was getting a handle how many signatures there actually were. My estimate was there were probably about 100,000 in late April. Now, my opinion was there was no way we could get there in July without a massive paid effort, which would have to get us between 75- and 100,000 signatures a week out in the street, supplemented by at least 4- to 500,000 signatures through direct mail, all in May and June. And that's why we had to put together. . . .

BORENSTEIN: To get for November, or to make it at all?

GILLIARD: To make it for fall. It's kind of a chicken or egg thing here. The fact that the money came in, and all of a sudden, people at every grocery store and every Home Depot saw a table led to the excitement. And then that played into what talk radio and everybody else was doing.

BORENSTEIN: But what about Mark's point that maybe we wouldn't be here now, we'd be here next June or next March?

GILLIARD: I didn't really care about next June or next March, I was only focused on July, so I didn't look beyond that.

CHANCE: The impetus for Steve was Darrell Issa's political aspirations.

SMITH: True.

RUSSO: Let me answer something that's pronounced in what everybody's been saying, and that is, there's a decided bias in favor of big shots, and it worked to our advantage. People think that only big shots can do anything. And as Dan Walters has said, we go through this thing every 12 years in California, from Reagan's election in '66, to Prop 13 in '78, to term limits in '90, and now the recall, where people actually make some effort to take their government back. And none of those were big people, generally, playing the lead. The biggest advantage we had in defeating Gray Davis is the fact that they didn't take it seriously. I'd love to have somebody tell me what really happened, but I'm sure somebody said, "Let's go talk to Brulte and Dave Cox, the Republican leaders.' Both of them said, "Oh, no, nothing's going on. This is a nutty thing." Somebody said, "Let's go talk to Duff Sundheim and Mark Brasco, the National Committee Chairman and the State Party Chairman." They talked to them, they said, 'Oh, no, nothing's going on." "I know Karl Rove. I'll call the White House." They called the White House, the White House said, 'Nah, nothing's going on." "Call Bill Hauck at the Roundtable, call Jack Stewart at the Manufacturers, call Alan Zaremberg at the Chamber." They all said, "Nah, nothing's going on."

CHANCE: Is that what happened, Steve?

RUSSO: One more anecdote. There was a story very late in the campaign. Ventura County was a hot bed of signature gathering because we have competing candidates. We had more signatures coming out of Ventura . . . they were pouring out. There was a story in the *Ventura Star Press*, where they were quoting the head of the County AFL/CIO. And the question to her was: "Are you going to go out and fight the recall in your county?" And she said, "We're ready to go. As soon as we see any signs of it, we'll be there." We had already exceeded our goals in Ventura County. Completely clueless. I called one of my friends in the labor movement and I said, "Is this a secret strategy to shock the grassroots, you know, the troops, so the rank and file would say, 'Holy smokes!' or is this person completely stupid and clueless?" And they said, "I'm afraid to say that it's the latter." Without that being asleep, we wouldn't have done it. If Gray Davis had followed the advice a lot of the labor guys gave him to act like a governor in January, act like a governor in February, act like a governor in March, we never would have had a recall, because people don't like recalls. By March it was done.

SMITH: There was an assertion that the whole reason for the recall was the budget. That was the trigger, that was the anger point, there is no question. Had the energy situation not happened two years earlier, it would not have been what it was. You could have had either one; you couldn't have both.

ABERNATHY: That's right. I agree with Steve.

SMITH: That's why there was no anger, and then there was anger. And I absolutely agree with you, no question. That's when we went over the line, and it stripped away any Teflon and he was vulnerable to any arrows. And then the budget showed up and every arrow hit, and that's what happened. In terms of the "take it seriously/not take it seriously/when we took it seriously," and did we call all the Republican leadership? No, we didn't call all the Republican leadership. I, frankly, can't imagine calling Duff, but that's totally beside the point. When we took it seriously was when Darrell Issa's money showed up. And I've got to tell you there is no way it would have qualified earlier, and I am highly skeptical that it would have ever qualified without Darrell's money. There is a thing that happens in initiatives. The chart does go up. That's what happens in any signature campaign. But you need critical mass for the chart to go up. They had not achieved critical mass to get the chart to go up. It just wasn't here yet. Would they have gotten there in July 1? Maybe. I can't say; that's why I'm skeptical, but I'm not saying it couldn't happen, because they could have achieved critical mass. At some point, though, they would have had to cross some line in the signature world that all of a sudden, the thing takes off and goes by itself.

ABERNATHY: Steve is right about the critical mass, and we weren't there yet, but we had plans to make it there. I don't want you to be in denial, still, about this, Steve, but back in February. . . .

SMITH: I've been in denial for years.

ABERNATHY: . . . when we first started on this, and you were deciding whether the governor should even respond or not, the governor said, "No, it's going nowhere. There's a couple of right-wing kooks out there." And that was the beginning of the denial I saw, and it continued all the way through.

GILLIARD: Let me add one thing about something we haven't touched on. We did a focus group shortly after we started Rescue California. We brought Frank Lowens out from the East Coast, because I wanted somebody not from California to do this. And he started out the group by asking everybody a one- or two-word impression of Governor Davis. Now, this was a group that was aimed at swing voters. All 28 responses were negative, including the 15 Democrats were negative.

And then the other thing that came out in this group that was very interesting to me is people felt that the last election in November wasn't valid. They didn't feel they had a real choice. They didn't like their choices. And people volunteered in a focus group, which I had never seen before, about the negative ads that Davis had run against Dick Riordan in the Republican primary. And they volunteered that they deprived them of a choice in the November election. And that made them much more open to the recall than they would have been if they felt they had a real choice in November. If they had felt they had a real choice with a real campaign and two candidates they liked, or at least one they liked, then they would have not have responded as positively to the recall.

WILLS: At the risk of sounding like we split the difference, what came to my mind in this conversation is motive and opportunity. Voters had a motive to recall Gray Davis. The talk radio folks, which Sal touched on, and, as somebody who had his eyebrows singed by these folks, I can tell you was a very powerful force in sustaining the anger. The anger was the result of a situation in the governor's negatives in all the things. But sustaining the anger was in large measure a function of how effectively talk radio used the medium. What Darrell Issa's money did was it gave those angry people opportunity. Downloading a petition and signing it, putting it in the mail, that's several steps that most ordinary people eventually get to the point where they go. "Oh, screw it." They were very successful. But what the petition signature gatherers, the actual people on the ground did was give those people who maybe heard about it on talk radio a place to go and an easy way to sign those petitions.

So I tend to agree that it would have been much harder, all other things being equal—in other words, if Bader doesn't show up, if there's no professional signature gathering firm, that somebody else doesn't come in with a lot of money to put bodies in front of people at a critical point—then they wouldn't have gotten to that critical mass, and it would have been a much more laborious process.

CHANCE: At what point did you decide to turn Darrell Issa into a Nazi McCarthy?

SMITH: That's an interesting interpretation. Let me do one other thing real quickly, and then we can move into that. Somebody just referenced back to the illegitimate election in '02. You know, it's interesting to look at '02 not just here but across the country. The reality is there were 17 open governors' races in '02; every one of them changed parties. Right? Five Democratic incumbent governors across the county stood for election—three of them fell, two survived, one was this guy. If you read the tea leaves the way they should have been read, we probably should have lost in November of '02. The only reason we didn't is because we had a hapless opponent and a horrendous campaign against us—all due respect, but you know, it was just crazy. That being said, you don't start your second term with a whole lot of turf to work with. We knew that.

I just wanted to lay that as a basis. We took it seriously when Issa got in. We had two missions, essentially. We were behind the eight-ball on the polling from day one. There were 50-55 percent of the electorate that were gone from before the signature process began. And what made it worse from my perspective is 90 percent of those 50-55 percent were hard locked, and the ears were closed. They weren't listening anymore. So we were playing in a margin that's tight. As a result, we were throwing long balls from May.

The 'block the signature" was "if they have the money they'll qualify," because if you've got money in a signature campaign you do. So we had two missions: one, was to make it more difficult, close them down to the degree we could, which is why we did the "alternative signature" campaign; and, two, was, frankly, to dry up the money. And two things happened that made Darrell Issa the target: number one, he became the only checkbook in town, so if you were going to dry up the money it was a very singularly focused drying of money; and, number two, he did what I thought was just insane: he took out the full-page newspaper ad about a week or two after he did the money and announced that he was running for governor. It completely delegitimized a legitimate use of the signature process. And it made him a target. It gave us the perfect opportunity. Now, his own past, it turns out, provided more targets than we could have ever dreamt of at the start.

BORENSTEIN: Did you play that card too early?

SMITH: Well, in some ways, we didn't play it early enough. At least Congressman Issa didn't get the message early enough. Had Congressman Issa realized 60 days earlier that he was not going to run for governor of California, that he was not a viable candidate, would he have put in the $2 million?

CHANCE: Would he. . . ?

SMITH: I don't know, but our goal was to cut it off.

BORENSTEIN: Dave?

GILLIARD: I can only speak on the recall side of this because I wasn't running his campaign, but I think that the answer to that is probably no, he probably wouldn't have. On the other hand, one of the things we talked about early on before he put up the first $100,000, I said, "You're going to have people all over you. You're going to be the target, and you're going to have to have the guts to stick through this, and you're going to have to keep giving me the money or we're not going to do it." And he understood that, and he kept to a schedule. I know you guys were looking everyday to see how much money Congressman Issa was putting in. I had a schedule of when he was supposed to put it in, and he kept to it all the way to the very end. In fact he called me after we ended up with more signatures than we thought, he said, "Thanks for buying the landslide for me." I said, "Sometimes you can't control these things."

RUSSO: I've got to tell you, I wondered about that conversation.

GILLIARD: In fact, if you guys hadn't raised the car tax, we might not have done it. That's one thing we didn't talk about here. We were getting about 100,000 signatures a week out on the street, and our direct mail was performing the way we thought it would. The week before the car tax stuff came out, we had slipped down to about 80,000. And I thought it was just the fact that we were kind of, you know, you get the easy ones first. And all of a sudden, that came out, and we were back up instantly, and that thing gave us a boost in the street signatures that we could have never gotten on our own.

BORENSTEIN: Let me summarize one key point here. It sounds like we wouldn't be here today, maybe we'd be here in March, but we wouldn't be here today if not for Darrell Issa's gubernatorial ambition.

GILLIARD: That's correct.

RUSSO: I agree with that. The one thing, though, I think, that Carroll touched on that I think needs more amplification is the importance of talk radio and the Internet. The numbers are astronomical. Remember, we're just one website, although I think we were probably the most active website; we had 25 million hits to our website. We were the number one ranked website in politics until Schwarzenegger got into the race and passed us. We had a half-a-million downloads from our website alone. And we worked with all the talk radio stations, and most of the talk radio stations had links either to us or a download petition on theirs. There was a multiplier effect. So out of our half-a-million downloads, there's probably a couple million petitions that were printed and out in the world, as a consequence. And this was continual driven by talk radio.

The big difference, and we talked about at our last conference here, was Melanie Morgan did the MTBE thing in a big way. And Dick Mountjoy, the most conservative senator in the Senate, wins in the San Francisco Bay Area. That woke me up and said there is something powerful going on here. And that's exactly what we used that to beat Dick Riordan in the primary in 2002, we united all the talk radio stations and focused on a single agenda. And that was what our goal was in this thing, is to have every talk radio host talk about the recall everyday. And Melanie Morgan and Eric Hoag and Roger Hedgecock were the leaders, but by the time we got to the end we had a newsletter that we called *e-Call* that went out to the talk radio hosts. We had 45 radio talk show hosts that were taking our material and using it every single day the entire course of the campaign. And that is what was causing the multiplier effect.

And so, as Mark said, it was growing exponentially. And to the extent that it would ever falter a little bit, we had the car tax, or we had the drivers' license bill. There were always things in the news that would create the spark. And we had enough people that were prepared to donate a lot of money to the campaign, as did Ted Costa.

CHANCE: Steve, at any point did you guys say, 'We better just start looking ahead to the election because this is going to happen. We better stop fighting this and get on." It struck me that there wasn't this sense from the Davis side that, "Hey, we should be really looking at Arnold Schwarzenegger.' Did you guys just overlook him?

SMITH: No. About the second or third week in June we began to look at it and say, "You know what? It's there. It's only a question of which ballot." And it began to look worse and worse. As a matter of fact, I knew this campaign was completely whacked-out on both sides from a press perspective when on one day on a street corner in Los Angeles, on about 45-minutes notice, we called a press conference. I don't even remember what we talked about at the press conference. But there were 12 cameras. And this wasn't the governor, this was me standing on a street corner in Los Angeles. And I didn't say anything, and there were 12 cameras! And I'm going, "Wow! This is a whole different kind of thing. This is like New Hampshire." And then to make it even better, the next day somebody from Issa's campaign handed Ted two boxes of signatures and there were 12 cameras for that event. I thought, 'Oh, good, we can just hand signatures back and forth." It changed this campaign from that moment forward.

About mid June all of a sudden everything went off the rulebooks by any normal campaign. We looked at it and said, "We are probably into an election." We began looking at candidates. That's when we began locking in the election strategy.

BORENSTEIN: So what were the communications going on between your camp and the Davis camp, and the other potential Democratic candidate?

WILLS: Well, the primary focus in that area came from labor, and it was predicated on the polling, as well as the common sense analysis, which is that if there are no Democrats on the ballot that makes it better for the governor, because it then becomes the governor against what at that time still looked like a collection of people who were to the right of California. So labor, in particular, Dan Perry, my boss—we were pretty much the most visible people on the no side. The week before the campaign launch I was defending America's heroes at a solemn memorial ceremony at the Capitol, and a week later I'm the guy at the Cubs game who got in the way of the ball. I go from defending the people with the highest approval ratings in the world to the politician with the lowest approval rating in the world, and everybody was calling. Right from the get-go that was the moment when I said that the media was going to go towards this in a way that they hadn't before. It was history, and it was doable. I think early on the media sensed that it was history and it was doable.

CHANCE: Did the governor provide any leadership there, or was he holed up in a bunker in denial?

WILLS: At some point, it becomes a conscious strategy, but at the outset, as Steve said, the decision to start the campaign was really genuinely driven from the outside. At some point, you say to yourself, "No matter how interested he may be in it as an observer, we can't let him get close because there can be no hint that the governor is pulling the strings on this campaign." It's essential to the message that we were trying to put out that this is not the governor's campaign.

BORENSTEIN: Were you talking to Garry South?

WILLS: I never talked to Garry South once.

BORENSTEIN: Steve?

SMITH: Yeah, sure.

BORENSTEIN: How often did you talk to Garry?

SMITH: During that phase? Oh, maybe once every 10 days. I had been part of the Davis crew for a while, so I talked to a number of those folks, sort of randomly, individually, "What do you think about this?" But we didn't put what I would call a strategy team together until right when we're doing the transition between the two organizations. And partly for legal reasons. There was one great scene coming into a Holiday Inn on a Saturday morning. It was actually the meeting that the AFL decided they were going to try to back all these folks out. I was in there to brief them on what was going on. The governor was coming in about 40 minutes later to pump up the troops, essentially. I was leaving as the governor is walking in. Now, this is a guy who I've talked to four times, five times a week for years, and he takes one look at me . . . and we haven't talked since I took the lead, because that's just appropriate. Right? I'm walking out of the hotel, he's getting out of the car, and he looks at me and says, "Get away from me! I shouldn't be talking to you!" "Fine, boss. I'm gone." That's really the way it was. At that point, it was fairly self-evident what was going on. That changed very shortly.

CHANCE: Well, was there some discussion that perhaps he needed to go out with a message to the people to address this anger that was going on?

SMITH: In the early days if there was it was inside and I wasn't part of it. And once we got into the Taxpayers' phase, I honestly don't know.

BORENSTEIN: Until you guys did the transition and Gray Davis and his folks really got involved, which was after it qualified?

SMITH: When it became absolutely clear it was going to qualify.

BORENSTEIN: At that point there was no formal strategizing or planning that seemed to have been going on from the governor's team to stop this thing?

SMITH: No, absolutely nothing was going on. There were informal conversations, but there was nothing serious.

BORENSTEIN: So there was no discussion of what the governor might do to go forward and do a *mea culpa,* or do something to slow this thing down?

SMITH: I don't believe there was a lot of that conversation. The folks who were working around the governor the closest at that point, Larry was off doing his business, Griz was off doing his thing, Garry was off doing his thing. So I don't even know who could answer that.

BORENSTEIN: So, basically, until the last couple of months, there was no real Gray Davis organized effort having to do with the recall, in terms of strategizing and planning?

SMITH: No.

BORENSTEIN: Is that really possible?

WILLS: Let me give you an example, some evidence to support that. And that is, there was another antirecall group that formed out of the California Labor Federation. I forget what they were called, you know, "Californians for Not Those Guys." And they were basically on our message, but they had their own ideas about the strategy; they had their own ideas about what we would do, and whether or not that was working, and, specifically, they had their own ideas about the petition drive that we did. I don't think that if there had been a coordinated disciplined head at the top of this campaign that you would have had these satellite operations.

CHANCE: But just to make sure that we closed full circle on Issa, at what point did it dawn on Darrell that he wasn't going to be the guy? And he actually dropped out on August 7.

GILLIARD: When he dropped out, He did not signal that to his consultants, he did not signal it until really 24 hours before the day that he was actually going to drop out. And I think he really didn't make the final decision until he was driving down to the registrar that day to file his papers. And he was very conflicted about this, and the final decision probably wasn't until then.

CHANCE: Did you give him some advice on that?

GILIARD: You know, I've given him advice over the years, and he hasn't really followed it, but I told him that I felt that he couldn't win the governor's race, and it would make no sense for him to file, and to be a spoiler, that he had already done himself a tremendous amount of good by funding the recall, putting it on the ballot, that he would be a hero inside the Republican Party, and he could maybe use that in the future to run for something else.

BORENSTEIN: Did people call you, telling you to give him that. . . ?

GILLIARD: No. Actually, there was no pressure like that at all. In fact, we talked a little before about White House involvement and all that. I had one conversation with Karl Rove during this whole period, in which I kept trying to bring it around to the recall, and he kept trying to talk about something else. There was no interest, zero, in this recall effort out of the White House. Dave Cox, Assembly Leader, called me and said, "What are you doing? You're crazy. You're ruining our plans for taking over the Assembly by doing this. The Party is going to be in ruin when you're done." Jim Brulte called and said, "Is it real? Is Darrell's money real?" And I said, "Yes." He goes, "Well, don't screw up because if you do the Party is going to be ruined." Same message. I mean, they were afraid of this recall.

BORENSTEIN: There was no help from anybody?

GILLIARD: There was no help at all. This was really done with the people here, and Darrell Issa's money, and the grassroots, and the talk show people.

ABERNATHY: I'll relay one thing to that, and that is an incident in February, February 22, I talked to both Jim Brulte and Cox, and I made a point to go and speak to them. And they have both been out to the media and said, "This recall is a bad idea, and we're against it." And I went to each of them and I asked them, "Please, don't say that publicly. And if you have to say anything, just say it's a matter between the people and their governor, and legislators are staying out of it." They both assured me on that day that they would stop bad-mouthing the recall.

Now, the total number of signatures that were gathered—these are a couple of things that have been erroneously reported—was 2,160,000 signatures. As a result of that, Dan, you mentioned how we were planning the up-ramp. Well, it up-ramped, and as Dave mentioned, it keeps right on going. So 1.6 . . we turned it, we knew it was way plenty when we turned it in, and let's go with it. But there were 2.16 million signatures that were eventually gathered. And that was before August 1.

You could take all of the signatures—we said it didn't matter whether Issa paid for those signatures or not—you could take all the signatures that Issa paid for in the paid signature gather, about 900,000 signatures, and we could put those in the dumpster and we would still have been qualified in July. So those are cold, hard facts. And Steve I see you're still in denial. But those are the facts, and it is because of what Sal has mentioned about this thing just gets bigger and bigger, and the radio people. And I want to really mention Eric Holt, because when we first filed the first petition that we had to take over to file in the governor, a couple days before that, while Ted Costa went on the radio on that very show, and said . . . you know, we have to have signatures, he said, "We need people that will sign this thing to recall the governor." And Ted was on the radio, they were talking about it, and he said, "Come on down to Ted Costa's People's Advocate office, Arden Way in Sacramento. There's a Krispy Kreme Donut there. Just pull into the donut shop and you could sign this petition." And before long, there was a traffic jam out there—there were 300 cars trying to get into the parking lot, honking their horns, and trying to jam in there to sign those petitions. So, you know, Ted called me right then after that and he said, "This thing is really going to go."

When we got the first petition on March 25, finally, Ted took the petition out to a Wal-Mart, and after about an hour, he called me on his cell phone and said, "Mark, they're lined up 30-deep to sign this thing. You know, they're running across the parking lot to sign it. This is going to be a prairie fire." He said, "I've never felt anything like this since Prop 13. This feels like Prop 13."

Chapter 9

The Recall:
The Legal Challenges

JERRY LUBENOW: The moderator of our next panel, Karen Getman, is the former chairman of the Fair Political Practices Commission. We are very fortunate to have Karen here at IGS as our executive in residence for the year. Karen will introduce the panel.

KAREN GETMAN: This is the panel on the legal challenges and issues that arose during the recall litigation. Steve mentioned he thought there were something was like 12 lawsuits. We counted about 20, although the AG's office has told me about four that we didn't even know about. So there were about 20 to 25 lawsuits filed challenging various aspects of the recall, which was just extraordinary, given the shortened timeframe. And what you have up here are the people who played major roles in those lawsuits.

   I want to start by welcoming Steve Coony, chief deputy attorney general. He is going to be talking a bit about his office's representation of Kevin Shelley, the secretary of state. To Steve's right is Tom Knox, who is a commissioner of the Fair Political Practices Commission. The chairman pro tempore, Liane Randolph, had wanted to be here, but I'm pleased to announce that she's the mother of a brand new baby boy born a couple of weeks early, but they're both doing fine. To my right is Tom Hiltachk of Bell, McAndrews, Hiltachk and Davidion. His office represented Ted Costa and Rescue California in the initial litigation, and now serves as counsel to Governor-elect Schwarzenegger. Robin Johansen, of Remcho, Johansen and Purcell, has been a long-time counsel to Governor Gray Davis and was the lead litigation counsel for the governor in the recall litigation. And, finally, we're pleased to have Mark Rosenbaum of the ACLU in southern California, whose lawsuit over the punch-card voting machines actually stopped the recall election for eight very long days in the middle of last month.

This is an unusual panel because we've got lawyers. And I hope you appreciate that to some extent they're going to be constrained by an attorney-client privilege in a way that your last panelists were not, although we can talk about a lot of things now that the privilege was blown in the last panel.

I want to start by asking them how politics and legal issues were intertwined here. Robin could you talk a little bit about how the governor's legal challenges to the recall played into the political strategies that we just heard about trying to defeat the recall?

ROBIN JOHANSEN: The biggest issue that we had representing the governor was not trying to look as though we were going to do away with the recall. And as those of you who are familiar with the lawsuit that we did file on behalf of the governor know, we didn't ask the Court to stop the recall, we asked the Court to do two things: one, move it to the March ballot; and, two, allow the governor to run as a candidate on the second question. That was a constraint born of some legal realities about our assessment of whether there was a way to stop the recall. But there's always this downside that we as lawyers who are election lawyers have to face, and that is, if you lose and you tried to keep the people from voting, you're going to look pretty bad. So that was a major issue. It was an issue that we resolved in favor of bringing one lawsuit in the California Supreme Court, asking for those two things. And in our view, it would have made it a fairer election.

We at the time were looking at what everybody else was looking at and saying, "This is going to be a debacle." And to a certain degree, we were wrong. When we look at how the registrars managed to pull that election together in that kind of time and with those few resources, I'm just amazed. And it wasn't as much of a debacle as we thought it would be. I think there were a lot of votes that didn't get counted, and I still believe that very strongly, that there were voices that were not heard because of the punch-cards. And Mark can talk about that. But it was not the kind of train wreck that in some ways we predicted it would be.

GETMAN: Do you think that there were challenges that, in fact, could have knocked the recall statute out, could have prevented the recall at all that you didn't bring more for political reasons than for legal reasons?

JOHANSEN: No. We're dealing with a state constitutional provision that had never been tested, but that was fairly simple in its design. It was terrible in implementation, and there's a lot of room here for some strong improvement, legally. But when you stop and look at it, it's a state constitutional provision, so the only things that are going to trump that are general constitutional issues, and those are kind of narrow when it comes to a state issue like recall.

GETMAN: Tom, yesterday you reminded me of something that I think is important, which is that in most of these lawsuits Ted Costa was not named as a party, and yet Ted Costa intervened in virtually all, if not all of them. Can you talk about what that strategy was, and how that played into his political strategy to qualify the recall?

TOM HILTACHK: We were largely playing defense. We were not named in any of the lawsuits. So from our perspective. . . .

GETMAN: Was that deliberate, Robin?

JOHANSEN: For the most part. I was only involved in one, but there was never any idea that we would try to keep Mr. Costa out.

HILTACHK: We had three things we had to think about with every new lawsuit that was filed. One was a practical decision: did we have the resources? And by resources, I mean, manpower, womanpower, and money, because we thought as a strategy going in probably as early as June that they would try to break our bank with litigation. Second was just a legal analysis as to whether the lawsuit was something that we needed to be a part of for a variety of reasons. So the lawsuits that we did ultimately join, we had made a legal calculation that we had to be part of that lawsuit. And, third was the political opportunity, if you will, to continue to make the case that we were trying to make at the time.

On the political side, with every lawsuit that we would intervene in, we had four principal objectives that we were trying to articulate with our getting into the lawsuit. The first one was to characterize all the lawsuits as being an attack on the voters, and to characterize ourselves as defenders of the voters. So for all of you in the media, whoever talked to me, and most of you did numerous times, I always started with 1.6 million—"1.6 million people turned in signatures, signed petitions, and we're here to defend those 1.6 million." Every one of our briefs first line was: '1.6 million people signed petitions. They deserve to have their recall."

The second thing, and this is a little more subtle, and it goes to the point that Robin made, is we very much tried to promote the county clerks as good, competent, civil servants, whom we trusted to do a good job. We never attacked the county registrars in any form or fashion, because we knew that they were our best allies.

Third, we were concerned about Secretary Shelley. And one of the reasons we would promote the county clerks was to continue to put pressure on Shelley to be a public servant and not a partisan. So while we tried not to ever attack the secretary, we were always trying to put pressure on him to say, "Look, there's a process. Just follow the process. Don't let politics play a part of this. And just let this happen as it's going to occur."

And the last thing we did is we wanted to pin every lawsuit on the governor, no matter who filed it. . . .

JOHANSEN: We knew you were going to do that.

HILTACHK: . . . no matter what was going on. This was Gray Davis. This was planned, orchestrated, and this is just the first of many more to come, or the second, or the third, or the twelfth of many more to come. That was our political message that we were delivering any time we made the legal and practical decision to get involved.

GETMAN: Since the governor was being tagged with all of the lawsuits anyway, why didn't you get involved in more of the litigation?

JOHANSEN: Well, for one thing, you want to be able to say, "Hey, that's not us. That's somebody else." More than half of these things sprang up, and the first thing I knew about it was I read about it in the paper. It was just extraordinary. Other times, people would call me and say, "Hey, I've got a great idea!" These were usually lawyers, and I'd say, "Okay. How does that help the governor?" And they would go on about some legal theory. Some of these points made it into the lawsuits that were filed in the California Supreme Court, the one about choosing the wrong number for the signatures to file as candidates. Basically, as I saw that one, it would push us into a two-election cycle, where you would have the recall, and then you would have the replacement election. The idea was that Kevin Shelley was using the wrong number of signatures to qualify to run as a replacement candidate. And I just said, "Well, how does that help the governor?" I couldn't quite figure that one out. So we didn't have much to do with many of these, almost none of them.

HILTACHK: Maybe that's a lesson we can learn from this. In the first panel we learned that there probably wasn't a vast right-wing conspiracy. We were convinced there was a vast left-wing conspiracy on the lawsuits, and we believed these to all be orchestrated, all timed, and all largely funded.

JOHANSEN: I think he thought I was the puppet master here.

GETMAN: It must be a different Democratic Party that you were thinking of.

JOHANSEN: Yeah.

GETMAN: Steve, we asked Kevin Shelley to send a representative to the panel. He declined. He doesn't want to make any public statements about the recall after the election. Your office must have been in something of an awkward position. Were you counseling Kevin Shelley on the decisions, or were you simply defending whatever he did in the courts?

STEVE COONY: I have to open with a three-part disclaimer. First of all, I was a registered spectator, who was dragooned for this panel a little while ago when I found out that the attorney general was going to be late this morning. He should be here; he may join us during the panel discussion. The next is that I'm the chief deputy attorney general for administration and policy. I am the non-attorney in the group this morning, so I won't be rendering legal opinions, but I will do the best I can to express the position of our office. The third constraint I have is the one you just hit on that many members of the panel have, and that is that the office represents as a client the secretary of state. Any election has a long tail as far as litigation is concerned; not only am I constrained in terms of the pre-election discussions to talking in very general terms, but because the secretary of state still has actions that might be subject to future litigation, I can't talk too much about what's going on right now. And that's why I think Secretary Shelley couldn't join the session as a panelist or as the speaker.

Having said all that, at one point or another every member of our government law section was engaged on one of these, one or more of these two dozen lawsuits in which the state was on the receiving end, or had to participate in some way, many, though not all of them directed at Secretary Shelley. For about two solid months there was a task force involving the attorney general's staff and the counsel for the secretary of state, who were basically in 24/7 contact one way or another, whether they were e-mailing, conferencing, meeting directly, exchanging briefs, and so on. Operationally, we had to develop over a period of time, and on the same kind of hyperbolic curve from the certification of the signatures through this intense litigation, more and more involvement of folks, working and trying to develop a consensus not only about what the law itself meant, but what the appropriate way to express the state's position ought to be so that in both appearance and in fact we would be speaking with one voice.

GETMAN: Were there times when that threatened to break apart?

COONY: Well, Tom probably hit on one of the two main elements that made this a less than scholarly discussion, and, first, is that so much of it was carried on virtually in full view of the public. The media interest on every iota of information or opinion about this race from June on meant that you were seeing an awful lot more of Secretary Shelley, who became quickly aware that the only other secretary of state who had gotten that kind of attention was the secretary of state for Florida, Ms. Harris, and he took that as a cautionary note. So there was intense media scrutiny and there was understandable partisan suspicion of both offices. And I will say "partisan" in terms of recall supporters, most of them Republicans, and they may have had some concern that all of the constitutional offices were held by Democrats. We understood that concern.

Coming to a conclusion on the legal strategy for people who were defending the state of California and the constitution and the recall statues actually was fairly simple. And I would like to think that it would have been the same no matter who was in office. As someone pointed out, the constitutional provisions and the recall statutes are not all that complicated. They are basically a prescription for speed: do it as quickly as possible once certain threshold criteria are met—signatures, election, calling the election.

But there is an area or two where some judgment on the part of the secretary of state, for instance, has to be made as to whether the petitions were adequate or so on. It was difficult, given everything that was going on at one time, for the secretary to make those decisions carefully and thoughtfully. We simply tried to provide as much assistance as we could to make them confident that they were operating constitutionally and in accordance with the statute. There were from time to time conversations directly between the attorney general and secretary of state, and a lot of ongoing conversation at the staff level. That's sort of mechanically how we dealt with things.

GETMAN: Let me ask you about another source of potential conflict. Bill Lockyer has made known his intentions to run for governor in 2006. There was a lot of speculation about whether he would announce as a replacement candidate. How did that factor into what was going on?

COONY: It was something that the office was certainly aware of, and professional attorneys were certainly aware it might become an issue. At one point, we were advising the lieutenant governor on his responsibilities should the recall qualify a few days before he became a candidate. And that's another opportunity for that kind of concern to come into play. But those folks who are senior management in the attorney general's office knew from beginning to end of that speculation there was no chance that Bill was going to declare. What we had to deal with was the concern that other people had that he couldn't possibly be telling the truth, that this was an opportunity that somehow one couldn't pass up.

GETMAN: That never changed, that never wavered?

COONY: I can tell you, as somebody that's close to him that he's thought from beginning to end that, separately from his responsibilities, but as a political matter, he did not think it was fair to use the process this way against the governor. And he did not want to participate in this kind of an election for a variety of reasons. That had to be separated from how we approached providing legal advice in his view. And in the view of the office, as I said, that was a fairly simple matter. But communicating to folks who believed that everything operates off of people's political self-interest and nothing else, convincing them that we were trying to be the best legal counsel for the state that we could is not always an easy matter. I think we were convincing only in retrospect. He didn't run. And I think we did a good job of defending the state of California.

GETMAN: Mark, when did the ACLU decide to bring its lawsuit, and why did you decide to jump in? There's a lot of speculation that you were coordinating with the antirecall forces. What was really going on within the ACLU in making that decision?

MARK ROSENBAUM: Well, as to your last point, when Governor Davis leaves office, I may have to layoff two of my lawyers because we're not going to have enough work to do. We had no discussions with the antirecall people, and this lawsuit didn't start with the recall. We filed a lawsuit in 2001, when Governor Davis was the governor. The consent decree in that case was issued May 9, 2002. It gets rid of prescored punch-card machines throughout the state of California, and that's seven months before anyone even had a glimmer of an idea about the recall itself.

The reason we became involved in the recall is because the evidence that had been amassed in that case, which had come, as everyone knows, on the heels of Bush versus Gore. The real problem of Bush versus Gore wasn't just the lack of recount standards, but as the Supreme Court acknowledged, it was the use of these punch-card machines that made the actual operation of the recount so difficult and so problematic from county to county. We became involved in the recall because the consent decree that we had entered into, which was quite deliberately entered into so that the statewide election in March of next year would be a statewide election that could go forward with machines that wouldn't disenfranchise voters, that that apple cart was upset. It snowed in Los Angeles County since 1921 on three occasions. That's three more times than we've had recalls in California. And we were taken by surprise, as everyone was, that this election was to go forward—132,000 people were disenfranchised in the last presidential election because of these machines.

This for me was one of saddest experiences I've had in terms of litigation, because I think Tom is exactly right—they wrote their briefs, and they organized their litigation the way a political consultant would. They represented voters, I suppose, they certainly represented the pro-recall people, and that's perfectly legitimate. But we represented individuals who were going to be disenfranchised. I don't know if they were for or against the recall, and I don't know if they were for or against 54 or 53. I think this election was a train wreck. We now know, based on Dr. Henry Brady's data and certain data that's come out of Harvard, that 176,000 people in the six counties were disenfranchised; their votes didn't count.

GETMAN: Didn't count at all?

ROSENBAUM: Did not count at all. We were lucky; we dodged the bullet. The margin of error here was two percent. If the election had been close then this election would have been determined by the votes that were not counted, rather than the votes that were counted. I think that's a tragedy. And that was extraordinarily upsetting. Every vote ought to count—which was, in fact, what the Republicans argued in Bush versus Gore, and is right, and is at the heart of a representative democracy, and is, in fact, what the American dream is, that on election day, at minimum, that's when we're all equal, that's when we know that all our votes have the same opportunity to be counted. That principle was ignored. And that didn't get played in the papers that were being filed. And no matter what side of the fence people were on in the recall or on these initiatives, everyone should have stood up for the principle that all people ought to be using machines that work. The secretary of state was straightforward on this in his papers, the secretary of state for the first time in the history of California tossed out these machines, not because they weren't spiffy enough or because they weren't the newest model; he did it because they didn't work. They were error-prone. They didn't meet the minimal legal standard of being adequate. They were defective under the law.

GETMAN: Then how come you let them be used in the November 2002 election?

ROSENBAUM: That's a terrifically interesting question. And another way of asking that question is when a court issues an order saying that schools are seg-regated, how come you don't go in the next day and say those schools have got to be desegregated? And the answer is you have to be practical. We were really unhappy with the November 2002 election. We held our nose. That was not a constitutionally acceptable election. But what was the alternative? We checked out replacement machines in the six counties, and they weren't available, and they weren't going to be available for some period of time.

GETMAN: But that was also true this time around.

ROSENBAUM: But they're two different elections. In November 2002, if we had moved to enjoin the election, then you would have had the entire delegation to the United States House of Representatives from California, you would have had all the elected executive officials in California, you would have had 80 as-semblypersons, and 20 state senate persons with vacancies. And a court would have either had to say, "Stay on the job for a year-and-a-half, or appoint some-one." It would have been an impossible situation. That's why elections typically are not enjoined. In this case, with the recall, it was happenstance. If the secre-tary of state had certified the election, if the lieutenant governor had certified the election a month-and-a-half later, it would have been in March. The state law says it can be up to 180 days. There's nothing holy about 50 or 60 days. The law permits it up to 180 days. And if that had been the case, Initiatives 53 and 54, which aren't supposed to take effect until 2005 or 2006, and were originally certified on the March election of next year would have gone back on that ballot.

The recall is a tougher question, Karen, but it's not the same thing as saying that people who haven't been elected should stay in office. That's a close ques-tion, but where it's a matter of another month-and-a-half and where the reality is that 176,000 people are going to be disenfranchised, that's a constitutionally flawed election, and it ought to just gag anyone who says that they're committed to a democracy. And so you hold your nose a little bit, but you say at least eve-ryone is going to have an opportunity to vote, and that's a real democracy and that's a real election. And that's the difference between the two sets of elections.

JOHANSEN: The point that Mark is making about the 176,000 people is the important one. That is the part that I really believe was the train wreck. And it's not a question about what the margin of victory was. We know that we would be in litigation right now, today, if that had been a close election. We all know that. But even without that, those 176,000 people have not had their voice heard, and those voices are being looked at very carefully by every single elected official in California today. They are examining how the people voted down to the precinct level in their own districts, and they're tuning their message and their policy-making to whatever they think they can glean from this last election. So the fact that we didn't have a close election and, therefore, no harm, no foul to these people is absolutely wrong. Those voices were not heard. And if they had been heard then their elected legislators and their congresswomen and everybody else might be looking differently on how they're going to plan their political future.

ROSENBAUM: I want to give you a sense of what this is about. 176,000 votes—that is more than the population of 31 counties in this state. In Los Angeles County one out of 11 votes—one out of 11, imagine that—were not registered for the first question on the ballot, which is dramatically different as to what happened in other counties that did not use punch-card machines. And there the conversation gets really distorted. It's really important to point out that this number could have been decisive. And now, in terms of reform of infrastructure, California, not Florida, is exhibit A.

But where I really think things get distorted is I don't care if those 176,000 wanted to vote for Gallagher or Gary Coleman. The point is we ought to be saying that is the most precious commodity in a democracy, those votes, and not ask would it affect the outcome of the election, would it change the election. That's terribly interesting and important. But the more organic question to a democracy is how can we just willy-nilly say those votes can be sacrificed as if they don't really matter?

GETMAN: Tom, were you guys shocked by the 9th Circuit Panel decision? Were you prepared for it?

HILTACHK: We anticipated and prepared for a punch-card lawsuit very early on. I can remember the day I was sitting in my office when it occurred to me. We sat around and we said, "Okay, what would we do if we were in their shoes?" And I remember vividly the day when the punch-card lawsuit came into my mind, and said, "Well, that's what they would do." We were surprised that the governor filed it first. We were surprised that they filed it under California State Supreme Court. That was something we didn't anticipate. But I don't want to dive into numbers and who was disenfranchised and who was not disenfranchised. The ACLU didn't have a problem with disenfranchising half-a-million people who had already voted.

ROSENBAUM: Well, they weren't disenfranchised. They were going to vote. The 176,000 people, their votes would never be registered, and that's a different story.

HILTACHK: You weren't concerned about the November 2002 election, because if you were concerned about the November 2002 election, you wouldn't have entered the consent decree in the first place. You would have litigated it and found out whether punch-cards were a valid voting system or not. You didn't do that. You chose to accept a consent decree. . . .

ROSENBAUM: That's not factually correct. The secretary of state capitulated the day before we were supposed to take the deposition of the official in his office, who was a very decent guy and a straight-shooter about the accuracy of the machine. The secretary of state decertified the machines as incompetent, and we thought long and hard about enjoining that November election. But what were we going to do, walk into court, get an injunction, which we would have gotten, and we would have gotten a constitutional statement that the machines were inadequate, and then do what? Wait a year-and-a-half and let nobody be in the House of Representatives in the state of California? It's just a nonsense scenario that no one rationally could have accepted.

HILTACHK: You didn't have to wait until weeks or months before the November election; you could have continued that litigation. You could have forced a change, if that's what you wanted to do.

ROSENBAUM: We should have filed a lawsuit saying, "In case there's a recall. . . ."

HILTACHK: No, no, I'm talking about November 2002. The recall didn't happen overnight. It started in February. And the ACLU didn't file the lawsuit in May. . . .

ROSENBAUM: Because it would have been thrown out of court.

HILTACHK: . . . they didn't file it in June, they didn't file it in July when it was certified. They waited until the last possible minute.

ROSENBAUM: We waited two weeks until after the certification.

HILTACHK: To affect the outcome of the election. Early on, we researched on the punch card about what were the counties going to do. We knew they were changing the voting systems. And it all played out that when the ACLU came in, and their relief was, "Put this off until March," their motivation was revealed, because almost all the counties would have dumped punch-cards and were prepared to dump punch-cards by November. We were shocked that the ACLU didn't come in and say, "All we have to do is hold this election off a month, just hold it off a month. . . ."

ROSENBAUM: That is what we said. We tried to get that information, quite frankly, and the registrars wouldn't tell us. We tried to get that information, and the secretary of state wouldn't tell us. We did not say what you said, Tom. We said, "The election can be tomorrow. As soon as the secretary of state and the counties have the machines in place, the election should go forward." We did not seek—and you can read any paper we filed—postponement until March. We sought a postponement until the earliest possible date that the machines were ready. And the L.A. registrar and other registrars were publicly saying they weren't going to be ready any time soon. We didn't know if that was true. We desperately sought that information. If you knew that information and didn't come forward with that information then you did not give the Court the benefit of that information. We were told by registrars, and we were told by the secretary of state, that they either didn't know or that they wouldn't be ready earlier. We filed the case virtually the minute we could. We obviously couldn't file a case when there's no recall. The judge would say, "This is purely hypothetical." But we filed it as soon as we could, and we specifically said, "Have the election go forward at the earliest possible date."

The one thing the ACLU was involved with was opposing Proposition 54. Proposition 54 went down in flames. I don't know what would have happened if it had gone to March, when there may be the driver's license initiative and other initiatives, I don't know what is going to happen. We've heard conflicting things about the governor's race and who would benefit from it. I don't know that. But nobody asked that question, because this was just a continuation.

GETMAN: Let me stop you there, because, Robin, one of the things that surprised people was that when you lost in the California Supreme Court you didn't go into Federal Court, particularly on the punch-card issue. There was nothing until the ACLU went in, which they didn't do until after the California Supreme Court denied review of the petition. What was your thinking then, why didn't you go into Federal Court?

JOHANSEN: Two things were going on. One, the governor had a race to run. He had to say, "All right, it's time. This is going to be an election, and let's just get on with it." And that's what he said. The other thing was that we knew about the ACLU's suit, we knew that the consent decree was there. So we knew that they were thinking about going in. And, frankly, having them go, the question is why didn't you help him? Well, we helped him by not going with him. If we had been in there, or tried to move in to intervene, it would have looked very partisan. It just wasn't the place. And so, God bless them, they went ahead and they picked up the banner and carried it forward, and that was the right thing to do.

GETMAN: So from that moment on, no more talk of lawsuits from the governor. It didn't matter. There wasn't going to be any more litigation from him.

ROSENBAUM: They were done.

JOHANSEN: I have to say one thing here. I know Tom was surprised that we went into the California Supreme Court. Remember, our lawsuit was two-pronged. There was the punch card—and it was much more than just the punch cards: it was closing the polling places, it was they can't be ready in time, a whole bunch of stuff that we put into our lawsuit that Henry Brady helped us with as well. It wasn't purely California law, because we were arguing on a federal constitutional provision. But we were basically saying this is something that a California court should address first. And our view was that a federal court was not going to intervene to make California handle its recall process differently. It just was much more likely that the California Supreme Court would feel that it had the stature, and, frankly, the responsibility to do that, and we wished they had felt that.

GETMAN: Let me get the Fair Political Practices in here. As if there wasn't enough controversy, they had to set the campaign finance rules for the campaign. And there were several controversial decisions, one of which allowed the replacement candidates to have, in essence, ballot measure committees with no contribution limits. The commissioners are appointed by different parties and different authorities, was there political pressure being applied to the Commission during that time?

TOM KNOX: I'm the only Republican appointed by a Republican, and he's out of office, so I don't know where the pressure would have come. I don't think there was any political pressure from the inside. That is, Attorney General Lockyer I don't believe called the commissioner he appointed and asked him to do something or other, and I don't think that happened to anybody else. There was a series of campaign advocates who appeared before us and urged us to take actions that they thought would aid their campaign. With respect to the contribution limitations, we ultimately concluded that the target official, the governor, could raise money into his antirecall campaign without limits. We concluded that the replacement candidates were all subject to campaign contribution limits, but we further ruled that committees formed to support or oppose the recall could raise money without the campaign contribution limitations, including such committees that were controlled by replacement candidates.

We got there in some instances because a statute said it directly, in other instances by sort of melding together case law and statutes and reasoning by analogy. And in connection with that discussion, predictably, the Davis advocates showed up and argued to us that the candidate-controlled committees that supported the recall should be subject to limits. The Schwarzenegger advocates showed up and urged us to conclude that contribution limits did not apply to the replacement candidates at all. There's always sort of a low buzz of politics in our deliberations in terms of the witnesses who appear before it, but, clearly, like everything else, it amped up substantially during the recall campaign.

GETMAN: Arnold Schwarzenegger is out there saying that he's going to fund his campaign himself, and he's not going to be beholden to special interests. And yet he's in front of the Fair Political Practices Commission urging that there be no limits on the amount of money that he can pour into an Arnold Schwarzenegger Total Recall Committee. What was going on?

HILTACHK: Well, the governor made it very clear that he wanted the ability to use unlimited funds to attack any of the replacement candidates. And our position was if the governor was going to raise unlimited funds to defend his record that the statute provided for that, but if he was going to use unlimited funds to attack any of the replacement candidates then we're basically tying the hands of the replacement candidates behind their back, because they were going to be subject to limited funds. Basically, we were looking for a level playing field. Our position was impose limits on everybody or take limits off of everybody, but let's have a level playing field. I think the commission ended up splitting the baby.

GETMAN: But at that point you knew that, in fact, despite the talk about self-funding, you were going to be out there raising substantial funds and needed to do away with the limits.

HILTACHK: That was a mischaracterization of what he said. He never said he wasn't going to raise money. He said that he was not beholden to anyone because he didn't need their money.

GETMAN: I'm going to do the press a favor and leave the follow-up to you on that one.

HILTACHK: The campaign always anticipated raising funds from day one. And so what we were looking for was a level playing field. What the commission ultimately did in splitting the baby, basically, was they probably killed Cruz Bustamante. He was the candidate who was in the position to receive unlimited funds to support his candidacy from the Indian gaming money and the union money that ultimately, in my view, led to his downfall.

GETMAN: Let's get back there. The question is did the FPPC kill Cruz Bustamante? Did he kill himself? Richard Ross will answer that, I'm sure, this afternoon. But it was not a shining moment for the commission either, because there seemed to be a lot of back and forth, there's a lot of doubt about what the commission was really saying and wasn't saying, a sense that you weren't going to go into court and then you were going to go into court. You had a lawsuit against Ward Connerly, but you wouldn't bring a lawsuit against Cruz Bustamante. Was that because there was division within the commission about what to do? What was going on there?

KNOX: Clearly, we did not do Bustamante any favors. As the world now knows there is a Sacramento Trial Court ruling that says the commission got it wrong when it ruled. Statues limit the ability of a candidate to raise money after an election into a campaign committee for the election already concluded.

We adopted a regulation that said that limit didn't apply to pre-Proposition 34 committees. The commission made that decision well before the recall was on anybody's radar, more than a year in advance, after a fairly spirited discussion, and it passed by a 3 to 2 vote.

Clearly, though, that issue, the Bustamante issue, was the biggest burr under the commission's saddle, and probably under the lieutenant governor's saddle, too, during the campaign. And it engendered the most partisan comments and criticism of the commission—that plus the commission's decision then to actually sue Ward Connerly in advance of the election. Tom Hiltachk showed up and said that if we didn't immediately run over to the courthouse and sue Cruz Bustamante, we would be countenancing a violation of the law. His partner, Ben Davidion said that by suing Connerly, but not Bustamante immediately we were engaged in the rankest sort of hypocrisy and partisanship. And Ross Johnson showed up at our commission meeting about two weeks or three weeks before the election, and told us that if we did not join him in running down to courthouse and suing Bustamante, we would show that we had "no better than room temperature IQ." That was actually his statement.

GETMAN: I want you to know these are volunteer commissioners. Tom gets $100 a meeting for doing this.

KNOX: Well, he spoke with a man who knows a room temperature IQ when he sees one. With respect to Bustamante, there's no doubt we adopted a regulation that said: you could raise money into a pre-Prop 34 committee without regard to certain limits. And that, ultimately, is what the Sacramento Superior Court judge said. We got it wrong, and what Bustamante did was, therefore, a violation of the statute.

What we never said was that you could take the money out of that pre-Prop. 34 committee—Bustamante's 2002 committee—and roll it into his 2003 gubernatorial committee. We were very clear in a number of places by way of statements, facts, and fact sheets that that was not permissible. In fact, in an advice letter to one of Bustamante's lawyers that preceded the recall, we made that clear as well.

GETMAN: Then why not take him into court?

KNOX: Because we are we're not really a rapid response agency. We're not a political . . [audience laughter] I meant that without irony, actually. We're a law enforcement agency. A complaint comes to our attention, we investigate it, we interview witnesses, we look at the law where it's not clear—and maybe parts of Prop 34 are ill-defined—and ultimately we do whatever we're going to do after, when the violation has a certain magnitude, the commissioners have been consulted. We're not suited, nor do I think it would be right to be running into court based on yesterday's headline, when, clearly, the very fact of filing a legal action becomes then a factor in the campaign itself. And, probably, in turn encourages campaigns in the future to come in and make getting FPPC action against an opponent part of their political campaign plan. That's why we didn't go in.

HILTACHK: If I could. I agree that the commission is sort of in a pickle, particularly right before an election, and historically has declined to intercede. The difference was, one, that in this case we thought we had a violation of limits, we never had limits throughout the commission's history. And, two, there really was no need for an investigation. The public record showed that. Even if you accepted the commission's decision about raising unlimited funds, as Commissioner Knox has said, they always took the position that you could not essentially launder it through that committee into a new committee. Well, the public disclosed that that's what was going on. Campaign reports were being filed that clearly indicated that the money was coming in designated for governor through his lieutenant governor committee, and being transferred. So the public record was there. And then the kicker for me was the Prop 54 case. That case had been languishing at the commission for a year-and-a-half, and on the same day that the commission's staff was telling me and telling my friend Dan Morain here, that "We don't sue before an election. We don't get involved. Historically we've never done an injunction before," within minutes they were putting out a press release announcing their unprecedented act of obtaining an injunction against Prop 54.

GETMAN: And why did you do that right before the election?

KNOX: The Connerly case and the Bustamante case were very different. With respect to Bustamante, the facts, whatever they turn out to be, and I have to be careful here because the matter is still under investigation by our enforcement division, but whatever the facts are they had erupted very shortly before the election. The case that we ultimately filed against Ward Connerly had been in the works for months and months and months. It actually came up from the normal processes. The commission approved filing a complaint if we couldn't reach a settlement, and there had been careful settlement discussions that went nowhere. And, ultimately, in the normal course of the decision process, the matter came to, "Is it time to file a complaint?" At that point, the election was admittedly near at hand. And then the question to which we tried to give a principled answer was, "Should we let the proximity the election date actually lead us to postpone a lawsuit we were otherwise willing to file?" You can debate whether we made the right answer or not in that regard. But, what we decided in that context was we would simply go ahead and do what we would have done anyway on the date we did it, without regard to the election. We weren't going to let the election date either accelerate or retard what would have been our normal process to file a complaint.

GETMAN: Now that we've been through the very first gubernatorial recall, tell me the two things that you would change about the law or if you think something needs changing. Steve, why don't I start with you.

COONY: Speaking on an official basis for the office, of course, we defend the law. And there have been a couple of changes as a result of court actions, so the law won't be the same, wasn't in this election and won't be in future elections, as far as the matter of whether or not you have to vote in the first election in order to vote in the second. But speaking separately for Bill Lockyer as someone who is interested in policy, and given the fact he doesn't make those policies anymore because he's not in the legislature, I think we feel that California ought to take a serious look at raising the initial signature threshold to something considerably more than twelve percent, which is if not the lowest, among the lowest in the states that have recalls. If you put this in terms of employment law, if you're talking about firing somebody, basically, without having to have a cause, then maybe it would be better if you had to get one in five of your fellow employers to sign that petition, rather than only one in eight.

And although having 135 people actually make the ballot still sounds somewhat excessive, I don't think Bill feels that making the ballot less accessible to candidates in a statewide election, especially making it financial inaccessible, either through high filing fees or signature requirements that are impossible to meet unless you have a lot of money is a good idea. So on that, he'd probably fall on the side of let's keep the ballot as accessible as we can.

On the other hand, one significant element in our recall constitutional provision and statute is the sudden death nature of the current recall law, and maybe that deserves a look. The process that we have certainly helps attract a crowd of candidates, some of whom simple wanted to be noticed. And it's a process that, for a majoritarian like Attorney General Lockyer, really diminishes majority rule further, because this extraordinary election notwithstanding, the current process is really stacked toward producing only a plurality candidate every time in a replacement election.

So even in a shortened timeframe, I think Bill's view would be there's no reason why we couldn't have a recall primary and a recall runoff election with a lieutenant governor assuming the governor's duties during the runoff period if the recall is successful on the first ballot. Those are the significant changes I think the attorney general would sponsor.

GETMAN: Tom, should I change campaign finance rules and make something separate for recall elections?

KNOX: Yeah, I think they should. Clearly, the campaign contribution limits are really a crazy patchwork. In this case, there were no limits on the governor's ability to raise money. The challengers were subject to limits. But committees to support or oppose the recall that were controlled by candidates weren't subject to limits. As I've said before, you get there by putting together statutes, constitutional law, and arguing by analogy from a number of statues. I have said we have to take a look at just taking the limits off, at least in the context of a recall election, because I don't know how else you really do level the playing field. There's a constitutional dimension that prohibits you from imposing limits as to some of these players, or there may be a constitutional limit, and a constitutional restraint. And accordingly, the only way you get everybody to that level playing field is to take the limits off entirely.

GETMAN: Mark, now that there won't be punch-card issues anymore, does that take care of your concerns, or is there something else that you think as a result of this experience needs to be changed.

ROSENBAUM: I think the focus needs to be changed. It's true that, as we said, the punch-card machines disenfranchised 176,000 persons here in California. Broken down even more, the counties that were affected were disproportionately communities that had citizens of color—46 percent versus 32 percent that used the nonpunch-card machines.

So the broader agenda now is to take seriously the integrity of the infrastructure of democracy. That's what the voting machines are, and that's what the general systems are. California is through with punch-card machines, but Detroit test-drives automobiles more thoroughly, more strenuously than we test-drive voting machines here. We ought to look at the existing machines in California, and we ought to see whether or not they disenfranchise the disabled, what is the ability of individuals to vote, and to check their votes, so that they don't inadvertently get disenfranchised because of the quality of the machine. And, certainly, punch-card machines throughout the country belong in the scrap heap immediately. I agree with Tom, it's not the problem of the registrars, it's the problem of the state in not appropriating enough money, and certainly the problem with the federal government, in not making this a sufficient priority after Bush versus Gore.

The other procedures go to the same point. In this past election, the number of voting places were reduced by one-quarter. In Los Angeles County, they were reduced from 5,000 to around 1,800. That disenfranchises people, particularly working people and poor people, who have more difficulties getting to those voting places.

So the message here is that what Bush versus Gore did, and what the Florida experience ought to have done was to say to us that the principles that we talk about with respect to voting rights, that we tell our kids are the essence of a democracy, the dreams of patriots, that we say to them if we're really serious the entire infrastructure needs to be examined. We need to have stringent standards, and we ought to take the voting machines and the voting procedures and treat them with the same degree of care as we say do the vote and our democracy.

GETMAN: Robin, having represented the target of a recall, what would you say did not work and needs to be changed, other than the fact it can happen?

JOHANSEN: I agree with Steve about the need to raise the number of signatures. We had an example here of another rather pernicious aspect of the entire initiative/referendum/recall process, and that is, people were gathering signatures who really weren't qualified to do that. And there was litigation about that, and whether the secretary of state should be checking the declarations of these signature gatherers. There was evidence presented in one of the lawsuits about all kinds of people who were trucked in from out of state to gather signatures. That needs to be tightened up.

Frankly, when the target is the governor, we would probably all be better off just having an automatic succession by the lieutenant governor. That's why he or she is there. Why bother to have one if we're not going to use him? It would have made this entire process a more rational debate. I don't think that, in this political climate, necessarily, I would have wanted that, but as a structural matter it's a better way to go.

GETMAN: Tom, I want you answer the question from the point of view of Governor Schwarzenegger, and I want you to assume that he puts in a budget in January that makes it clear the deficit is even bigger, and there's massive cuts to Social Security, and a rich Democrat comes along, and January 15 we've got recall petitions circulating, and we've got some money behind it. Is he willing to go through the exact same legal process that Governor Davis went through, or do you think that something has to change?

HILTACHK: I don't think there's anything fundamentally flawed with the process. I think there are some technical things that need to be done in the elections code. Those of us who walk through the elections code from day to day know that it's not a model of clarity in any respect, much less in the recall context. And when we get into these situations, we learn how vague it can be, and how poorly written it frankly is, and that needs to be taken care of.

But, as we learned this morning, the recall has been tried dozens and dozens of times. In my view, this was a unique circumstance and a unique time, you know, almost a perfect storm.

GETMAN: But if it happens to repeat next year. . . ?

HILTACHK: I'm not concerned about that, because I don't believe it will, and not just because of the results of this election. The voters are very reluctant to sign recall petitions. They tried to recall Gray Davis in his first term and got nowhere. Nobody's got close. Something unique was happening here, and it's up to us to try to figure out what that was. But I'm not sure that's going to be repeating itself, and the fact that some wealthy Democrat might come in and decide to pay circulators doesn't mean people will come up to the card table and sign. People stood in line to sign these petitions—155,000 received them in the mail, signed it themselves, got their neighbors and the little league captain to sign them, and returned the petitions. That's unprecedented. The only thing I've ever seen anything like that was the Three Strikes Initiative right after the Polly Klaus tragedy, where people would stand in front of the Wal-Mart, and there would be a line of 50 people desiring to sign petitions. I don't think that's likely to be duplicated any time soon.

I read the inaugural address in 1911 when we instituted the recall. And it was described as something we'll probably never have to use, but it's good that it's there. It's something that everybody's got to keep in mind. After nearly 100 years, it became obvious we had to use it. And it will probably just sit there dormant again, as a power that the voters have to keep people in check. So Hiram Johnson was right, except for the fact that it needed a rebirth, a renewal, and that's what this was about.

Chapter 10

The Recall:
The Race to Replace Gray Davis

CARLA MARINUCCI: Let me introduce our panel: Wayne Johnson from the Simon campaign; John Feliz from the McClintock campaign; Don Sipple, media guru for the Schwarzenegger campaign; George Gorton, strategist for the Schwarzenegger campaign; Sean Walsh, communications director for the Schwarzenegger campaign; Garry South, senior advisor for the Davis campaign; Larry Grisolano, the campaign manager for the Davis campaign; Richie Ross, campaign manager for the Bustamante campaign; and Tyler Snortum-Phelps from the Camejo campaign. Thanks for being with us.

MARK BARABAK: We're going to start by asking each of you in about 60 seconds to get your candidate into the race. There was a lot of discussion—Riordan was going to run, Riordan wasn't running; Bustamante wasn't going to run, he ended up running—give us the back story on how your people became candidates.

WAYNE JOHNSON: Well, Bill Simon had been the nominee in the previous cycle. He was concerned whether or not he should jump into the race and thought it might be too soon, and that was probably the case. Early polling showed that he ran very strongly. He was sort of the institutional Republican candidate. But then when he delayed in making the decision—I thought he should have jumped in immediately—but by coming in third or fourth into the race on the Republican side, I think he lost some of that. Particularly after Schwarzenegger came in, he became the institutional candidate and sort of sucked the air out of the environment for Bill.

JOHN FELIZ: Tom McClintock decided to get in the race soon after he believed that the recall was going to be qualified. He felt that he had a statewide antitax constituency and a track record of leadership in running statewide, since he had just finished the controller's race and could have very well won. We had a major strength in the fact that we had a statewide constituency, and a major weakness that we did not have a large finance base. We figured we were going to change that, and things happened in the race that totally and absolutely were unanticipated.

DON SIPPLE: Mine is real easy. It was a total surprise. He got in the race based on his own compass, at the last minute, and in a very untraditional way.

GEORGE GORTON: It was pretty exciting going back and forth as to whether or not he was going to get into the race. He did not believe that there was going to be a race until very late, and did not focus on it until very late. He kept saying, "George, the *L.A. Times* said this isn't going to qualify." In the end, there were a lot of discussions as to whether he would run or Dick Riordan would run, as you all know. I was the most surprised person in America. I was backstage with him at Jay Leno, and the story is absolutely true. The last thing he said to me was, "Come on, let's do it," which I thought meant the statement that was in my pocket (which said he wasn't going to run). And he went out and shocked me.

RICHIE ROSS: Cruz actually had been pretty firm all through the summer about not considering getting into the race. And Tuesday of the last week before that, word came out that Senator Feinstein wasn't going to run. You looked at the field as it was shaping up at that point, with Peter Ueberroth, and Bill Simon, and Arnold Schwarzenegger, and you said, "Hmmm . . . Tom McClintock . . ." Even if it's a down year for Democrats or a down time for Democrats, you know, the advertising slogan for the New York State Lotto is, "Hey, you never know." I think it was based on a sense that somebody should probably do it, and nobody apparently was going to do it, and so he made a decision that he would take his shot.

TYLER SNORTUM-PHELPS: The minute the petition started circulating, Peter started thinking about entering. We knew we wanted to have a Green voice in this campaign. We wanted to get our platform out there. We wanted to build on the success from last year's campaign. So that was less of a question for us than what attitude do we take toward the recall itself. And that came from the fact that a lot of Greens had mixed feelings about whether the recall was a good idea. So that was where the major debate was. Everybody said, "Of course if this is going to happen, Peter should run. But what do we say about the recall?" And we went through a lot of discussion about that at a lot of different levels. Ultimately, the state party ended up taking no position on it, and Peter himself personally came out in favor of it. But there was really never any question that he would be the candidate and that it was a good idea for us to run.

MARINUCCI: Garry, the day after the recall qualifies, Paul Maslin is quoted in the paper saying, "The worst of all worlds is to end up with a semi-candidate, a two-tiered question. Then we are assured the recall passes." Is that what happened in your view?

GARRY SOUTH: Yes, it is. I said that publicly, privately, on national TV, and in every newspaper in America, pretty much. Obviously, we didn't have anything to do with our candidate getting into this race. That decision was made for us by the people who signed the petitions. I was telling Democratic donors and Democratic officeholders for months that the only way to beat the recall is to beat the recall. And to harbor this fantasy that somehow you could allow people to come out and throw the existing Democratic governor out of office and replace him with a Democrat, whomever that might be, and everything would be hunky-dory was simply not going to happen, because that's not the way recalls happen. The "No on Recall/Yes on Bustamante" formulation was a nonstarter to begin with. The classic rule of thumb in politics is you do not convey mixed messages to the voters. That was a textbook case of a mixed message—as well as being disingenuous, I might add, on the part of the formulators of it.

LARRY GRISOLANO: As these folks made their decisions to come in, the very best thing that could have happened to Governor Davis's effort to defeat the recall is if somebody had initially emerged as the alternative on the second ballot, and the worst thing that could happen was if there was all this splintering that you see represented at this table, with all these different options. And the fact that it took so long to work itself out and for somebody to emerge, and that so many people got in and divided the attention and the vote on the alternative side for so long also worked to our detriment.

BARABAK: Now, just to admonish you, this is literally being written for the history books; young, impressionable minds will be reading this. So spin aside, we want as true an account as we can get. And we want to follow-up with you because there was a time when it looked like Dick Riordan was going to get in the race with Arnold Schwarzenegger's backing, and that didn't happen. How did we get from there to what happened?

GORTON: Well, Dick and Arnold are great friends, and they talked a lot. I was privy to some of those conversations. And one of them would say, "If you run I'll support you," and the other would say, "If you run I'll support you." And Dick, right up to the end was saying, "If you run, Arnold, I'll support you." And, in fact, Dick was saying up to the end, "I would prefer that you run." And Arnold did, and surprised us.

MARINUCCI: We had a week in which we kept being told Arnold was going to give a press conference, and, "He's strongly leaning against." There was day after day of strongly leaning against.

GORTON: Well, I don't think I said "strongly," but I was taking his temperature everyday, and being his spokesman, I was just telling the truth. For a long time, I thought, and I said, "I think Arnold is running." And that was my take on it. And then one day, it didn't seem like that anymore to me, so I said that.

BARABAK: How did we get from leaning against to the *Tonight Show* announcement? Something happened that changed him from leaning against to announcing. . . .

GORTON: You'll have to ask him.

SIPPLE: I don't know for sure. I think that if we reconstruct that day, the Feinstein announcement that she was definitely not going to be a candidate probably factored into that.

BARABAK: Would he have run if Dianne had run?

GORTON: I had the feeling that he would definitely run if Dianne had run.

BARABAK: He would have run?

GORTON: Well, I really don't know, but I've asked him about it, about his decision making. I walked out of the front of the Jay Leno show and looked at him. And he just looked at me like he thought it was really funny, the look on my face, which was staggered, as some of you know who were there. I think he just made up his mind he was going to run.

MARINUCCI: I have to ask about the *Tonight Show* appearance, because he gave a five-minute talk, in which he hit all the major talking points of what would be his campaign: "We're mad as hell and we're not going to take it anymore." "The politicians are fumbling and fiddling away." and "My opponents are going to throw everything at me." He didn't consult with any of you guys? Did this just all come out . . . ?

SIPPLE: At the point where there was an exploration of the candidacy, there were some discussions that probably were reflective of that, but not a briefing paper before the *Tonight Show*. It was a cumulative sense of his from discussions we had had prior to this time.

WALSH: That's right. He had come back from the *Terminator 3* European promotional tour and met with Mayor Riordan. He had numerous discussions with other folks, doing the due diligence. And as Attorney General Lockyer pretty much summed up Arnold's attitude through the entire campaign and part of the due diligence, at least from my exposure in those early days, was hope, opportunity, "Can I make change?" "Can things happen?" And so he talked to people. They went through and said all the negative sides of what would happen if he ran. They went through the positive sides of what he could actually do. And, probably more than anything else, there was his desire that he could actually take it. And the more people said the harder it would be, the more he got enthusiastic about taking the challenge.

GORTON: That's Arnold.

BARABAK: So who knew? If his top political strategists did not know, who knew? Obviously, he knew. Did he say something to Maria?

GORTON: Maria.

SIPPLE: Maria knew.

BARABAK: He and Maria were the only two?

GORTON: Right.

BARABAK: And is this the way the campaign operated? He'd go out and you guys would say, "Hey, look what Arnold did today? What a surprise."

GORTON: Did it look like that to you, Mark? Sorry, but it was not that way.

SIPPLE: Some historians and archivists would point to an incident in 1980, where he had been in training for *Conan, the Barbarian*, the movie, and there was a body building championship in Australia that he was slated to judge. And instead of being a judge, at the last minute, he became a participant and won. I don't know if there's a connection, but, obviously, he had a dramatic entry into the race.

MARINUCCI: One more question and then I want to get back to the Democrats. It was said that Riordan was blind-sided by this announcement. And Maria had said publicly that she advised him very strongly against running. He did not take her advice, obviously. Who can tell us about that?

GORTON: Maria was very supportive of him running before he decided to run, and I can say that for sure from conversations. She was very supportive. I also know he had lots of conversations with Dick Riordan, including the day before he decided to . . . where Dick Riordan said, "You know, Arnold, you should run, not me."

BARABAK: So Maria came around in the last 48 hours, or in the Green Room?

GORTON: Well, since I don't know when Arnold came around, I don't know when Maria came around.

MARINUCCI: Just as Arnold is about to announce, on the Democrat side there's chaos with Democrats like Loretta Sanchez calling for other people to be in the race; Bustamante is considering it, and there's a summit meeting in San Francisco, with a bunch of political consultants, yourself included, Richie. You were called together with Willie Brown. And Randy Shandobil interviews you as you're about to go into this meeting, and you said, "Sometimes people stab in you in the back in politics, and sometimes you need to look for people to stab you in the stomach." Were you at that point going into that meeting thinking, "Yes, he's going to do this?"

ROSS: The phrase was, "Stab you in the front." Mr. Brown invited several of us to come together. We went to the meeting to have a discussion about ways to defeat the recall. I think that meeting was on a Monday. Later in that same week, other people, whom we won't discuss, had different points of view about the need for an alternative candidate. Those discussions took place over the week-end. I did not raise any of those discussions with Cruz. And then on Tuesday, when we heard that Senator Feinstein wasn't going to run, I felt an obligation to at least share with him the other discussions that were taking place, and that I was party to, and that he had a right to know about, and to put those discussions into whatever calculation he was going to make. And he asked me point blank that Tuesday evening, "Well, what are my odds?" I said to him, "Cruz, you know, 1 in 5, 1 in 6." He said, "Well, those aren't very good odds." I said, "No, but I think you have to evaluate those odds, compared to the odds that you might have at another time in a different circumstance." And he said, "What's your recommendation?" And I said, "I'm not going to make one. You ought to make a decision predicated on if you ran and lost would you regret those thoughts more on October the 8, than if you didn't run and never knew?" And the next morning he called me up, he had discussed it with his wife, and said to me he was going, and I began to communicate that with people, and it happened just like that.

BARABAK: I want to follow up with Garry. Garry, you're someone who is known here for your subtlety and light touch.

SOUTH: Why, thank you.

BARABAK: What efforts went into clearing the field and establishing the race that you guys wanted to have, which was just a straight yes or no on the recall? Behind the scenes, what were you doing?

SOUTH: Senator Feinstein actually had more to do with the attempt to clear the field than the governor did. Senator Feinstein talked to the governor in mid July, I believe, and said, "You have to fight this thing. You have to get off the dime; you have to stop acting like this is not going to happen or that it's not happen-ing. You have to stop being governor, and stop going around signing bills and doing photo ops. You have to start directly, specifically, aggressively, fighting this recall." And she told him that she was going to talk to all the other seven Democratic statewide elected officeholders to implore them to stay out of the race. It's interesting that of all the folks that were out there agitating to have a backup candidate, the one who was most opposed to that was the one who, herself, had fought off a recall. None of the others have. And Dianne was adamant from day one that Democrats, regardless of their view of the governor, had to bind behind the no on recall, and that to waste effort and time trying to find a so-called backup candidate not only in the final analysis would not work, which is what I had been saying for months, but that it would impede our ability to make this thing a clear cut choice between no on recall and whatever was going to happen on line two. So Dianne really was the power behind the attempt to try to keep the field clear. The governor did very little of that, if any, that I'm aware of.

BARABAK: Richie, did Cruz hear from Senator Feinstein? If he did, please feel free to betray any confidences.

ROSS: I'm not aware that he did.

SOUTH: She talked to Cruz.

BARABAK: She did. Well, do tell.

SOUTH: I wasn't privy to the conversation. I know she talked to all seven statewide officeholders.

BARABAK: Betray any confidences you may care to. Do you know what was said?

SOUTH: I do not know what was said. But if you take the senator's public comments, which were pretty aggressive about this matter, you can probably assume that's pretty much what she was saying when she was talking to the statewide officeholders.

BARABAK: And just to pick up where we left off, where was the governor's head at on all this stuff, around this period? Angry? Upset? Concerned?

GRISOLANO: What period?

BARABAK: Well, we're talking about when the field is still unclear. He knows there's going to be a recall, but it's not clear who he's going to be running against. What was his mindset?

GRISOLANO: Well, he was certainly concerned. I don't think he had gotten to a point where it had gelled with him how he was going to attack the thing, and what the appropriate response was. It took a couple of weeks. And, certainly, he got advice, he talked to people, and he kind of cleared up in his own head how to organize a response to this, what kind of campaign is necessary, and I think that was what was going on between qualifying and filing with him, sorting all that out.

SOUTH: When the recall reared its head, I think in the governor's own mind, it presented a dilemma to him. He had, as has been reported, basically forsworn fundraising for 2003. He had kept a small officeholder committee open. He had agreed to a budget for that committee which was fairly small, and had told all of us internally that he did not want to raise money even for that committee until at least September. He wanted to get the budget behind him; he wanted to get some governing behind him. He's a realist; he has two ears and two eyes; and he knows that he was hurt in the 2002 campaign by the perception that he was a nonstop fundraiser, that governmental functions, at least in some people's criticism, were suffering because he was spending all of this time on the campaign trail raising money. So he was aware of all that, and he simply didn't want to get back engaged in a campaign.

So when the recall reared its head in February, I think he was hoping against hope that it would not qualify so that he did not have to get back into full bore campaign mode, and bring back upon him all of the criticisms that had been leveled on him in 2002 about the connection between fundraising and government action and on and on and on. Internally, with some of the people that were advising him, there was the sense that the signature-gathering had been stopped. But there was a division inside the camp about whether or not a blocking action could be mounted to complicate or thwart the gathering of the signatures, or whether or not that was a waste of money and energy.

BARABAK: Okay, the recall is on. Arnold shocks the world, including his advisors, by getting in the race. Did Bill Simon say to himself, or did Tom McClintock say, "Holy smokes! Here's this big movie star. What do I do now?" or were they just full speed ahead?

JOHNSON: Well, Bill got in after Arnold did, he announced Saturday, the last day; filed his papers the same day that Arnold did. So, he had time to reflect on that. I think the assumptions in our camp was that we were running a primary first, and then it would turn into a general election, but first one of the Republican candidates had to break out of the pack. And I think there was an assumption that somebody would take Arnold down. We thought the guys at the other table over there might jump on him right way. We thought that he would come under a lot of criticism. As it turns out, the way we read it, they simply weren't on the same page. The Democrats were fighting an internal battle over whether to oppose the recall or support Cruz or whatever.

BARABAK: Did Simon get in this race thinking, "I can run, and I can win," or is it just "I'm going to run, and maybe this will help me down the road?" Did he get in thinking, "By, golly, I can be the next governor California"?

JOHNSON: Absolutely, he was running.

BARABAK: John, what did McClintock think? Did he say, "I see a clear path around Schwarzenegger, and I'm going to be the next governor?"

FELIZ: Well, first of all, I made the wrong assumption that this was going to be a mediocre turnout election. That was the first thing I discussed with Tom. If that were so, we figured we had about a million-and-a-half identified voters throughout the state of California, and that would get us about 26 to 28 percent of the vote, which I thought would be enough to win the race. I felt like Mr. Johnson, that the Davis campaign, or the Bustamante campaign, or whoever was going to do it, was simply not going to give Arnold a free ride, and that they would begin the campaign very early. So many things did not happen the way we thought that it created a constant roller-coaster throughout the campaign. If Dianne Feinstein had decided to enter the race, we probably would have not run.

BARABAK: Why not?

FELIZ: Our numbers that we took, initially, showed that she would be very strong, and you would have to have one candidate emerge to defeat her. Also, it would ensure that Davis would be recalled. So I'm agreeing with Garry that the best way to beat the recall was essentially to go with no Democrats in the race. That was the best way to do it. Once a Democrat entered the race, we felt whoever it was outside of Dianne would come in third, maybe fourth, and that other Republicans might actually beat them. We figured that the Republican victory number exceeded 60 percent. As it turned out, it did. So that assumption was correct. We just didn't know how it would be put together.

MARINUCCI: So let's set the stage for the next part of the campaign. Arnold declares. He goes down and files the candidacy. An incredible media scene, hundreds of reporters when he and Maria show up. And then you go through some rough days. . . .

WALSH: Let me stop for a second on the Dianne side. In our focus groups in San Francisco, she was very, very popular. But in the focus group we did in L.A., she didn't really register that much. There's this perception that Dianne was this be all/end all giant slayer, and I'm not convinced.

SIPPLE: Playing off what Dave said, I don't think there was enough appreciation in the political communities how unconventional this whole process was and how unconventional this campaign was going to be, and how the electorate hungered for something different. So the notion of Davis or Bustamante attacking Schwarzenegger from the get-go—I mean, politics as usual was on trial. It was a change versus status quo election. So anything they did that was consistent with politics as usual or same-old/same-old was going to hurt them, not us.

That's the backdrop to this discussion; that's where the people were on this thing.

BARABAK: Was it anti-Sacramento? Let's say, Feinstein had got in. Would it have been the Washington establishment, or was it an anti-Sacramento thing? Could you have run an anti-government. . . ?

GORTON: We did a poll in June, and that was the first time we were able to get Arnold's attention. He didn't think there was a possibility that he was going to run even in June. But there's a group of people, Joe Shumate and Dick Dresner, who did the poll, and Sean, and John and I, and we've had the opportunity, the three of us, to work with Arnold. So we were really testing Arnold. The first thing you have to understand, the whole strategy of this thing was Arnold being Arnold. And two-thirds of the people in our poll who describe themselves as very conservative, in spite of push questions that we used against Arnold, ended up for Arnold. So we knew there was something really magic about it. And we ended up with huge support among people described as very conservative, and what have you. As far as the poll related to Dianne Feinstein, she did very strongly against Arnold in northern California, but in southern California she didn't do that strongly at all.

BARABAK: Bringing it back to Carla's question: he's in the race, you have a rough few days if you believe the *L.A. Times*, which said there was some staff tension.

MARINUCCI: You had the Warren Buffet comment, you had the story about Arnold's voting record, and he was pretty much dark for. . . .

WALSH: Well, we didn't know that this was going to happen. We didn't. So even though you've got a team of people around Arnold who have some experience, after you go on the *Tonight Show* and announce, phones and faxes and computers don't appear magically with pixie dust overnight. You don't have an office. You don't have an infrastructure. You don't have a staff. You don't have anything.

GORTON: I couldn't make an outgoing call for three days, except on my fax machine, because my phone would be ringing, ringing, ringing, and I had three lines at home.

SIPPLE: We were trying to build a battleship while swimming, and it was a very difficult process. But we knew, given the way things happen, and that there was no structure, that was going to be good. We had five or six days of coverage from the phenomenon factor, which was a blessing, as we were able to put some pieces in place. Now, we viewed this as a football game, and I figured the first half was going to be kind of sloppy, just by the nature of it. It was like a presidential campaign that was happening in the borders of California, which was totally different. And the needs for the, quote, front-runner, somebody of his stature, were immensely more than a typical governor's race.

WALSH: The press corps got annoyed with us early on; you wanted to knock on the front door, have somebody propose, talk about kids, and seal the deal on the first day. We had a timetable and a schedule. Arnold is as infectious in a room with five people, projecting hope and his views, as he is with 15,000 or 7,500 in Bakersfield. And we had to build a structure around where he wanted to go and what he wanted to do. And the structure was people, the structure was policy staff, the structure was what proposals are you going to do, and how are you going to face-off Gray on economy and the budget, etc. Because he's larger than life, and can drive a lot of messages, that covered us. But until he could put all that infrastructure in place, it doesn't do you any good to go sit down with the *San Francisco Chronicle* and the *L.A. Times*: "So what's your eight-point plan to solve the budget?" Well, you don't have an eight-point plan to solve the budget. You've got to let all of the infrastructure build up over a period of time until you're ready to go and formally launch. You wanted everything from us right away—you wanted one-on-one interviews, you wanted retail campaigning, you wanted everything when we didn't have offices, phones, and faxes. The first couple weeks was just building that technical side.

MARINUCCI: Let's get some reaction from the Democrats. You're watching the media insanity go on with Arnold. Are you thinking, "How do we counter this? How do we play this?" Garry? Larry? What do you do?

GRISOLANO: Well, out of the box, the Schwarzenegger campaign didn't necessarily look like it was going to be the dominant force in this race that it ultimately ended up being. There was some reason for hope when it started out, and the lack of specificity was something that people in our research noticed immediately about this campaign. And our focus people were saying, "You know, I'm willing to give this guy the benefit of the doubt, and I'd like to know more about him. But he's going to have to pass over a bar here with me. He's going to have to demonstrate that there's something that he can do to solve problems, that there's some kind of plan behind him." And, in the early going, there was no reason to believe that he was making it over that hurdle.

Part of what Sean is talking about, in all due respect, was not that they needed time to actually formulate that eight-point plan, but they needed time to create the insulation around him, so that he could avoid ever giving that eight-point plan. And that was what was going on at that time, we were seeing how the electorate was responding to a candidate that they had some doubts about and who wasn't addressing those doubts. And that's where the hope was. We knew that if it became a charisma-fest that we had some problems on our hands.

SOUTH: Again, with all due respect to my friend, Sean, it isn't like Arnold Schwarzenegger popped up out of the duck blind in July of 2003 and decided he wanted to run for governor. Bob White told me clear back in early 2001 that

Arnold was having conversations with the Wilson people about running for governor. He publicly came forward in February of 2001, two-and-a-half years ago, to say, "I may run for governor in 2002." We all know the story of what happened there; he decided not to do so. This was not about getting fax machines and phone lines put it. This was a calculated decision that you could run this sort of candidate without the kinds of position papers, specifics, plans, proposals that a mere mortal candidate would be held to. And this is not from a lack of planning, or a lack of advance notice, or a lack of forethought that he was ever going to run for governor, because this stuff has been going on since 2001.

GORTON: I appreciate that Garry thinks he knows more about what we were thinking than we do, but I've done a lot of campaigns. I have never done a campaign that went from zero to 60 that fast.

WALSH: Zero to warp speed, really.

GORTON: Zero to warp speed. And I don't care what you say, if you don't have a plan of attack, or what voters you're going after, or any kind of concept about things, it takes time to put it together. And it especially takes time to put together if you've got this intense scrutiny from everybody in the world, not just the country, the world, and your phones are ringing so much you can't make outgoing calls.

BARABAK: But what about what Garry said? If there was an inkling he might run, why not have the phone bank set up so you're not talking on your fax, and why not have that infrastructure ready just in case?

GORTON: Why not indeed? But we did not.

WALSH: Past politicians fighting amongst themselves—Cruz versus Gray, puke politics—Bill Lockyer kind of set the tone and boxed you guys in early on by saying that if Gray goes the puke politics route he's going to get hammered.

SOUTH: That was before we knew Lockyer was a Schwarzenegger partisan.

WALSH: We had the conference here at Berkeley at the end of the Simon campaign, and we talked about how the pay-to-play, the taking the campaign contributions, etc. did hurt you guys, and did leave a lasting impression. And you said that all politicians do that and the public accepts that. I think that there was such a hangover from that and people were tired of partisan politics; they were tired of all the stuff in Sacramento. Bill Simon did talk about pay-to-play, and he said this budget is going to happen, and right after the election the huge budget stuff blew up. And so when Don and George were talking to Arnold early on conceptually about what it takes to be a be a future leader of California, change versus status quo, a lot of those things were formulated. But having those discussions, doing the focus groups, and doing the polling doesn't mean that Arnold is there yet. Is it '06? All of these discussions happened, all the intellectual framework was done, but not the structural framework. And I'll be honest with you, too, I think we all underestimated, I know I certainly did, how quickly this would take off and the intensity level. As soon as he announced, it all came crushing down on top of us.

So, yeah, he was talking about it. Yeah, he was thinking about it. But putting together what your overall, intellectual, conceptual campaign is going to be are two different things. You have the war plan of the war college, but making sure you've got the generals, the colonels, and the air support and ground support is different.

What I want to know at the end of this thing is I think Garry South is one of the most talented strategists in the state, and I don't know why you weren't more publicly involved in the Gray Davis campaign, because I think it would have made a big difference.

MARINUCCI: But didn't the timeframe make a big difference? Did he acknowledge to you afterwards that the short campaign season was an opportunity to not pass up?

WALSH: Arnold was the anti-Gray.

BARABAK: But talk about the timeframe and the fact this was a 60-day snap election.

SIPPLE: Look, Arnold Schwarzenegger is a gentleman who had risen to the top in two very competitive industries—body building and the movie business. He has a keen sense of marketing, because he marketed himself. And we revisited that somewhat during the campaign. He is a positive imager—he doesn't game things out in the traditional political way, but his positive image was that a short campaign probably benefited him.

BARABAK: How and why?

SIPPLE: You'd have to ask him that. But given the environment, which is distinctly antipolitician, anti-establishment, he's the embodiment of change. And if you take my analogy to a presidential race, there's a lot of symbolism in this campaign. It wasn't about eight-point plans, because there wasn't time for it to be about eight-point plans. It was about symbolism, messages, and messengers. And I think he had all of those things line up in his favor for his campaign.

BARABAK: Was he advantaged by a short campaign, George?

GORTON: I think he was advantaged by a short campaign, because he was somebody that was well known and well liked. He had a tremendous positive favorable. The question was could it be translated into votes? But I'll steal a line from Don Sipple when he says, "Arnold Schwarzenegger wasn't a wannabe, he was a wannado." When I started talking to him about doing this thing, I said, "Arnold, you know, this is a huge problem." And he said, "George, huge problems make for huge solutions." And he said, "I'm not going up there just to balance the budget. I'm going up there to make big change." This is him. He didn't just become the top of the world in two professions, he made one profession, he created bodybuilding. And he thinks and he believes that he can go up there and make major changes and do the things that California needs.

So you come down to this idea of specifics, and people have had specifics for years and years and years. What they wanted was somebody that would actually do something. For God's sake, there's the Little Hoover Commission, there's the Constitutional Commission, there's this commission and that commission. We all know what needs to be done, but nobody has done it.

SIPPLE: The two things that people knew about Arnold Schwarzenegger was that he was the embodiment of the American dream, and that he sets goals and achieves them. What do you want in a governor? Somebody who sets goals and achieves them, right? And he's done that in his personal life. And they gave him a big break on a lot of the substance stuff because he sets goals and achieves them. The guy's a winner.

MARINUCCI: Let's follow up on something that Don just said, which is they gave him a big break on a lot of things because they knew who he was. But I talked to a lot of you guys during the campaign. You thought he would be a lot easier to take down than he was because of the personal stuff. You had even mentioned it in *Premier Magazine*. . . .

SOUTH: Oh, sure. Throw that in my face.

MARINUCCI: When you were talking about a possible opponent to Davis, you were saying between Riordan and Arnold, Arnold would be easier to take down. Am I right?

SOUTH: No, I never thought that Arnold would be easier to take down. I thought Riordan would be more of a conventional candidate if he had been the Republican nominee or the main Republican candidate. But, Arnold was outside the box; that was the problem.

MARINUCCI: But did you think from the start that the tabloids and everybody else would start kicking in as soon as he declared and the celebrity thing started happening?

SOUTH: I thought that would be the case because that's what the tabloids generally do, until I found out that the tabloids, rather than taking off after Arnold, were actually combining to put out glossy magazines glorifying Arnold's career to try to make money at the newsstands. So that part of the equation simply never came into being.

But in any campaign, trying to deal with a nontraditional candidate is a lot more difficult than trying to deal with a traditional sort of in the box candidate. And Arnold was clearly going to be in that category.

MARINUCCI: Richie, talk about the developments that went on with Cruz, and as all of this was going on. The stories that developed about MECHA, the Hispanic student organization that he belonged to, created a tremendous amount of news. And he didn't really seem to address it or apologize. Can you explain what went on there? Why didn't he directly confront it?

ROSS: Well, he was never going to apologize for being a member of MECHA. Irrespective of what the consequence of that would be, he was just not doing it. So that was not anything that we tortured ourselves over in any way. We knew he was just going to take his lumps for it, and he was prepared to do so.

BARABAK: Why wouldn't he have ever apologized?

ROSS: He didn't think there was anything to apologize for. We all had funny hair, funny clothes, said funny things, were members of funny organizations. No disrespect to the Republicans, but a lot of us were part of a lot of 1960s student lunacy. And, it was kind of a healthy part of our lives. I got a kick just walking over here, seeing that it was still alive and well on the campus. So we just didn't feel we were going to engage in that, and he was prepared to take whatever the consequence of that refusal was.

MARINUCCI: Why didn't he distance himself from the news stories that talk about the racist motto of the organization: "For the race, everything . . . ," why didn't he distant himself from that?

ROSS: He did not believe then, does not believe now that it is a racist organization. It was a lefty, 1960s student organization. It was an important part of his life. He ran for student body president at Fresno State, as part of the MECHA student movement. He was not going to walk away from that, or renounce it. And if people don't accept it, that's fine. That's the consequence of public life.

SOUTH: Since this is a historical record that we're constructing, I would be remiss if I did not point out a couple of things about the lieutenant governor's decision to get into this race that I happen to know. First of all, it's well and good to try to pose this as a last minute, selfless, sacrificial decision, to get into this race because Dianne Feinstein opted out and to save the party. But the fact is clear back in the spring, it was well known that the lieutenant governor was making inquiries of attorneys about whether or not if the recall qualified and it fell to him to set the date of the special election, whether that would be a conflict of interest if he then, in fact, decided to run in that election. It was well known in July, even before the thing qualified, that he had asked the attorney general's office for a legal opinion about whether or not he could declare the date of the special election, but declare as part of that that there was no need for a candidate election because California had a constitutional provision that determined very clearly that when the office of governor was vacant, the lieutenant governor automatically succeeded.

So, this was a long process that the lieutenant governor was going through, thinking about this, not just talking to his wife the night before. That is disingenuous.

BARABAK: This is why it was box lunches, no cutlery, no sharp objects. Richie, is it disingenuous to say he was thinking about this the whole time?

ROSS: Garry is entitled to his point of view. There's no reason for me to debate his point of view.

MARINUCCI: Do you dispute anything he said?

ROSS: I have a different construction of what went on. There's no reason for me to debate someone else's point of view.

SOUTH: I'll take that as a no.

BARABAK: I want to ask Tyler the same question I asked of McClintock and Simon's people, did Peter Camejo get into this race thinking, "By, golly, I'm going to be sitting in the governor's office, I'm going to be governor?"

SNORTUM-PHELPS: Our whole campaign is very different than the other folks here, in that Peter represents a party, and a party with a very clearly defined platform that is trying to move into power in California. And, that party represents a movement, and we are looking to become the electoral expression of that movement. So our goals always were to advance that growth, and to put the Green Party on the map, and to put our platform out there. I don't think we had great hopes of putting Peter in the governor's mansion. It certainly wouldn't have been the end of the world, but our goal, really, was to challenge both of the major parties and to tap into the anger that the voters had with politics as usual as has already been discussed, by letting them know that there was a clear alternative with the laid-out positions and platforms that we had.

BARABAK: Not that Peter Camejo would have been elected, but might he have done better if it had been a bunch of conventional candidates running?

SNORTUM-PHELPS: Yeah, it's entirely possible. Particularly Schwarzenegger entering the race had an impact on us. It shifted the focus, with consequences for everybody, but it definitely shifted it for us. One of the only ways we tend to get attention is through the spoiler factor. We, of course, have a whole point of view on that and how it could have been solved by the two parties in power over the last 10 years quite easily by putting a runoff system in place. But that was one of the ways that we got media focus. And when you had Arnold out there so strong, that issue was no longer there. So then we had to actually ask the people to just pay attention to Peter, based on what he was saying, which doesn't always work with reporters.

MARINUCCI: About this time in the race, we've got two important events going on: Schwarzenegger announcing his economy recovery team, and Davis about to give an important speech at UCLA, which is billed as an apology. So let's go to you first and talk about that, because as it turns out it was not an apology. Did you want him to give an apology? Did you advise him to say *mea culpa,* and he just didn't deliver?

SOUTH: Well, that's a state secret.

MARINUCCI: I take that as a yes.

SOUTH: I think people got out of that speech what they wanted to get out of it. I think there were differences of opinion inside the Davis camp about whether that speech did everything it was intended to do. Part of it was just the format of it, with cheering supporters and that sort of thing. The atmospherics of it, the optics of it, if you will, didn't particularly look, at first glance, if you just saw a clip of it on the news, didn't look like a *mea culpa,* it didn't look like somebody who was particularly abject in seeking people's forgiveness. So, partly, it was the format and the way that it was done. But if you go back and read the actual text of the speech, there was a fair amount of contrition in the speech.

BARABAK: Was it necessary for him to go out and be abject, or was it okay what he did? Should he have said, "Golly, I'm sorry. I screwed up, and I'm really sorry about that," and said the "S" word in some fashion? Would it have been a difference?

SOUTH: He was in a position in this race, for all kinds of reasons that most of us understand, where he was damned if he did and damned if he didn't. If he took the apologetic route, people in focus groups would say, "Well, too little, too late." If he took the defensive route, saying, "Good things have happened. We worked our way through the energy crisis, the budget deficit is not my personal fault, it's part of the national context of the recession and job loss," then people would say, "There he goes again blaming somebody else." So if you are the governor, which tack do you take, knowing that neither one of them is a slam-dunk with respect to rejuvenating yourself with the electorate to the point that they're not going to throw you out of office?

GRISOLANO: There's an important context to the speech that explains why he did what he did, and whether or not it was perfect was beside the point. He went through this qualifying period where events were out of Gray Davis's control, out of the campaign apparatus' control, out of Democratic control. Events were being driven by our opponents. Then, during the filing period, there was extraordinary drama. Mr. Schwarzenegger gets in; Dianne Feinstein gets out; Mr. Bustamante gets in And there's nothing you can do about these things; they're out of your control. Now you're in a defined period from the beginning to the end of the campaign, and Governor Davis was in real jeopardy of being passed over as though he wasn't part of this drama. The point of the UCLA speech was that he had to introduce himself back into the storyline, and say some provocative things—how provocative is secondary—he had to say some provocative things; he had to ask people to take another look at him before they focus on all the other things that are going on in the campaign. And to the degree that was the goal, and that was a point in time where the recall may have been a foregone conclusion, that's what the speech achieved, and that's what he set out to do.

BARABAK: I was going to save this for the big dramatic finish, but, as you look back, was this hopeless? Could Gray Davis have withstood this and not been recalled, or was it preordained from the start?

GRISOLANO: I think the chances from the beginning were very bad. And we've had some friendly discussion here about the lieutenant governor's involvement, and I think the hardest thing for the Democratic Party had to do with question number two. You hear the word "discipline" a lot in campaigns, and a campaign ought to be disciplined, and the party ought to exercise some discipline. The easiest time to be disciplined is when the options are obvious and the hardest time is when you've got to choose between a bad choice and a worse choice. We started in a bad place, but those who advocated getting a backup candidate offered a worse choice. As fluid as events were, as tumultuous as this process was, there may have been a break where he could have busted through, he could have made his way above 51%. But he was in a bad place from the beginning, and as events played out, I don't think there's anything he could have done to break through the ceiling.

BARABAK: Was it hopeless, Garry?

SOUTH: This was basically a mathematical calculation. How do you get 50 percent plus one of the voters to vote for somebody with a 26 percent job approval rating? That's the dilemma. And in our tracking there were only two occasions where we got yes on the recall below 50—one was a three-night track in the middle of September, where it came out about 49 to 46, still with yes ahead, but below 50; and then the Saturday night before the election, where the tracking actually had this thing about 49 to 49. On Sunday night and Monday night, it bounced back because, frankly, I think the Schwarzenegger campaign to their credit did a very good job of fighting back on the *L.A. Times* charges. They had set up the case well in advance that they're going to do this to us, "We're warning you they're going to do this to us." They seized on Lockyer's comment, as could be totally expected, and used that to say, "Even Davis's friends are telling you that he's going to run a puke campaign." The charges took a couple days to soak in, and once they did, this thing went pretty much even-steven in our tracks. But by the time Sunday night rolled around before the election, it was pretty much back up to 53-44, or somewhere in there, but pretty much back up to where it ended up. So was it impossible? No. Did there have to be some earth-shaking thing happen in order to get 50 percent plus 1 no on the recall? Absolutely, yes.

BARABAK: Without really saying it, you very strongly imply that Gray Davis was basically sold down the river by his fellow Democrats. It was Cruz and it was comments by the likes of Lockyer that basically screwed the guy.

GRISOLANO: They weren't helpful.

SOUTH: They were not helpful. Honest to God, they were not.

GRISOLANO: They were harmful.

SOUTH: And, with all due respect to the attorney general of California, if you go back and look at the senate races that were run when he was president pro tem for his candidates, you would be pretty hard-pressed to say these campaigns were any more lofty or high purpose or less negative than any other campaign in California history. Sanctimonious posturing is all well and good, but the fact is it was not helpful.

MARINUCCI: Richie, did you sincerely think that your candidate could run a no on recall/yes on Bustamante campaign? Was that not a mixed message?

ROSS: It was totally a mixed message. Mark called me three weeks before the election, and he said to me, "Well, what has to happen for you guys to win?" And I said, "Mark, the same thing is going to have to happen in the next three weeks as we've needed to happen all along. We're going to have to get incredibly lucky." Our calculation always was, and we all . . . you know, Garry talked about their polls, and all of these fellows decided that you need to hear your own polls, don't get confused by anybody else's. Well, ours always showed us that the governor's position was enormously difficult, enormously difficult; and we never saw wide fluctuation in the recall. I think we did 14 polls in a row, and when we asked voters a generic question, "Who would you rather see in the governor's office, a Democrat, a Republican, or an Independent?" from the very beginning the word Democrat never got beyond 36 percent. That was stunning to us.

So we looked at that and said, "Okay, the only way for this to happen, and we agreed with John Feliz, would be for Tom McClintock to get into the mid 20s, and then you catch a break, and Peter Ueberroth stays in the race. And so we were always looking at kind of that great race the governor ran in the primary of 1998, where they had to play that split and get through. Our calculation was always about the way the Democratic primary electorate was split. Could we just be in the right place, kind of at the right time, play the splits, appeal to the Democratic base, hope there wasn't massive drop-off or work to control the degree of drop-off between questions 1 and questions 2, try to control that number, work to reduce it, and then? It took a long time, a little over a month, so about half the time for us to get to the point where a majority of people in the Democratic Party finally endorsed it. The AFL/CIO, the State Labor Federation finally endorsed it. So it took a while to get credibility and to have people come to a conclusion, and then, ultimately, what happens is the Arnold Schwarzenegger campaign just catches fire. They make all of the right moves to fuel some advantages that they had going in, but they made a lot of terrific strategic decisions, and it collapsed around everybody but them.

BARABAK: Okay, so you guys have three of the great minds in American politics working for Arnold Schwarzenegger, but it's not enough. You bring in Bob White; you bring in Mike Murphy. You stumble with Warren Buffet. He has his economic summit where Arnold isn't speaking to substance, he's dodging reporters, he does 45 minutes in the parking lot. . . .

MARINUCCI: Don, you said the economic summit was a critical part of the campaign.

BARABAK: Walk us up to that point.

SIPPLE: We were still building the battleship. There was the Buffet thing, the Prop. 13 controversy. But there was a net plus to Buffet's involvement, because it signals to everybody that Arnold Schwarzenegger has access to the top talent in the country, if not the world. That's very important, from his position. So Prop. 13 was dying down; Shultz, Buffet and the rest came, and the subtext at that point of the campaign was that Arnold has no substance, he's afraid of debating, da-da-da-da. He faced 47 cameras that day and 45 minutes of questions; and he held his own. In fact, as I watched him, he took control of that room, and he got bigger with every answer. So he passed a very big bar, and the campaign did, too, that day. And I think anybody who was there was very impressed with his performance.

GORTON: Warren Buffet was a net plus to the campaign, but was almost a huge minus because he shook the resolve of the Howard Jarvis Taxpayers Committee to endorse us. We had to really walk them back in off a limb, and we needed that to anchor us on the right.

BARABAK: Warren Buffet is a great marquee name, but Prop. 13, what did that do?

JOHNSON: We saw it as a huge opportunity, obviously. When he made the comment, I thought it was interesting, but when Warren Buffet talks to the *Wall Street Journal* stocks go up and down, companies rise and fall on what this guy says. He's careful what he says, so we thought it was believable that they were floating the idea of a tax increase. We cut a little radio spot, spent $40,000 to run it in the Valley. I heard it once on radio; I heard it three times on national television. It just got caught up in this whole thing. We polled four days later and asked, "Which candidate had an advisor who proposed raising property taxes?" Forty-eight percent of the voters said Arnold Schwarzenegger. We asked the follow-up question . . . "Who is going to keep your taxes low?" Arnold Schwarzenegger. So, I mean. . . .

BARABAK: How do you explain that phenomenon?

SIPPLE: It was Warren Buffet talking about it, not Arnold Schwarzenegger. I'm watching a poker game here. Richie is describing how he's trying to draw to an inside straight, and everybody else is trying to improve their hand. We had a good set of cards in this campaign, and the best candidate under the circumstances. Everybody goes through these machinations about "Warren Buffet, this and that," and, "The advisor said such and such." It was not Arnold Schwarzenegger. Had Arnold Schwarzenegger said that, it would have been a different kettle of fish.

BARABAK: Your take on the Prop. 13 thing, John?

FELIZ: It was a huge mistake to have him say that, or not vet him properly. I don't think anybody would disagree with me on that, Here's one of the most left-wing financiers in the entire nation coming aboard a campaign that hadn't gelled as far as what direction they were going to go. I thought that was a mistake. However, we tracked right afterwards, too, and saw Bill Simon literally tank as a result of the attack, and he said, "The last thing that I'm going to do is attack Arnold Schwarzenegger on these lines, until I figure out how to do this."

The most important thing I learned out of this whole thing was that the media took control of the campaign. The candidates were essentially players in this play that was going on. And talk radio to network or cable TV news, and the *Los Angeles Times* essentially determined the direction of this race at various points in time. And, no disrespect to Mr. South or Mr. Gorton and the strategists, but I'm a little bit stunned that some of the most incisive consultants in the entire world were amazed that this race was going to take place and were not prepared for it. I think what they were not prepared for was the excitement that took place. I don't think anyone was prepared for that.

WALSH: The media never took control of our campaign. We always decided where we were going to go, and for the most part, what we were going to do, even when we took a lot of public criticism, number one. Number two, with regards to Warren Buffet you say left-wing financier, most people when you mention Warren Buffet's name, he's perceived as one of the great economic and business minds in the world.

FELIZ: You're talking about perception, though. Not reality.

WALSH: I'm talking about looking at the election results and what Arnold Schwarzenegger drew from across the state.

GORTON: And, third, you're acting like it's bad that instead of paid media driving a campaign, free media was important to the campaign.

FELIZ: I'm not saying that it's bad. I think it's great.

WALSH: He drew Warren Buffet, who is a very prominent Democrat. That sent a very strong message across the board that he's going for the best and brightest, and not just Republicans. He drew other people who were supportive of Governor Davis, who came to that conference, and it was a very big group. So it set a very clear tone about change, and it's not going to be a partisan, status quo type of campaign. And Don is absolutely right. He brought in very bright people. People were amazed that (a) he could get a Democrat, (b) he could get Warren Buffet, and (c) they could all come together at the same time. He went out there, brought them all together—Schultz, Buffet, and Schwarzenegger. And he took that podium and he took control.

BARABAK: When did you all learn about the Prop. 13? Did you go to the website? Did you get a phone call? Did you pick up the *Wall Street Journal*?

WALSH: I got a phone call from the *Wall Street Journal*.

BARABAK: So you knew that was coming?

WALSH: Late in the afternoon, yeah.

GORTON: It was definitely not a trial balloon.

WALSH: No, it was not a trial balloon; it was a no-brainer. Arnold said, "That's not where I stand, but I'm going to bring people in." And he didn't want people who are "yes" men, he wants people who are going give him tough ideas and different perspectives. And it's not just them and it's not just the attitude, that's the way the guy approached the campaign.

MARINUCCI: This raises the media strategy issue. Arnold at this point was going on talk radio, conservative talk radio and Howard Stern. And yet a lot of the folks out here didn't get those one-on-one interviews. Explain what the decision making was.

SIPPLE: There was a conscious decision and an article of faith in the campaign that the campaign and Arnold was going to play to the people, not the press. In a traditional campaign, the press tail wags the dog, in many cases. Well, Arnold

Schwarzenegger was a well-known cultural icon; he didn't need that. In order to be able to say what he wants to do and put forth his agenda, we had to go outside the mainstream media, and do it successfully, and it was in keeping with the unconventional nature of this election, and the desire to have an unconventional campaign, because he was an unconventional leader/nonpolitician. So it was a conscious strategy of the campaign to do it that way.

FELIZ: The Economic Recovery Summit was brilliant. It was a home run. It cast the race differently. It changed the Buffet phenomena and factor. And, the Schwarzenegger strategy was brilliant. They essentially cast themselves as the antitax conservative in the race. Some of the mistakes that were made by the McClintock campaign only assisted them. And trying to cast Cruz as a left-wing candidate ended up making Cruz scary, which actually cut our own corner. The conservatives were saying, "We can't have scary Cruz elected as governor of California. We're going to have to have somebody that is acceptable." And that's Arnold.

BARABAK: Wayne, there was an event in Placer County and Simon and McClintock were both there, and McClintock got a much, much better reception than Simon. Were you guys surprised that there was not more of a residual Bill Simon vote or support for him out there?

JOHNSON: Well, they were shooting your commercial for McClintock that day. And that was his crowd. But that was probably the surprise of the whole race, not that event, but the way the oxygen got sucked out of the room for us. We think of ourselves as running the conservative candidate, and the press thought of him as the conservative candidate. Before the candidates all filed, the Simon base was the institutional Republican—people who went to the polls and voted for Dole, voted for Bush, they voted for whoever ran last time, the institutional Republican vote. And that all disappeared and went not to McClintock, but to Schwarzenegger. And that's what took the oxygen away from us.

FELIZ: One of the things that was the most disconcerting for the Schwarzenegger campaign was how they couldn't get us to withdraw from the race after Simon withdrew, after Issa didn't get in, and after eventually Peter left. If I've answered once, I answered a thousand times, when people asked, "When is Tom going to get out?" I felt that the strategy of making Arnold the acceptable candidate, and then saying, "Tom can't win, he's a spoiler," and having the press carry that for them was really our greatest frustration of the race.

BARABAK: With all due respect to Wayne, we're going to get Simon out of the race at this point. Can you just tell us when he came to that decision and how difficult it was for him?

JOHNSON: We obviously were disappointed that we couldn't get any traction. We started everything up and running, we had residual staff ready to go out and cherry-pick from the campaign that they had done last year. We were up and running, we were all over the state, we were everywhere that first week. And the local press saw us everywhere. So we were feeling pretty good. We felt the mistake with the Warren Buffet thing might be the first crack in the armor because we didn't think Arnold had gelled yet. But we took a survey, we went out and did an analysis that just took the whole electorate apart, put it back together, showing what kind of candidate they would vote for. We gave them all the attributes, and there was no way they were going to vote for somebody that held all of Arnold's positions. And then when we came back and we put Arnold's name in, they voted for Arnold. It was pretty obvious that nothing traditional we could do was going to crack that. For every 10 points that we could knock off of Arnold, we got 3-1/2 of it, Tom got 3, and Ueberroth got 2-1/2. So all we could do was equalize things. We had to attack. And I don't think Bill was prepared to go out and attack Arnold.

GORTON: Although we definitely wanted everyone out of the race from the Republican side, we did a lot of modeling about what has happened in past races, and what could be expected to happen in this race. And we came up with a pretty strong projection that Tom would lose about half his support toward the end. And we watched that, it was one of the questions we did in our tracking poll. So we felt that even if Tom didn't get out of the race, we were going to win.

FELIZ: He's absolutely correct. We should have been up around the mid 20s or high 20s, and Tom lost about 10 or 15 points because of the *Los Angeles Times* groping story. That's what collapsed us. And it was the most frustrating experience of the entire race. I have no idea what were they thinking getting involved in the race in this fashion. But the real key to the whole thing goes back to something I read in a *Los Angeles Times* column by George Skelton. And what he had written regarding the previous race in 2002 for governor was that the people never got a chance to have a race; they felt that they got cheated out of a choice by either negative or sleaze campaigning, or no campaign, or no issues at all except negativity. And this race was being cast as something different. It gave me heart that if I had a candidate that could be principled, had vision, and stayed above the fray, maybe that would break through. As it turned out, they liked Tom, they thought he was a great guy. He ended up with some of the highest positives that any candidate running in a statewide race under this intensity probably had ever amassed, and the lowest negatives. The fact is he didn't get the people to vote for him, because they had another alternative.

MARINUCCI: Let's get to an issue that affected both McClintock and Bustamante, the Indian gaming money. Richie, I think this is something that everybody wants to hear. Explain the donations from Indian gaming, why they went into Cruz's campaign instead of an independent expenditure, what was the thinking?

ROSS: The legal advice that we had, and we believe today that the legal advice given to us at the time was sound legal advice, was the best advice our attorneys were able to give us based on the facts they had. They believed that these, quote/unquote, old pre-Prop. 34 committees, would be allowable, and, in fact, the FPPC had set up a very elaborate system for handling these contributions. So it wasn't actually a scheme that we invented or thought of, they just came to us one day and said, "You can do this." We said, "Oh, okay." It was just that simple. Had they come to us and said, "You know, this is an iffy proposition. . . " but there was nothing in the law, or in anybody's frame of reference at the time that indicated that this would be a problem.

Now, we always knew that, politically, you're going to have a perception issue. We know that Indian contributions could be a source of controversy. We understood all that. But we also knew that for us—Don talked earlier about us trying to draw the inside straight—they were in a literal sense, table stakes, that the only chance we had to get Democratic establishment figures to find the whole notion of Cruz being an acceptable alternative would require people perceiving that, "The tribes might fund this guy, and he might be real. And, we don't want him to win without us." So there was a lot of us trying to get people to believe that, "Okay, if you don't support us, they will, and we'll win without you."

BARABAK: When Cruz was thinking of getting into the race, did you guys have a budget in mind? And, where did you figure that money was going to come from. Did you say, "We're going to get $4-8 million from the Indian tribes?"

ROSS: Oh, no. We had no basis for saying it. Dan Morain called me; he was the only one who spotted it. A couple weeks into the race he said, "You know, this $10 million you're going to be getting from the tribes? I think you're bluffing." I said, "Oh, okay."

MARINUCCI: The widely held perception was that one of the deciding factors in doing it the way you did was, as a consultant, you would profit quite heavily, that you would get a cut out of the deal.

ROSS: I don't think, in the 30 years I've been involved, anybody has ever been able to make a credible case or an honorable one that would suggest that I've made a series of business decisions to the detriment of the candidate, to the persons, or causes that I've been hired to represent.

MARINUCCI: But that one was to the detriment of the candidate in the long run? Didn't it kill him?

ROSS: I believe that had all the money been spent in an independent effort, the issue on the table would have been, "Why won't you, Cruz, tell the Indians to stop spending millions of dollars on your behalf?" And it would have been a legitimate question that would have been posited by our opponents, by the press, and by other legitimate sources. It was not an illegitimate question to have raised in the course of the campaign, and there was no good answer to it.

BARABAK: You have a dynamic where you have a very, very unpopular incumbent who is seen as always having his hands out, raising money, and being pay-to-play, and fast and lose, fair or not. What were you thinking when you said, "You know, we're going to use this loophole in the campaign finance law to bring this money in?"

ROSS: Well, you've got to remember, given the number of people who have such committees, it was not perceived by us to be a, quote/unquote, loophole. Now, subsequently, a judge disagrees with the FPPC advice that we were basing it on. And, ultimately, I think when all of the legal record is established through the appeals process, it will be pretty clear when people from the FPPC are deposed that they will have to say that, "Yes, they did give us that oral advice." As the generic answer to the question, "Who would you like to see as governor?" we were always in the mid 30s. So we're looking at this thing pretty cold eyed and saying, "We need to just hang onto a vote that's in the mid 30s, and then hope that the Republican candidates split the difference." That was the operating assumption.

BARABAK: I can see where, technically, your lawyers told you this, but did you not have a concern of how the public would perceive using this loophole?

ROSS: We understood that the public would have a serious question about us receiving large amounts of money from Indian tribes, we knew that going in. And the question on the table for us wasn't what account it went into, or whether it was an independent or not. We know going in if they spend substantial numbers of dollars promoting our candidacy, we're going to suffer a consequence from that.

BARABAK: So the bottom line was you needed the money.

ROSS: We needed the money.

MARINUCCI: Garry, did this have blow-back on your candidate?

SOUTH: The Indian money thing?

MARINUCCI: Yeah.

SOUTH: I don't think it had any affect on Gray that I can think of. It certainly had an affect on Bustamante. In our focus group, I have never seen any—even the so-called Oracle scandal stuff in 2002, which Simon used pretty effectively against us—"fundraising scandal," quote/unquote, ever penetrate as deeply down to the bottom of the electorate as this Indian money laundry.

BARABAK: And why?

SOUTH: Because of the high visibility of the race. This may be something you can get away with when you're running a legislative campaign that is below the radar, low visibility. You can't get away with this kind of scam when you're in the most highly covered race in the history of California, and everyone is watching it under a microscope.

BARABAK: Yeah, you're all nodding your heads, yeah.

SIPPLE: I think that it was an intensely important issue for Arnold Schwarzenegger, because the fact is that the entire political establishment in California has been up to this time addicted to their cash. Okay? We found that it was one of the best symbols of what's wrong with the status quo in Sacramento. And so we went with a spot, where I think Arnold was kind of defined as governor in that commercial, to be honest. Because everybody else would pander to him, and there was a meeting in August, where Davis, McClintock, and Bustamante all pandered to Tanaga, and then there was a bunch of information that came out in the *Times* about what level of funds people were getting from them. And so I think what distinguished us was that, in a change versus status quo election, it made us the sole person who was not playing that game.

BARABAK: My understanding is that there was some debate internally with the Schwarzenegger camp about how to handle the Indian gaming money issue. What was that dispute-discussion, call it what you will, and what were the two sides, and why did you end up coming down the way you did?

SIPPLE: I don't think we're going to talk about what happened behind the curtain. We came down where we did, and I think that's the important thing.

WALSH: To lift the curtain a tiny bit, I think, part of the decision making with Arnold was the California Teachers Association endorsement—what we would pledge to do or not do, etc. Arnold went in, made his pitch about why he should be governor to the CTA. He said, "But I won't fill out your questionnaires. I'll sit down at the table. You'll have a position at the negotiating table. I'll work with you in good faith. We did it on 49. But no promises, no favors. I don't want your money." And so that was his attitude right from the start, and that attitude carried over to the tribal gaming stuff. He was going to have to sit down at the bargaining table and negotiate a compact with them. And so that attitude with CTA moved over to the Indian tribes. And that was his attitude.

FELIZ: Tom's position was that these are sovereign peoples; you don't have to negotiate. It's like us negotiating with Nevada over gaming. You don't have to do that. And we didn't pander to the Indians, we told them our position about that meeting. If anyone was there covering it, we could have covered it afterwards. The thing about the Indian money, we tested as being neutral. It was failing to follow the rules that made it poison. And, interestingly enough, the next individual that took the big hit from that was Davis, because it went back again, failing to follow the fundraising rules, as people perceived it. And it hurt Davis as much as it hurt anyone else who was getting Indian money.

WALSH: It hurt Cruz because, like or not, the Oracle stuff and all the pay to play stuff, which we had hammered on in my prior life had a residual effect. When you guys did the Prop. 34 stuff and the Indian stuff, and Ross Johnson— and I've got to tell you, the legal team that surrounded Ross Johnson were brilliant in the way they dealt with that—kept it in the earned media day after day after day. So the pay-to-play stuff that was on Gray, that residual carry-over, got transferred to you. So you, basically, got radioactive with it. And it hurt you, and it lasted so long in the earned media, there was so much earned media attention here, that it really, really hurt you badly.

SIPPLE: Cruz Bustamante's unfavorable was in the low 20s when we first started testing, and it ended up almost 60. And I don't think there was a negative ad run against Cruz Bustamante.

GRISOLANO: It took Gray Davis six years to get that high.

SOUTH: Yeah, the fact is at the end of the campaign in our tracking, their favs and un-favs were pretty much within the margin of error.

BARABAK: We're going to talk about the debates. The decision by the Schwarzenegger campaign is that you're going to do one and only one, the Super Bowl of debates. You chose to skip the first debate. You did the second debate. Talk about the debate strategy.

SIPPLE: Mike Murphy did an immense job for the campaign, running the road show and driving the free media message. Mike had a big role in the debate and the debate prep, and the whole schematic for it. And, while we took a short-term hit early on by not playing, we thought we would get a long-term benefit, because the bar would be very low, and he would be very ready to debate at a time of our choosing, and he would acquit himself very nicely under the circumstances. That was all part of the strategy. And if we wanted to play a typical politician role, and we were not a typical politician, we would have debated everyday. We didn't want to go there, and it was part of the unconventional campaign to do debates unconventionally. And he did. The bar was low. He did very well. And I think the campaign took off after that.

WALSH: And, again, that was not letting the media or outside influences drive us. Don is absolutely right. Mike came in about five weeks out, and played a very critical role in bringing everybody together.

MARINUCCI: Is that the single-digit factor, the high point of the campaign, do you think, the single most important element?

GORTON: I think every time Arnold Schwarzenegger did something important, it was a big factor. It was Arnold Schwarzenegger's performance. When he did the debate, it was Arnold Schwarzenegger's performance. And when you have Arnold Schwarzenegger out doing things, we went up in the polls.

BARABAK: In the one debate that Gray was a participant, the one here in Walnut Creek, did he help himself, hurt himself, did it matter?

SOUTH: I don't think it had any chemical effect on the campaign. I do think that the town forums and the town halls that he did, for those people who saw them, or who saw clips on them, or who saw stories about them, thought he actually performed quite well under a great deal of stress. I wish we had been doing that for the last five years.

MARINUCCI: Did you see the debate as a sort of psychological turning point for the voters? Did they need to see Arnold being able to perform, or why do you think it had as much affect as it did?

SOUTH: Well, I think that debate on the 24th for the governor was important because up until that point Cruz's position in the candidate field had made it impossible for the antirecall effort to gel this thing down, to boil it down to here are the two choices: you can either retain Governor Davis or you're going to get Arnold Schwarzenegger. And there were spots produced that went in that direction, and focus groups were very resistant to them, because they weren't ready to go there yet. They thought there were other options. And some of the questions that came up in the focus groups were, "Well, what about Cruz? How can Davis say this is about him and Schwarzenegger when you've got the lieutenant governor in the race?" And in that debate where Arnold performed—I wouldn't say it was an Academy Award-winning performance, but it was adequate, and he was strong, and Cruz was almost not there—people then came to the conclusion that this was going to boil down to either retaining the governor, or you're going to get Arnold Schwarzenegger. That's the effect it had on the antirecall.

BARABAK: Can I jump back to the time when you guys started doing the conservative talk radio? McClintock was in the race, Arnold was in that wonderful middle ground area, but he did move right to some extent for a time. Was there any concern that moving so far right you're going to start alienating people on the left, or was Cruz such a weakened candidate on the left?

GORTON: Our strategy from the beginning was to go up the middle. Based on the polling data we got back in the June poll, which we worked out in July, we felt that Arnold would just pull away and work from the right-hand side. We did feel we needed the Howard Jarvis Taxpayers Association as a symbol on the right, but we never. . . .

BARABAK: A symbol of what?

GORTON: That Arnold was a conservative. But we ran up the middle. I don't know how you define right or left, to be honest with you, but the budget and the economy were such crushing, overriding issues with people. The economy in L.A. is not as bad as up here, but the perception in L.A. was still that it was very, very bad, and worker's comp, all those issues, were really front and center on people's minds. And running to the right on a conservative economic message, or taxes, is not really running to the right, it's just running on those specific focused issues.

MARINUCCI: John, on the debate, your guy came out with the highest ratings, and Peter Camejo scored very high. A lot of the pundits said these guys did the best actual performance in the debate. Do you want to talk about that a little?

FELIZ: There were two measures of the debate. The first measure was how the individuals supported themselves in the debate—facts, to the point, and how well they came out. The second one was survey research. In every one of the debates that Tom attended Tom won in both dimensions. In fact, that was one of the reasons he gained such a very high favorable. Technically speaking, we won every one of the engagements. But what happened, what was the real key? And I'm going to have to agree with the Schwarzenegger campaign on this one. Brilliant campaign strategy, once again, of letting Arnold carry it. The day of the 24th at the CSUS was a turning point, I believe, for the campaign. It created the acceptability factor. Arnold came across as doing fairly well; he didn't do terrible. He came across as the type of individual people wanted him to be. And I think at that point in time, despite the fact that survey-wise, as well as from a technical standpoint, we beat him, we lost it there.

BARABAK: There was a sense going into that debate that Tom McClintock would go after Arnold Schwarzenegger, and argue, "I'm the true conservative in the race." He did not do that. What was the decision behind his debate performance?

FELIZ: We looked at both sides of that, and I probably shouldn't talk about it too much more. We felt that in a free-flowing environment such as that debate, which really wasn't on debate points more than anything else—if you noticed, Arnold and Arianna didn't follow the rules as they were meant to be followed—we would really take a beating. Arnold was far more capable of delivering incisive one-liners, and Tom would react to those in the fashion that he does. So we decided just to stick to the debate.

GORTON: I looked at the two measures, the pundits and the polls, and all the polls I saw Arnold won. Maybe with the pundits, some were one way and some were the other. But if you ask the voters, they liked Arnold.

SNORTUM-PHELPS: Yeah, the first thing I'll say, before going a back to what the debates meant to us, is that I think that Arianna's decision to attack Arnold helped him. We think that there was certainly less substance to Arnold's responses than other candidates, particularly, Peter and Tom, but he didn't end up getting judged on that, he ended up getting judged on how he handled the attack, He was calm and poised and smiled and said the nice, little, quips back to her.

The Walnut Creek debate was a watershed moment for the Green Party, that was the first nationally televised debate that a Green candidate had ever been in. Remember, Ralph Nadar didn't make it; they wouldn't even let him be in the audience. So that was a huge moment for us. And what do you expect a voter might think of a third party candidate, don't have a lot of experience listening to a third party candidate—that they're there going to be shrill, that they're going to be single-issue, trying to get attention, very hyper. So our job was to present, Peter as the ambassador of the Green Party. And, of course, the calm part was the hardest one for him, if anybody has ever seen Peter. But I think we really decided to focus on issues and be calm, and keep the personal attacks down.

Now, before the 24th in Sacramento, we actually thought, "Well, we did so well in Walnut Creek, so many positive comments, maybe it is time to take it a little notch up and go after Arnold a little bit." And we had a lot of discussions about that, we had a liaison committee with our state party leadership that was advising Peter throughout the process, and we made a very crucial decision not to get personal. Peter's wife had something to say about that as well. And I think it really helped, because afterwards we heard the exact same thing that McClintock heard, "Boy, your guy was great, he was clear, he didn't get into the mudslinging, he was effective." And we saw polls that rated Peter as top in some of these debates. And that continued all the way through the end. Now, Peter got a little funnier, and a little more relaxed in those later debates, but nobody was watching those anymore. After the 24, that was it.

GRISOLANO: The reason Schwarzenegger won the debate was, number one, because it wasn't about the issues or whether McClintock could say his plan well; it was about Arnold Schwarzenegger, and is he going to make it, and how is he going to comport himself. And the clip that showed every single day for a week after that debate, where they said Arnold Schwarzenegger handled himself well, was not McClintock saying, "You don't know the budget deficit from a hole in the ground," was not Camejo saying, "You don't understand the tax structure," and him saying, "I've got a role in *Terminator 4* for you." It was a strident personal attack, which he was well suited to deal with. If there had been the kind of action that these guys were saying that they declined to engage in, there may have been a different result of that debate; it may have been the bar that he couldn't get over. But since the whole media coverage was about this sort of personal attack back and forth in which Arianna looked awfully strident, he handled it extremely well, and it was how he got past the debate thing without exposing his inability to talk about the issues of the day.

BARABAK: Okay, so Arnold Schwarzenegger gives a speech, the first hundred days of his administration, and the *Los Angeles Times*, publishes the accounts of seven women who say that they were subjected to untoward behavior by Arnold Schwarzenegger.

MARINUCCI: What kind of insanity was going on the morning that that happened?

WALSH: Well, we knew about it the day before. The *Times*, in this instance, actually gave us the opportunity to try and address some of the issues brought forward in a timely manner. And these date back 35-odd years. So we did our due diligence to go back and try and find observers that would be there at the same time, and could either refute or provide some corroboration for the charges made in the *Times*.

MARINUCCI: As a fellow journalist, I'd like to hear the *Times* response. You heard this campaign many times during the course of the campaign say that the *Times* deliberately held this story to affect the Schwarzenegger. . . .

WALSH: I don't think anybody from our campaign ever said the *Times* deliberately held the story.

BARABAK: I'll momentarily take off my moderator hat and put on my *L.A. Times* hat, and just say a couple things. This is a pretty politically sophisticated audience, and I think a lot of people realize that if you want to work with the premise that the *L.A. Times* set out to destroy Arnold Schwarzenegger's candidacy, we would have published these articles two or three weeks earlier, before people had really made up their minds and opinions had settled. It's obviously a lot harder to turn people back when they're supporting Arnold Schwarzenegger than when they were kind of sitting on the fence.

The second thing, and the most important point I will make, is that the electoral results validated precisely what we did. The stories were published not a minute earlier or later than when they were ready to be published, and we did what newspapers do—we put the information out there and people could then decide. "I think it's a hit piece and it's irrelevant." "I'm really bothered about this, I'm not going to vote for him." Or "It bothers me, but I dislike Gray even more, so I'm going to vote for him." That's what newspapers do. We put the information out there, and the notion that it was a late hit, you know, we don't live in the day of the Pony Express, where Arnold Schwarzenegger had to write out his response by hand, put it in a saddle bag, ride it across the country to a telegraph office in New York. He had five days. Five days, plenty of time to respond to it. And I would lastly say he didn't deny it, he said it was true.

It came down to a matter of timing. I think we put it out in a timely fashion. I think he had plenty of time to respond. And more to the point, I think the people had the opportunity to process the information and then vote on it. I don't want to turn this into a debate, but let me put back on my moderator hat and ask you a question. You were quoted in that original article basically denying it. The next morning Arnold Schwarzenegger basically said, "Where there's smoke, there's fire." He admitted at least part of it.

WALSH: Well, the issue was there were specific instances brought forward in the *L.A. Times.* We went forward and dealt with those on a case-by-case basis, as we did in every instance that came forward. With regards to those specific instances, we either denied those instances, specifically, or we said there was no recollection, etc. But as we later moved forward, there were some instances where there was some bawdry behavior, crude humor that was used in an instance where the specific allegation never occurred, but there was some instance of interaction there.

But let me go back a little bit. When we did our focus groups going into this election, Garry had already sent the *Premier Magazine* article around two years earlier, people had been spending 20 years going through the grocery lines in the supermarkets, seeing the *Globe*, the *Enquirer*, etc. When questions were asked about Hollywood-type behavior, what did the public think about it? Most people shrugged, "That's the way things go in Hollywood." So through 20 years of walking through grocery stores at checkout stands, people have seen these types of stories about Hollywood people, not just Arnold, but others, and there was some inoculation on these types of things. So where in the *Times* or other people in the media, it was a huge, huge deal to them, some new breaking revelation, those issues had been floating out in the consciousness for a long time.

GORTON: I just wanted to say the most extraordinary number I ever saw in a poll anywhere, anytime was Thursday night. We changed the tracking poll questions every single night so we could judge what was happening in the campaign with regard to any particular issue. I put on, "Are you aware of this thing?" And 94 percent the first night were aware of it. And I hadn't heard of 94 percent of the people being aware of anything in one night. And yet our polling numbers stayed high. And they stayed high Thursday, Friday, and they crashed on Saturday.

BARABAK: Why did this basically roll off his back?

WALSH: I don't think people ever took their eye off the fundamental premise of the election. Again, and it sounds hackneyed, but it was change versus status quo, and they wanted a fundamental change. And if you look, most people made up their minds 60 days out or before that; these types of issues didn't bother them. What bothered them was the perception of government being held by special interests, the pay-to-play stuff, whatever the problems were in Sacramento, and this type of stuff didn't.

FELIZ: If I could put my journalism hat on for a minute, I teach journalism at CSU, my feeling about what the *Los Angeles Times* did was not only extremely risky in the approach that they took, but certainly in respect to the entire polling that the *Los Angeles Times* had done throughout the election, which was way off all the time for whatever reason, indicates to me that there was divided loyalty here in the story. I will absolutely tell you that what's been said here is correct. We were doing rolling tracks of the entire week, and we discovered as soon as this groping thing hit it hit to the top and collapsed Tom McClintock's numbers, that's why Arnold stayed high. We dropped down into almost single digits that evening.

BARABAK: Why did people flock away from fine, upstanding Tom McClintock to the guy who was facing these allegations?

FELIZ: The verbatims came back saying, "This is a dirty trick; the Davis campaign was behind it, and we're not going to let them steal this election."

GORTON: I don't know what happened with the *L.A. Times* poll, but it really set the *L.A. Times* up. In our tracking poll, Arnold Schwarzenegger was ahead from the very first track to the very end, he never got behind once. And there was a huge difference yes/no. I've talked to my Democratic counterparts, and their polls reflect a lot of the same stuff. So I don't know what happened.

MARINUCCI: The *Oui Magazine* article was out there a couple weeks before, in which he's interviewed about a lot of very unusual activity, and says he doesn't remember it at first and then he does. Why do you think that did not bother the voters at all?

GORTON: The state is in big trouble, and people's minds are focused on the fact that it's in big trouble. Even the attorney general, who is a Democrat, is focused on the fact that there is big trouble here. We need to all get together and solve this problem. And it's a lot less about those kinds of things than it is about the fact that, "Our spending is going to be cut, and it's going to hurt my schools, and it's going to hurt my police department, and my taxes are going to be raised. And it's because these people up in Sacramento screwed it up." That's what this election was about, and you can bring up anything else you want.

BARABAK: Garry, the *L.A. Times* story comes out. Did it work as well as you thought it was going to when you conspired with the editors . . . no, I'm kidding. That is a joke. Let the record show . . . don't pull it out of context, I was joking. The story comes out. Did you think, "Wow, this is going to change the whole dynamic of this thing," or "Boy, this is really going to cement the Schwarzenegger victory?"

MARINUCCI: Why do you think this stuff didn't stick?

SOUTH: First, let me go back and answer your question, specifically. I don't think the *Times* held this story and all this Republican clap-trap about how this was a last minute hit—I believe John Carroll, who said you didn't have the story ready to run until you ran it. But the fact that it hit so late did, I think, mitigate to some degree, the seriousness of the charges, because it allowed the Schwarzenegger camp to say, "Oh, here's the last minute smear we've been warning you about for weeks," which they did very well. And Schwarzenegger himself is all over national TV saying, "This is a Davis trick. This is a Davis trick," even though the *Times* itself said no other candidate had anything to do with this, and I can assure you the Davis camp did not. We saw this for the first time on the *L.A. Times* website the night before it came out. Larry paged me and said, "Get on the website because there's a big story about Arnold." We didn't source it. I don't know a soul who was mentioned in any of those stories, had nothing to do with it. But the lateness of the charge did allow the Schwarzenegger camp, which they did effectively, to call it a last-minute smear, ignore the specifics, look at the smear aspect, and the last-minute nature of it. And it allowed people who were prone to give him the benefit of the doubt anyway to say, "Oh, there's nothing to this, this is a last-minute smear."

But as a citizen, it still does astonish me that you could have a candidate for governorship of the largest state in America be hit with specific charges by 16 women, all of them corroborated by other witnesses that he has been a serial groper and a sexual harasser for 30 years, and the other side simply wipes that off. By the way, Sean, there were not specific refutations made of any of this stuff. That's historical revisionism. What Arnold said was, "Some of it is true. No, not all of it is untrue." There was never a point-by-point, case-by-case refutation of any of this stuff. And my suspicion is that Schwarzenegger now thinks he doesn't have to do that, because he is now the governor, and he will be encased in the governor's office. And the Republicans, unlike what they did to Bill Clinton for eight years, will be out there saying, "Oh, come on, people looked at this in the campaign, and it was put aside."

WALSH: The bottom line was that people who were either the directors or producers, or people in a position where these specific allegations occurred, who would have had eyewitness opportunity to do confirm these things, released statements saying that these instances did not occur. So there was an effort to follow up, it did happen.

BARABAK: The last thing we're going to do is give each of you a chance to ask someone on the other side a question, and keep your answers very, very short.

WALSH: Why weren't you more involved in the campaign on a public basis? You were Gray's public advocate and strongest driver of news and other sorts of things. But we almost never saw you, and I don't know why.

SOUTH: I'll take the Fifth on that. I came in the last six weeks, basically, to run the strategy calls, to give the governor a level of comfort that decisions that were being made or being proposed had my input in them. But I had a lot of other things going on. I hadn't been on the governor's payroll since January, of my own volition. I respect him. I worked for him for a long time. This is not something I was going to drop everything else I was doing and come back and run, with all due respect to the governor. And I made that very clear to him.

SNORTUM-PHELPS: I want to ask Garry and Larry about the possibility that they were so concerned that the Republicans were going to take over, was there a discussion of the governor resigning at any point? And what did you think would happen? Do you think the recall would have failed, especially in the early months, if the governor had resigned to prevent this Republican takeover that everybody was warning us about?

GRISOLANO: Well, there's something worse than a recall winning and the Republicans taking over here. The recall goes to the fabric of elections that hold us together democratically. And for all this talk about it's a great mandate for change, you had a governor with 25 percent positive ratings, you've got a 45 percent vote share. There was extraordinary ambivalence in this electorate about whether this recall was a smart thing to do, whether it was good for our future, good for our economy. For the governor to resign just so the Republicans wouldn't take over would have been irresponsible. The only responsible thing for Democrats to do was to do everything they could to fight this thing because it was dead wrong.

SOUTH: I totally agree with that. There was never any serious discussion inside the Davis camp about the governor resigning. I know this guy like the back of my hand. It is the last thing he would have ever done, and it was the last thing I would have ever advocated that he do.

BARABAK: Because?

SOUTH: Because this was a governor who was duly reelected in a fully free election in November of 2002, whether people liked him or did not like him. Literally, within three months of being reelected, a little band of right-wing fanatics, who had nothing to do launched this recall to raise money, because they're direct mail fundraising people and that's how they keep their organizations going. They had the good fortune, which the other 31 gubernatorial recalls historically did not have, of marrying up with a rich egomaniac who wanted the job himself, who was worth $100 million, and who financed the whole thing. You could put anything on the ballot in California with a million-seven. I mean, my God. And to give into that sort of illegitimate attack on a duly elected public official, to give into that and resign the office, would have led to using the recall, as I suspect it's still going to be used in California given this precedent, to try to harass, blackmail, and threaten public officials who fall into disfavor either with the public at large, or with some special interest group, hoping that you can get them to the point of resigning.

BARABAK: Does anyone have a final question?

JOHNSON: Yeah, did any of you guys sign the recall petition on Pete Wilson?

SOUTH: No, I've never signed a petition in my life.

APPENDIX 1: THE MONEY

Gray Davis's Top 10 Sources of Campaign Funds

Total Raised in 2002: $46,106,841 (8,942 records)

Total Expenditures in 2002: $64,210,563.67

Ending Cash: $1,420,384.59

1.   California Correctional Peace Officers Assocation PAC
     $1,066,000

2.   Service Employees PEA
     $1,000,000

3.   AFSCME PAC
     $750,000

4.   Operating Engineers Local 3 Statewide PAC
     $687,000

5.   Democratic Governors Association
     $650,000

6.   California Union of Safety Employees 1M Governors Fund
     $507,500

7.   Paine Webber
     $377,633

8.   Casden Properties
     $355,000

9.   California State Pipe Trades Council PAC
     $300,000

10. Jerry Perenchio
     $300,000

Bill Simon's Top 10 Sources of Campaign Funds

Total Raised in 2002: $26,871,839 (21,276 records)

Total Expenditures in 2002: $33,595,243.81

Ending Cash: $1,044,801.86

1. William E. Simon, Jr. (personal loan)
   $9,963,668.80

2. Republican National Committee California Account
   $900,000

3. Russo, Marsh & Associates
   $588,498

4. Joseph Coors
   $345,000

5. A.G. Spanos
   $331,695

6. California Republican Party
   $295,027

7. William E. Simon, Jr.
   $286,331

8. Frank E. Baxter
   $280,074

9. Peter J. Simon
   $270,000

10. New Majority PAC
    $226,971

APPENDIX 2: THE 2002 GENERAL ELECTION

Results by County

	Davis DEM	Simon REP	Gulke AI	Camejo GRN	Copeland LIB
Alameda	216,058	76,407	3,622	37,919	6,558
Percent	62.9%	22.3%	1.0%	11.0%	1.9%
Alpine	229	247	17	40	15
Percent	40.9%	44.2%	3.0%	7.2%	2.6%
Amador	4,437	6,997	338	740	246
Percent	34.2%	54.0%	2.6%	5.8%	1.8%
Butte	19,437	32,706	1,497	5,963	1,050
Percent	31.6%	53.3%	2.4%	9.7%	1.7%
Calaveras	5,052	8,104	489	875	434
Percent	33.3%	53.4%	3.2%	5.8%	2.8%
Colusa	1,243	2,996	118	131	48
Percent	27.2%	65.5%	2.6%	2.9%	1.0%
Contra Costa	140,975	94,487	3,905	16,676	5,894
Percent	53.3%	35.7%	1.4%	6.3%	2.2%
Del Norte	2,922	3,093	239	207	165
Percent	43.3%	45.9%	3.6%	3.0%	2.4%
El Dorado	16,402	32,898	1,203	3,418	1,072
Percent	29.5%	59.1%	2.1%	6.1%	1.9%
Fresno	59,019	85,910	2,214	3,508	3,560
Percent	38.0%	55.3%	1.4%	2.2%	2.3%
Glenn	1,685	4,268	200	187	96
Percent	25.9%	65.5%	3.1%	2.9%	1.4%
Humboldt	19,499	16,118	547	5,170	961
Percent	45.5%	37.6%	1.2%	12.1%	2.2%
Imperial	11,644	8,789	360	546	258
Percent	53.3%	40.3%	1.7%	2.5%	1.1%
Inyo	2,114	3,567	159	210	142
Percent	33.7%	56.8%	2.5%	3.3%	2.2%
Kern	46,250	82,660	3,002	1,965	1,839
Percent	33.7%	60.3%	2.2%	1.4%	1.3%
Kings	7,776	12,212	491	298	246
Percent	36.7%	57.6%	2.3%	1.4%	1.1%
Lake	7,424	6,459	451	965	336
Percent	46.8%	40.7%	2.8%	6.0%	2.1%
Lassen	2,429	4,512	317	155	166
Percent	31.6%	58.7%	4.2%	2.0%	2.1%
Los Angeles	953,162	594,748	25,160	72,886	39,934
Percent	55.9%	34.9%	1.4%	4.3%	2.4%

Madera	8,217	15,998	651	517	517
Percent	31.4%	61.2%	2.5%	2.0%	1.9%
Marin	49,512	24,520	917	10,710	1,502
Percent	56.3%	27.9%	1.0%	12.1%	1.7%
Mariposa	2,126	3,720	193	215	130
Percent	32.8%	57.4%	2.9%	3.4%	2.0%
Mendocino	10,832	8,331	680	4,119	581
Percent	43.5%	33.5%	2.7%	16.6%	2.3%
Merced	18,071	19,191	749	792	1,379
Percent	44.6%	47.4%	1.8%	1.9%	3.4%
Modoc	900	2,161	145	54	67
Percent	26.7%	64.0%	4.3%	1.5%	2.0%
Mono	1,064	1,552	76	154	64
Percent	36.0%	52.6%	2.5%	5.3%	2.1%
Monterey	47,052	31,532	1,402	3,794	2,191
Percent	54.1%	36.3%	1.6%	4.4%	2.5%
Napa	17,516	13,483	824	3,570	774
Percent	47.8%	36.8%	2.2%	9.8%	2.1%
Nevada	13,338	20,573	817	3,297	743
Percent	34.0%	52.4%	2.1%	8.4%	1.8%
Orange	222,149	368,152	10,393	16,670	14,668
Percent	34.7%	57.5%	1.6%	2.7%	2.2%
Placer	28,495	58,623	1,556	4,657	1,500
Percent	29.7%	61.1%	1.6%	4.9%	1.5%
Plumas	2,598	4,310	264	380	182
Percent	33.1%	54.9%	3.3%	4.9%	2.3%
Riverside	121,845	159,440	5,530	5,995	6,601
Percent	40.3%	52.7%	1.9%	2.0%	2.2%
Sacramento	129,143	147,456	6,245	22,232	6,634
Percent	40.9%	46.7%	1.9%	7.1%	2.0%
San Benito	6,049	5,163	208	504	275
Percent	48.9%	41.8%	1.6%	4.1%	2.2%
San Bernardino	116,757	142,513	6,884	6,754	6,485
Percent	41.3%	50.4%	2.5%	2.3%	2.2%
San Diego	268,278	342,095	11,246	18,184	13,742
Percent	40.6%	51.8%	1.7%	2.8%	2.0%
San Francisco	143,102	33,214	1,639	33,495	3,048
Percent	66.3%	15.4%	0.7%	15.5%	1.4%
San Joaquin	53,747	58,239	2,736	4,630	2,540
Percent	43.6%	47.2%	2.2%	3.8%	2.0%
San Luis Obispo	29,732	43,552	1,531	4,189	1,618
Percent	36.4%	53.4%	1.8%	5.2%	2.0%
San Mateo	99,803	51,497	2,144	13,537	3,205
Percent	58.0%	30.0%	1.2%	7.9%	1.8%

Santa Barbara	50,741	52,832	1,401	5,785	2,586
Percent	44.4%	46.2%	1.2%	5.1%	2.2%
Santa Clara	199,399	116,862	5,951	24,097	9,430
Percent	55.4%	32.5%	1.6%	6.7%	2.6%
Santa Cruz	43,469	20,598	1,166	9,409	1,777
Percent	56.1%	26.6%	1.5%	12.1%	2.2%
Shasta	15,292	28,625	1,664	1,283	942
Percent	31.5%	59.0%	3.5%	2.6%	1.9%
Sierra	420	805	50	72	67
Percent	29.3%	56.0%	3.4%	5.1%	4.6%
Siskiyou	4,972	9,112	440	437	386
Percent	31.9%	58.4%	2.9%	2.8%	2.4%
Solano	46,385	33,516	2,174	4,038	1,316
Percent	52.4%	37.9%	2.5%	4.6%	1.4%
Sonoma	73,079	43,408	3,529	19,599	3,097
Percent	50.4%	30.0%	2.4%	13.6%	2.1%
Stanislaus	41,908	46,091	2,732	2,967	1,385
Percent	43.6%	48.0%	2.8%	3.1%	1.4%
Sutter	5,782	12,024	463	620	242
Percent	29.9%	62.1%	2.3%	3.3%	1.2%
Tehama	5,000	9,010	537	361	254
Percent	32.5%	58.6%	3.5%	2.4%	1.6%
Trinity	1,833	2,421	165	272	140
Percent	37.3%	49.2%	3.3%	5.6%	2.8%
Tulare	21,294	37,172	1,180	1,090	1,208
Percent	34.1%	59.5%	1.9%	1.7%	2.0%
Tuolumne	6,846	9,251	476	773	328
Percent	38.2%	51.6%	2.6%	4.4%	1.8%
Ventura	83,557	91,193	3,733	6,563	5,787
Percent	43.3%	47.2%	1.9%	3.4%	3.0%
Yolo	21,983	17,484	842	4,934	543
Percent	47.5%	37.8%	1.8%	10.6%	1.1%
Yuba	3,447	6,904	373	428	249
Percent	29.8%	59.6%	3.2%	3.6%	2.1%
State Totals	3,533,490	3,169,801	128,035	393,036	161,203
Percent	47.3%	42.4%	1.7%	5.3%	2.2%

APPENDIX 3:

Attorney General Bill Lockyer—
Why I Voted for Arnold

This is an excerpt from a luncheon talk Attorney General Lockyer gave to participants in the IGS Recall Review on October 18, 2003. It was the first time he spoke in public of his vote for Arnold Schwarzenegger.

I want to talk a bit about the campaign, but more about looking ahead and what I hope we can do as a family. I really like people that love politics and love government, that like thinking about policy, that think it's important. To me, they're really extraordinary and interesting. Those of you that went through this last campaign, probably only on the Arnold side, felt that wonderful experience of comradeship, the sense of community of the foxhole. But it is an extraordinary experience that we've denied people in our culture, because we lead such unconnected lives. And it's one of the things that happens in politics that makes it very, very unique, and I envy those who had that experience this last year. I have had it on numerous occasions in the past with Robert Kennedy and George McGovern and other campaigns. It's a special thing, and I wish we knew a way to have people have that experience, because it's what they don't get in our media-dominated politics. And our crusty cynicism drives them away from the experience.

So I want to just mention a few things. We're all trying to figure out what it means. I guess I have cynical moments, too. And I would say, "Gee. Well, there are three choices here: the terminator, the masturbator, and the prevaricator.' You can figure out which is which. But I guess if I had a subtext for this comment it would be why I voted for Arnold. And I'm still trying to understand the meanings. For the academics that are here, let me mention that we really value your disciplined work and analyses, and we would like you to help us understand who voted, why they voted, what mattered to them, what does it mean. We'd like to know what is the new generation of voters thinking, what matters to them? Latinos, what really mattered or didn't? Things of that nature. So we hope that you will stay focused and do some of that work. It will be useful in thinking about these matters down the road.

I want to talk a little about Republicans and Democrats, and Arnold lovers and Arnold haters, and Gray lovers and haters, but you understand how difficult that group would be to measure.

First, there's a lot of stuff I don't think we are comfortable talking about, and we run our little partisan tapes. For Republicans, with all the momentum, all the glitz, all the excitement, the circus that they brought to town was as good as there has ever been, $80-90 million spent, and all those signatures on petitions, and so on. Nothing changed in 11 months. What the voters thought a year ago is what they thought coming out of the polling place. I don't know what that means. Basically, they started with the opinion, "Anybody but Davis." God bless him, poor Bill Simon couldn't qualify as "anybody."

Now, Republicans ought to reflect, because I hear a lot puffery about the message. And I think it's worth noting that more than half of the recall voters support domestic partner benefits, and more than two-thirds of them want women's reproductive rights to be protected. They should ask, "Well, what does it mean if 45 percent of the voters have an unfavorable opinion of the guy they just elected?' What about the large, large number, something like two-thirds, that thought Arnold was never specific enough about any kind of policy that might be contemplated.

For Democrats, it was sort of comforting to say, "Well, gee, this is really about Gray Davis, it's not about us." And a lot of us went through that exercise. There were a lot of visits, and I don't know how many phone calls you got. I guess I'm sorry we exempted political phone calls in the "Do not Call" bill. But there is a higher standard of constitutionally protected speech, for Barbra Streisand, and Al Gore, Bill Clinton, and some others that kept phoning us and telling us to get out and vote. And Democrats and Republicans ought to be mindful of the fact that only about 30 percent of the electorate describe themselves as somewhat conservative. So whatever the Democrats were doing, people were listening to some other tune. For me, it seems to suggest that for Democrats, the real problem here isn't these esoteric little splinters of how many African-American women voted for Arnold, or something like that, it's what happened with union households, what happened with middle-class voters, what happened with the 18- to 25-year-old group that a lot of them supported the recall, or they didn't show up at all, didn't vote at all, didn't think it mattered to them. Now, those are, for Democrats, our natural allies. For those of us who think that the two essential issues in politics are "with whom" for "for what," and that "with whom" is the primary question and "for what" is secondary and derivative, those people don't think they're connected to Democrats. We still have these huge majorities in Sacramento and the legislature, the statewide elected office holders and so on. But when you look at the "right track/wrong track" question on everybody's polls, you find 80-75 percent saying, "California, wrong track."

I think the truth here, and it's not a new idea, it's one we're all familiar with, but it's that in some profoundly significant way, anyone in charge is in trouble. The bull's eye is on anyone in power. It doesn't matter if it's the Catholic Church, the mayor, the governor, the president, the head of the labor union, people are profoundly worried and disturbed and anxious about feeling somehow that their institutional life doesn't respond to their needs.

For consultants, this should be a year unlike any other. Earlier, Steve Smith made the comment that he had a press conference and 12 cameras showed up. For a consultant! Every story written, the minutia about tactics and so on, kept streaming out in an unusual, maybe unique way, maybe not to be repeated. But I suspect that there will be spotlights on the consultant community in the future

But Arnold fans should keep in mind that something very profound occurred—83 percent of the recall voters made up their mind before Arnold even entered the race. Four out of five were for the recall before he was a candidate, and, of course, those two-thirds that were disappointed with a lack of adequate programmatic detail. At least they knew, well, he ain't Gray Davis. He was an appealing person, and they decided they should give him a chance. Dan Walters and people like that write about these things in interesting ways, that change and reform in California are like a resonating chord that we hear regularly, obviously going way back to these reforms to the initiative and referendum and recall. More recently, we had the full-time legislature, Prop 1A, in—what?—'64 or around that time, and term limits, and Jerry Brown's campaign reform efforts, and Prop 13. Well, I think that's what Arnold meant to people—hopeful optimism. They had the consummate technocrat, and decided that wasn't what they wanted. They wanted a leader that was just upbeat and was going to promise a better future.

For Arnold haters, I would just say that I think Californians are really interested in this particular ticket—they want to know where the ride goes, and how it's going to work out, and so it's interesting. A lot of us, including me, reflect on to what extent were people like Jefferson and DeToqueville right when they observed that the essence of the American political experiment is popular sovereignty, and this is an example of people really taking government in their own hands, good or bad, wisely or unwisely. But as much as we like to think of it that way, fewer than five percent of the voters were voting for the first time. Ninety-five percent were old hands like us. That doesn't make it seem populist, unless it's the mood change. The voter registration actually was lower as a percent of eligible voters. It declined over the last year. So when we look at October, the last election, 71.3, down to 70.45 when voter reg closed this time. So it's actually an eligibility pool dip. If there's a populist argument at all, it's probably one that most people would talk about in terms of intensity, rather than the peasant rebellion, and that is, basically, that Republicans came out in greater numbers than Democrats, that they were more motivated to get to the polls. And we see those in the various numbers.

I want to talk a little bit about 'puke politics." I was trying to change the rules a little bit by that comment earlier in the year. And while a few were offended, most agreed. We do these things to manipulate turnout, to try to keep some people from voting for somebody that you make seem awful. By the way, if you want a prediction about the next round of puke politics, it would be the Bush campaign, with tens of millions of dollars against whatever Democrat comes out of the pack, because Bush can't explain why he said, "I've given you a TV. Isn't that nice? Oh, I forgot to tell you, I put it on your credit card." He can't explain that, or anything else. And so they will have to shift to the worst kind of personal attack, "Puke Politics '04." Stay tuned.

But what distresses me about it is what it does to voters, because it turns them off. They aren't smart bombs, they're big explosions that hit your own constituencies, as well as the others, and it contributes to this mood of the electorate that nothing matters to them in politics, and no one is saying anything they care about. I want to see an end to the politics of subtraction. What happened to the idea that we want people to participate, not because they're afraid of something or mad about something, but because they think something good can come of their participation, that the values of civic culture and participation are essential, and that they should play a role. Well, there are these small lessons. People want somebody that can balance a checkbook without asking somebody else to pay the bills, and they want a state that can live within its means and get a dollar's worth of service for every dollar's worth of tax they pay. I understand that. But we all have to take some responsibility. Me too. I don't point the finger at others without it being at me too.

Think about it. This is the most extraordinary experience in human history. There has never, ever, ever been a people, a place, a time, when the fundamental principle of everybody counts, every voice matters, every person is important prevailed. There's never been a society that tried that before. It's never been done. And we're crapping it up with all the cynicism and tactical advantage-taking. And that probably won't change. But my job, at least today, is to say, God, I love you, you're my family. It doesn't matter what you are politically or philosophically, but let's figure out together how do we tell people that they count; they matter? It's never been done. It's an unfinished experiment. We still have to kick the can down the road, but what an incredible idea. And, unfortunately, our efforts to secure temporary advantage to win an election too often disregard the fundamental fact that we all believe that. It's what makes us really unique, because we know it matters. We know it counts.

Yes, I was strongly opposed to the recall. I think it's bad for the state. I voted for Arnold. The first time I ever voted for a Republican in my life for a partisan office. First time. I've done it for nonpartisan local office. In my own office in Sacramento, the management team, frankly, I think I've got more Republicans and Independents than Democrats. Justice shouldn't be partisan. That's how we ought to try to do these things.

But you know what Arnold represented for me? I looked at the list; it was a crappy list. And he represented for me what he did for others—hope, change, reform, opportunity, upbeat, problem-solving. I want that. I'm tired of transactional, cynical, deal-making politics. I want to see principled leadership. And, yeah, he may be naïve about that. But you know what? It's real. And I'll tell you, the little conversation that maybe made me believe this more than anything else was after the election I saw him, and I said, "You know, Arnold, I've never voted for a Republican for a partisan office before. This is the first time I've ever done it." And he said, "Bill, you listened to my heart, not my party." Now, how can you not love somebody that feels that way about it? I hope I'm not being conned. I think the voters hope they're not being conned, because we really want and deserve people that genuinely want to see that little Diego can live safely, and go to good schools, and have healthcare when he needs it, and live his dreams, not my dreams. It's simple. It's simple. We all want that.

So together, please, let's figure it out, as people that care about this, who understand how significant this American experiment is, the most noble, the most noble in human history, and it deserves our respect. Thank you very much.

APPENDIX 4:

1998 Gubernatorial Election Results—Davis vs. Lungren

Carrried by Davis
Carried by Lungren

Map courtesy of the Statewide Database.

APPENDIX 5:

2002 Gubernatorial Election Results—Davis vs. Simon

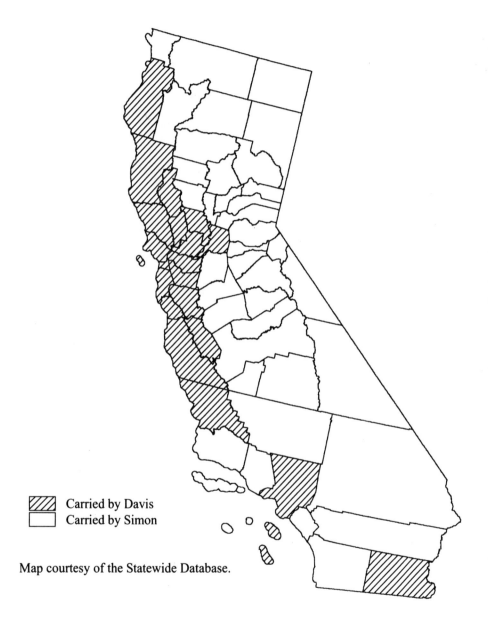

Carried by Davis
Carried by Simon

Map courtesy of the Statewide Database.

APPENDIX 6:

Recall Litigation, Update 12/8/2003

Federal Cases	Issue	Status
PARTNOY v. SHELLEY **Case Number** **03-CV-1460 BTM** **(USDC Southern District)** Lawyer: Shaun Martin and Sandra Rierson (Law Professors); AG[1]	7/23/03 Suit re: E.C. § 11382 is unconstitutional/violates 14th Amendment	Hearing July 29, 2003 —Granted. Judge issued order that voters will be allowed to cast a ballot for a potential successor even if they don't vote on recall. After intevention by Scott Raferty, subsequent Orders issued 8/21/03 (but Orders did not affect recall procedures)
SALAZAR v. MONTEREY CNTY **Case Number** **03-CV-3584** **(USDC Northern District)** Lawyer: Villagra/ MALDEF **OLIVEREZ v. STATE of CA** **Case Number** **03-CV-3658** **(USDC Northern District)** Lawyer: Rubin/LCCR; AG **Consolidated**	8/1/03 Complaint (Salazar) and 8/7/03 Motion for TRO (Oliverez) (Voting Rights Actions)	TRO issued 8/15/03 (preventing Monterey from mailing absentee ballots) 9/5/03: After clearance by DOJ, 3-judge panel denied motion for preliminary injunction and dissolved TRO

---

[1] This is only a partial list of attorneys; also doesn't include all amici and intervenors.

SOUTHWEST VOTER REGISTRATION EDUCATION PROJECT v. SHELLEY Case Number 03-CV-5715 (USDC Central District) (9ᵗʰ Cir. No. 03-56498) Lawyer: Rosenbaum/ACLU; AG	8/7/03 ACLU Complaint (suit against use of punch card voting machines)	8/20/03 USDC Order Denying TRO 9/15/03—9ᵗʰ Cir. Reversed and enjoined SOS from conducting election 9/23/03—En banc reinstated recall, after argument on 9/22/03
GALLEGOS v. STATE OF CA Case Number 03-CV-6157 (USDC Eastern District) Lawyer: Rubin/LCCR; AG	8/25/03 Complaint (Voting Rights Action, for other counties, Kings and Merced)	Moot due to outcome of other section 5 cases; plaintiffs filed voluntary dismissal without prejudice in 9/03

State Cases	Issue	Status
RECALL GRAY DAVIS COMM. v. SHELLEY Case Number C044487 (California Court of Appeal) Lawyer: Sweeney & Grant; AG	7/10/03 Suit re: enforcing Shelley to count and verify signatures on recall petitions	Petition granted 7/18/03

COSTA v. SHELLEY **Case Number** **03AS03887** **(Sacramento Superior)** Lawyer: Chuck Bell, Tom Hiltachk; AG	7/11/03 Suit re: County elections officials must count recall petition signatures without regard to extrinsic evidence or outside claims re circulators' status of CA registration or residency	Plaintiff Costa filed this suit but did not serve it; he filed a Request for Dismissal after California Supreme Court rulings
ROBINS v. SHELLEY **Case Number** **BC299066** **(Los Angeles Superior)** Lawyer: Paul Kiesel, Kiesel, Boucher & Larson; AG	7/15/03 Suit re: circulators not qualified	Lower Court denied TRO; Court of Appeal denied review on 7/23/03; Supreme Court denied review 8/7/03. After hearing, Court issued ruling 8/11/03 denying complaint.
FRANKEL v. SHELLEY **Case Number S117770** **(Cal. Supreme Court)** Lawyer: Falk and Mayer, Howard Rice, et al.; AG	7/28/03 Suit re: "if appropriate" issue (Lt. Governor succeeds Governor in recall election)	Petition denied 8/7/03
EISENBERG v. SHELLEY **Case Number S117763** **(Cal. Supreme Court)** Lawyer: Jon Eisenberg, Horvitz & Levy; AG	7/28/03 Suit re: Props. 53 and 54 should not be on recall ballot	Petition denied 8/7/03

BYRNES v. BUSTA-MANTE **Case Number S117832** **(Cal. Supreme Court)** Lawyer: Scott J. Rafferty, The Aerie Group; AG	7/30/03 Suit re: whether Article V, Section 10 establishes Lt. Governor as the constitutional successor in the event of a recall of Governor	Petition denied 8/7/03
BURTON v. SHEL-LEY **Case Number S117834** **(Cal. Supreme Court)** Lawyer: Mark Burton, Hersh & Hersh; AG	7/30/03 Suit re: SOS is not enforcing proper signature requirements for recall candidates (should be 1% of registered voters)	Petition denied 8/7/03; dissenting opinion of George and Moreno
DAVIS v. SHELLEY **Case Number S117921** **(Cal. Supreme Court)** Lawyer: Remcho, Johansen & Purcell; AG; Bell & Hiltachk	8/4/03 Suit re: equal protection; guarantee clause; election should be postponed and consolidated with March 2, 2004 primary election	Petition denied 8/7/03
JOHNSON v. BUSTA-MANTE **Case Number 03AS04931** **(Sac. Superior Court)** Lawyer: Sweeney, Grant; Lance Olson & Deborah Caplan; FPPC	9/03 Suit alleging that Bustamante accepted illegal contributions, or conducted illegal transfers of funds between his campaign committees (Gov. Code §§ 85303, 85316, 85301(c), 85310(c))	9/22/03 Ruling that Lt. Gov. must return to donors campaign funds in violation of PRA

CAMP v. SCHWAR-ZENEGGER Case Number 03AS05478 (Sac. Superior Court) Lawyer: Lowell Finley; Bell McAndrews, Hiltachk & Davidian	10/03 Suit alleging Schwarzenegger's $4 million loan violated Government Code § 85307, and that he solicited contributions in violation of PRA to pay off loan	10/02/03 Judge McMaster issued minute order denying application for TRO. Hearing on OSC set for 12/02/03.
McCLINTOCK v. SHELLEY Case Number 03CS01177 (Sac. Superior Court) Lawyer: Richard D. Ackerman; AG; FPPC	8/03 Suit seeking to require Secretary of State to publish McClintock's candidate statement in the ballot pamphlet even though he did not accept Prop. 34 spending limits.	8/26/03 Superior Court rejected McClintock's suit; 3rd Dist. Ct. appeal denied writ on 8/28/03. Cal. Supreme Ct. denied request for a stay.

APPENDIX 7

Recall Election Results

Shall Gray Davis be recalled?

Yes	4,972,524	55.4%
No	4,006,021	44.6%

Leading candidates to succeed Gray Davis as governor if recalled:

Arnold Schwarzenegger	4,203,596	48.6%
Cruz Bustamante	2,723,768	31.5%
Tom McClintock	1,160,182	13.5%
Peter Camejo	242,169	2.8%
Arianna Huffington	47,486	0.6%
Peter Ueberroth	25,125	0.3%